Sea of Bones

Her mind reeling, she instinctively checked its setting before jogging back toward the hut. She'd not quite reached its flooded porch when the soggy earth beneath her feet served to intervene, essentially tossing her airborne to land within a full dozen feet from lift-off, her lungs emptied with a resounding huff upon impact.

Zack had considered, ever-so-briefly, inquiring about the contents, the mystery ingredients tucked within that gradually bloating soda bottle as to decide on a proper plan of action.

That was, until, exchanging frenzied glances from the overturned cans to the soda bottle and back again, he was able to put two and two together, the severe twist in his gut nearly instantaneous as a reward for solving said enigma.

"Stoney, d-do not f-fear...I mean, how could y-you really, considering y-you w-were blown to f-fucking fragments y-years ago?" Chandler beamed, mustard-colored pus streaming down his cheeks to pool at his chin like bright yellow birth pods. When he actually locked eyes with Zack for the first time, it did very little to sooth the CO's splintering nerves.

"Well then..." the Aussie assassin codenamed 'Blaze' concluded with a playful wink, "...G'day then, m-mate...and I p-pray to m-my demonic s-sire it's the last fuckin' t-time for the both of us."

Initially, Zack lunged forward at the sight of Marquez Chandler leaning down with his mouth pulled wide to suckle the top of the sealed soda bottle, nearly slipping to one knee as he reversed field upon witnessing the bottle bloat to nearly twice its normal size.

He managed to clear the bedroom threshold in two leaping strides, diving chest-first into the middle of the kitchen floor when a massive shockwave threatened to bring the surrounding walls, drenched in fire, collapsing down on top of his sprawled frame.

Sea of Bones

Terry Lloyd Vinson

A Wings ePress, Inc.
Mystery/Crime Novel

Wings ePress, Inc.

Edited by: Jeanne Smith
Copy Edited by: Joan C. Powell
Executive Editor: Jeanne Smith
Cover Artist: TBD

Wings ePress Books
www.books-by-wings-epress.com

Copyright © 2017 by Terry Lloyd Vinson
ISBN 978-1-61309-712-0

Published In the United States Of America

Wings ePress Inc.
3000 N. Rock Road
Newton, KS 67114

Dedication

To my lovely wife, Liza, for her patience and understanding.

Prologue

Troubled Waters

The sleek, bullet-shaped cutter lurched wildly to the left, the wheel involuntarily jerking so suddenly and violently that Liza briefly thought her right shoulder at least partially dislocated. Despite her awkward stance—crouched to one knee with her back to the console—she maintained matching steely grips on the wheel at her back and the squirming form at her front, respectively. Strands of thoroughly saturated, tar black hair matted her forehead and cheeks, a few rogue stragglers even cloaking her left eye like plastered seaweed. The skies above alternated dark gray, fluorescent orange and swirling, churning plumes of midnight ebony, as if they were passing through multiple time zones simultaneously.

"Hang on, little lady," Barnes bellowed through the surrounding calamity, pointing past her toward the console. "Radar's lit up like Times Square on New Year's Eye! I...I do believe I'm fracturin' both arms just keepin' her upright. Now...do me...*us* both a colossal favor, bein' as this particular expedition into insanity was your idea to begin with...*face forward and man the damn console!*"

1

The radio blared in the background, the message being conveyed mostly lost in a barrage of static, the sea's fury and Mother Nature's building tantrum.

Legs splayed, breathing heavily labored, Barnes titled his head and regarded her with a deep frown.

"Now, as in this very fuckin' moment, would be *good*, woman!" he croaked, the bulging veins visible on his neck only a fragment thicker than the one streaking up his forehead like a fleshy, continuously expanding section of underground railway.

"*Sapat na*! I …I g-got it. Just l-let me get my footing, damn it!" she grumbled, though barely audible from the adjacent roar. Even many years past a last visit to the homeland, her Filipina accent held steadfast, never stronger than in times of great duress.

A brief scan of the console's navigational radar, followed by a series of turns of the rain-slickened steering column, and their course was quickly righted.

When next the radio screeched, the message doled out was clear and concise, and delivered in a frustrated tone that masked its building anger with a heavy dose of sarcasm.

"*Proteus,* do you read me? *Pegasus,* do *you* read? Damn it, Liz …Zack …Barnes? Whoever … pick up the mic and provide your present location as we…have…lost…you…lost you *both* on…navigational radar. Do you read? Over."

In lieu of steering the cutter through what appeared to be an endless army of battering waves while simultaneously resetting its course, Barnes fired a brief, intense glare Liza's way, who in turn shrugged off the request as if deaf to its existence.

"Master Correctional Officer Zackary Gorman …Officers Liza Gorman and Dylan Barnes, this is Atlantis CP, do you read? Does anyone read? Over."

"Swell. Sounds like Bowen's snatched the mic from sweet-cheeks Flores, and he ain't at all pleased!" Barnes howled, jerking the wheel hard to the left and then repeating the action in reverse.

2

Huffing, Liza reached up to clear away a sea-soaked hair-patch from both eyes while monitoring the vessel's in-dash radar screen, which pulsated like an aerial view of a massive Fourth of July fireworks show. As if to resent the very notion of shifting course yet again, the constant barrage of waves battering the bow appeared to ease off, even clearing a slim path for smoother passage.

"I take it a simple acknowledgement...that at least some of us are ...still wadin' *above* the waves is ...outta the question?" Barnes inquired between spats to clear his tongue of recently ingested saltwater.

"Why bother?" she countered through a fierce scowl Barnes didn't have to actually visualize to know was fully intact. "So they can order us back to base and string us up by our genitals? At this point, I'd rather constipatedly lost."

Fortunately, the storm easily drowned out his brief but unavoidable giggling fit, ignited by his new partner's latest language gaff.

"*Constapa*—yeah, um, right ...got'cha. Sounds ...like a pl-plan. Full speed ahead then balls to the wall."

"'Sides, we've been off the grid for almost forty-five minutes and even money says they locked 'er down a few ticks after we cleared the dock."

The cutter lurched violently to the left, forcing Barnes to wrestle the wheel with tightly clenched hands, his boots planted firmly atop the slippery deck but sliding involuntarily back several inches nonetheless. Nearly twice Liza's size, he was quickly finding his bulk a hindrance in such times. Flung back from the sudden jerk, he avoided a potential concussion only by ducking down at the last moment and dodging the sharp metal edge of a nearby supply cabinet. Despite an assortment of bruises and a deep gash atop his left forearm, he managed to pull himself upright and lumber toward the console even as Liza clung to the console's built-in handholds in a double-fisted death-grip.

"How far?" he barked, his normally gruff voice growing increasingly weak from the constant shouting.

Liza stared trance-like down into the GPS's glowing monitor.

3

"Fifteen to seventeen minutes. Maybe cut two or three minutes if someone would cease and desist stirring this damnable soup bowl!"

"Needless to say, turnin' back ain't an option, though I get the feelin' the boys at HQ might disagree somewhat vehemently."

Liza twisted around briefly, eyeing him somewhat curiously, as if he'd revealed some great universal secret instead of simply stating the painfully obvious. In lieu of greeting her perplexed stare with say, a stuck-out tongue, Barnes fired off a playful wink while forcing a smile that better resembled a pained grimace.

"Hey, chin up, lady. Bowen was already talkin' lockdown right before we shoved off, remember? No way they'll risk comin' after us in this squall."

"Yeah, well, maybe it's not such a bad idea, depending on who-what we run into out there," she countered, having already turned to bury her face into the monitor.

"Good point."

Following a rare, banter-free moment, Barnes inexplicably slammed the side of a clenched fist against the wheel while spatting forth a string of profanity mostly lost within the storm's continual screeching.

"Jesus, what *now*?" Liza more lipped than actually verbalized.

"Ya know, bein' the pessimistic type that I naturally am, this just hit me, and please feel free to correct any miscalculations. The flood rooms on those burgs are equipped with three life pods in case things really go to shit, weather-wise, right?"

Liza frowned, nodding sternly as if growing increasingly annoyed.

"Yeah, so?"

"Yeah well, never was great shakes at arithmetic, but that's definitely gonna leave somebody in the lurch when and *if* the time comes to tuck and cover."

As if to dismiss any and all impending, similarly problematic issues, she casually waved him off while shifting her gaze back to the glittering console.

"Hey, we'll torch that bridge when we cross it."

4

The radio blared just as Barnes had opened his mouth to correct this latest example of verbal butchery, a portion of the message being relayed lost in a series of echoing squelches.

"Crew of the —*oteus*...crew of...*Pegasus*...we are unable to pinpoint your respective locations. If at all possible, please respond, over."

"Ya hear LT's voice?" Barnes cackled, the knuckles of each hand shaded a dark purple from the constant pressure applied. "Talk about your classic glass half-empty. Sounds to me they've written us all off as floatin' chum already."

"Well, I'd say that's probably a *good* thing," Liza replied without shouting, thus the words were swallowed whole by booming thunder and thumping waves.

A fresh radio transmission interceded—so clear and void of interference as if conveyed across calm waters and clear, blue skies.

"Senior Officer Zackary Gorman...Officer Liza Gorman ...Officer Dylan Barnes, respectively, Please realize a storm of considerable magnitude, long since predicted to reach level four status, is being tracked at approximately forty-five to fifty-five minutes from this location. Radar currently tracks it twenty-one nautical miles to our west. You three were present at this morning's briefing, yes? Please advise, over."

"Bowen's radio etiquette needs some work, "Dylan barked, hunched over the wheel as if his ample midsection were practically sewn into it, "Un-o-fficial translation: Officer Barnes, you do realize such a reckless, jackass decision makes you solely responsible, financially speakin', for the possible loss of an Island-Class patrol boat? Again, if I'm speaking out of turn, please feel free to cut into this particular rant, but I'm fairly confident in thinkin' there's no place *in* or *around* Sector Two to safely prevent her from becomin' ocean debris while you three knuckleheads ride out the storm inside a reinforced hut. Please advise, knuckleheads. Over."

A long pause, void of static—what could've been labeled a dread, deadly silence if not for the churning, twisting, swirling chaos threatening to abort the mission with *or* without official permission to do so.

5

"Crew of the *Proteus*, ditto *Pegasus*, you may be looking at an extended span of forced segregation on or about Sector Two. We will attempt to maintain communications. Once the storm breaks, we'll fly recon your way. Upon your safe return to home base, expect a full board inquiry on this matter. Radio transmission from the site obviously won't be an option once the storm barricades the location, but please, if at all possible, maintain torso beacons for tracking. Atlantis out."

"Are they trackable at the bottom of an angry sea?" Barnes heard Liza chime in deliriously between transmissions, squinting over her right shoulder through the windshield's continuous spatter as a faint outline of Sector Two took shape on the grayish horizon.

"Doubtful. Those torso beacons flame out like candles in the wind as body heat ebbs away," he shouted in response, tongue planted firmly in cheek but doubtful she was even capable of detecting the sarcasm.

Having relaxed his grip at least somewhat while steering the cutter through what seemed an ever-mutating, endless legion of waves, he took a half-step to the left as she pushed back from the monitor and stood stiffly by his side.

"I...never thanked you for doing this," she said as their eyes collectively locked on the target point less than a half-mile to the north.

"I know you didn't...have to. It's a, well, you took a big chance."

"Yeah, and don't think for a minute you and that jar-headed hubby of yours don't owe me, *big time,*" he replied, nudging her playfully while careful to maintain a solid grip on the mist-coated wheel. "That is, if any of us survive to either collect *or* pay said debt."

With that, the pair of woefully mismatched partners shared a rare moment of semi-tranquility, perhaps the final such moment of peace either might ever experience.

As possible omens went, the single strike of lightning that soon lit up the raging, tar-black skies directly above the tiny island officially labeled as Hawk Island could hardly be construed as positive.

One

Decked out in a sleeveless green tee, beige parachute pants and flip-flops, a lanky, muscular man with a fluffy mop of hair stood with his hands on his hips as Zackary Gorman squeezed past with an armful of boxes. Once the Master Corrections Officer had vanished inside the hut's darkened interior, he turned his attention to the man's female cohort poised a few dozen feet to his left, her combat boots having submerged nearly to the ankle in moistened sand.

Stern, comically grim expression firmly intact, stocky of build—no doubt housing a layer or two of tightly-wound muscle beneath loose-fitting camouflage fatigues—he found the woman quite attractive despite the semi-butch overtones of her overall deportment. But then, he deduced with an inner smirk, two-plus years of incarceration had a way of chipping away at a man's standards.

Following a fierce morning squall that had, mercifully, passed in a matter of minutes, the waves rolled gently, pushed along by the gentlest of tropical breezes. As was the case, more-so during typhoon season, the local weather was of an extreme Jekyll-Hyde nature.

The short barrel of the taser curled into Liza Gorman's left palm appeared pointed directly toward his groin, while her right gently stroked the slick, black handle of an electric shock-baton. While there was no way to gauge her line of vision beneath a set of pitch-black, wraparound Wayfarers, he could practically feel the searing heat of her stare.

"You mind raising the sights on that thing, Officer G? I'd rather not be forced to pee from an IV tube in case your trigger finger gets an unexpected itch."

"Not to worry," she replied in a flat, android-like monotone, the aforementioned aim unaltered. "If so forced, I have a point of impact chosen already, and it doesn't involve genitals."

"Well, that's certainly a load off. Completely unnecessary, the entire practice. That is, if you don't mind my saying. All these months later, I certainly understand the limitations of this...*my* situation."

Once no reply from his stoic sentinel appeared forthcoming, he continued, albeit in a noticeably less sardonic tone.

"That is, even if I did manage to incapacitate both you and the senior officer, , it would serve little purpose save to perhaps force you both into an extended visit. Much as I'd enjoy the company, I'm not quite sure the toilet paper on hand would hold up. You'd think a level of trust would exist after these many months of interaction."

"Spare me, Hawkins," came Liza's curt reply, her lips curling slightly inward in the aftermath, "you'd croak us and go for that waiting cutter without hesitation, consequences be damned."

"Just to end up as barbecued chum for a passing school of tiger-sharks? Oh, you *severely* overestimate my level of desperation, to say nothing of pure, unadulterated ignorance."

The smirk of bemusement she wore spoke volumes compared to the minimal verbiage that followed.

"Says you, Slick. Just call me paranoid."

Shrugging, he heard Zack grunt, apparently upon finally lowering the aforementioned boxes somewhere within the hut's cramped living area.

"Hey, um, Doc, you mind checking the generator's battery for me? Hate to sound, to paraphrase your lovely spouse, *paranoid*, but on the outside chance it might decide to crap out the minute you two glide away, I'd have thirty days to bake to a crusty turn."

"Not a problem," he heard the big man reply following a resounding huff, "got a few more boxes to unload and then I'll snag the tester off the rig."

Tate Hawkins, almost upon being introduced to his primary sentinels *slash* supply saviors, had dubbed the hulking, higher-ranking of the two as *Doc Samson* after one of Marvel Comic's lesser-known doo-gooders. Being as the man was easily identified as the alpha male type and possessed roughly twice his own bulk, he'd felt it mandatory to at least attempt a bit of humor right from the get-go, if for no other reason than to lessen his own level of uneasiness.

"Appreciate it, big fella. Everything, in fact. More than you know."

"Just doing our job. Doesn't mean you've been added to our will," Liza chimed in sternly, suddenly chewing and chomping as if she'd magically regurgitated a jaw-load of chewing gum. In response, Hawkins shrugged weakly, twirling the ragged edges of a pencil-thin mustache he'd attempted to cultivate—with only minimal success—for the past several weeks.

"Still, the helpless, incarcerated masses cannot help but be appreciated for whatever they receive and by whatever means."

He leapt back playfully just as Zack reemerged from the shack with his head titled slightly downward to avoid a potentially nasty head-wound from the relatively low bridge entrance/exit.

"Damn, Hawk, you come up with that little jewel yourself or you been boning up on classic poetry again?"

Hawkins snickered as Zack trudged away, kicking up large clumps of sand in his wake with boots roughly twice the size as that of his petite partner.

"Monotony and the accompanying boredom does strange, frightening things to a man's mind, Doc. You find...new interests to fill the void. New horizons upon which to explore and find contentment."

To that, Liza cocked her head slightly to the left while elevating the Taser's aim to his upper midsection.

An 'XREP,' they'd explained during the initial brief upon his assignment some six months earlier, meaning *Extended Range Electro-Muscular Projectile*, a state-of-the-art wireless electro-shock projectile capable of either temporary nervous system paralysis or, at its highest setting, permanent neurological damage. From slight discomfort and full recovery to excruciating, inhuman anguish and twitching veggie, all depending on the desired setting and at the simple twist of a gauge no bigger than a digital watch-hand.

"I'm thinking a man who makes his living in your particular...specialty has little choice but to seek out those New Horizons, Slick. Not much choice really, unless you're able to track and eradicate the occasional sand-crab or sea-gull."

Tucking his hands at the pit of his back, he bowed just slightly.

"As usual, Officer G, I find your blunt honesty, however cruel, so wonderfully refreshing. Tell me, is this a character trait shared by the majority of your countrymen...and women?"

"I'd say about as common as sincere humility among mass murderers," she countered, tapping a forefinger to her right temple.

"Ouch. To that I can only say...touché. At this juncture it might be wise that we change the subject, least this strange arousal I feel mutates to a most...uncomfortable nature."

"Whatever blows your shorts," she replied without a semblance of humor, the Taser's stunted barrel making a beeline at the center of his slightly sun-burnt forehead. Crossing slim yet astonishingly ripped arms over an equally chiseled chest, Hawkins backed up several steps and leaned against a front wall.

"Um, are you able to recall any specific items from this month's inventory list?"

She used her free hand to reach up and scratch beneath the bill of her corporation-issued baseball cap, her dark brown eyes briefly scanning dark blue, utterly cloudless skies.

"Can't say I saw anything out of the norm. Usual toiletries, canned goods, bottled water, laundry supplies, daily supplements. Expecting something off the grid, were we?"

Shuffling his sandaled feet from side to side, his warped grin was laced with mischief.

"Well, if you'll recall, I did put in a request for some updated…um, entertainment items."

"You know porn's considered contraband, Hawk," Zack bellowed in the near distance, soon to swim into view and chugging slowly past his stoic spouse with an overstuffed duffel tossed over one bulky shoulder. As he rumbled past and through the opened door, Hawkins shot him a two-fingered salute before running splayed fingers through a thick wavy coif streaked in gray.

"Oh, so very sad. Yet another out of work Jester marooned thousands of miles from the nearest comedy club. Doc, you know very well of the items to which I refer."

Her aim unwavering, Liza side-stepped over several feet so as to acquire a more centered view of the hut's miniscule opening.

"Needless to say, the *cutlery* and/or *hammering tool* ban is still intact."

Showing the back of both hands, Hawkins stretched out the fingers of each and slowly flexed.

"That in mind, is a nail check in order? The toes have, admittedly, been a bit harder to keep gnawed down. As far as hardships go, I'd say being forced to cut meat with a plastic fork has become quite annoying."

Upon hearing the female officer's pained groan, he twisted about just in time to catch the conclusion of comically animated eye-roll.

"Master Officer Gorman, do us both a favor and appease Shakespeare here before he breaks out into medieval song."

Zack emerged a few seconds later, his breathing slightly labored but quickly stabilizing.

"Requested Blu-Rays present and accounted for, Hawk, as are the assorted CDs. That is, save one."

Hawkins cocked a brow, careful to maintain the required five foot minimum distance between himself and his assigned provider.

"That particular Pink Floyd disc had to be specially ordered. Next time for sure."

This time it was Hawkins whose eyes spun briefly upward, his lip puffed out in obvious disappointment.

"Ah, I was so looking forward to reacquainting myself with the haunting sounds of Roger and the boys, pre *The Wall* fame. Oh well, it isn't as if time is of the essence."

The larger man shrugged good-naturedly, flashing his spouse a tight-lipped smile.

"We thought about substituting some Jimmy Buffett, but reconsidered it as…well, inappropriate, considering the surroundings."

To this, Hawkins clamped the fingers of his left hand across his forehead and nodded, unable to fight off a silly grin of his own.

"Amazing. The hulking screw can yank a knee-slapping funny right from thin air. Again, such a waste of a natural-born talent. Of course, it goes without saying I'm thankful, truly thankful for the Discs."

As if to purposely shatter the sudden levity, Liza stepped forward with the Taser's aim once again leveled at his groin.

"What's with all the documentaries, Chief?" she inquired sourly as her professional superior and private partner rejoined her atop the soggy beachhead. "I mean, all that Kent Barnes' shit. Why bother smarting up at this point in the game? Seems a little pointless."

Hawkins openly winced, his eyes darting briefly to her superior, who in turn locked eyes with the sand-spattered tips of his own steel-toed boots.

"Um, that's Ken Burns, actually. And, well, smarting up? Pray tell, so rumor had it that upon capture and subsequent conviction and sentencing I wasn't the sharpest tack in the bag?"

"No such scuttlebutt I was privy too," Zack offered casually with palms out.

"Not labeling you an imbecile," Liza continued unabated, stone-faced and void any trace of good humor, "no doubt you possess a high level of skill and cleverness to have plotted and successfully executed such an impressive run of dastardly behavior."

Zack leaned in as if to whisper but was easily overheard in the relative quiet.

"Enough with the needle already. It's already past ten in the AM and we're running half an hour late for the next drop as it is."

"No offense taken, big fella. I understand your partner's …lack of fondness in being forced to assist one of my questionable ilk," Hawkins said, twirling both sides of his stash as if in direct response to the 'dastardly' reference.

"In all honesty, I've always been a student of historical fiction, no matter the media source. Despite an obvious lack of opportunity to swap opinions within say…a live or even on-line group discussion, I feel it mandatory to stay informed in matters of man's past mistakes and successes. Might sound strange considering the circumstances, but then, normalcy is a term with which I am no longer acquainted."

"Uh-huh, just your ordinary, average history nerd. Let me guess…" she concluded with a stern nod while holstering the Taser, "…your favorite historical references involve men named Wilkes-Booth, Oswald, Hinckley, Chapman. Role models, one and all, yes?"

"Really, Z, that'll *do*," Zack grumbled, applying a light tap to her left shoulder as he side-stepped by.

"Go warm up the beast and I'll join you momentarily."

"Yes, *master,*" she scowled, "pardon me all to hell and back for *oh-fend-ing* the inmate."

Just before she'd twisted about in a textbook about-face and trudged double-time toward the waiting lagoon, Hawkins had flashed a mock salute her way that went completely ignored.

"Pleasure to jaw with you too, Junior Officer Gorman!" he bellowed, both eyes temporarily glued to her shapely rear. It wasn't until he'd refocused on her substantially more intimidating better-half that the potential dangers of such an ill-timed ogling struck home.

"Um, Hawk, there is…one more thing," Zack half-whispered, seemingly oblivious to said infraction.

"Do tell, Doc?" Hawkins' grimaced, "not another of those pesky shakedowns? I swear to all that's holy, that I have not attempted to sharpen a single seashell or palm frond into a lethal, cutting edge instru—"

"Relax. Just a heads up…typhoon season is heating up and according to both short and long range forecasts, it's gonna be a record-breaker in both quantity and quality. That in mind, your gennie battery is still fully charged, but I left you a spare just in case. This bad boy…" he paused to whack a bare palm against a section of the hut's smooth, stone surface, "…is fortified for the mother of all 'canes, but just in case our next scheduled drop is delayed a few days, don't let it shake you. It's rare, but it does happen."

Hawkins replied while scanning the mostly blue skies, as if expecting an impending, instant mutation of said condition.

"Appreciate the concern, truly. Old city boy like me isn't accustomed to such phenomenon. As it is, this damned heat and humidity is still kicking my can on a daily basis."

Wincing, he nodded weakly toward the rear of the hut.

"Been forced to wait 'til sundown to sock the ol' hard bag, hardly leaving time for a suitable workout except on those rare nights when moonbeams reflecting off the sea provide adequate light. Oh, speaking of the gym set-up, my appreciation cannot be understated."

"No sweat, no pun intended. I noticed that permanent ravine you've dig around the island on those daily jogs."

"Indeed. The pedometer reading is up to ten point five miles per day and expanding. Oh, speaking of that magical little gizmo, please pass on my thanks to the powers that be."

"Duly noted, Hawk. Well, all right then, we're good for another calendar month. Sorry about the lack of info, legality-wise. Maybe next time."

"Not a prob, Doc. The wheels of justice turn ever-so-slowly and all that happy horseshit."

"You know it. Like scaling Pike's Peak on a trike with slashed tires."

Zack moved forward, his right hand briefly offered in parting gesture before snapping back to his side just as quickly.

"Take care. I know this....I can't imagine how such isolation can...what it can do to a man's state of mind... "

Perpetrating a serious breach of protocol, Hawkins stepped up, closing the gap between the two to reaching distance.

"I know you disapprove of my...methods, Zack, but, just between you and me, does...did my reasoning at least strike a positive cord?"

"I...don't...that is, um..."

"I've seen it in your eyes. Read it in your behavior. Night and day from your partner's, I've noted. Asian accent aside, her harsh words speak volumes. The woman does not take kindly of yours truly or those she categorizes as my ilk, no matter how noble the agenda."

"With Z...with Liza, it wasn't the agenda, but that...one major, grievous error tied to its final target. That is, the final target only because you were apprehended soon after."

Hawkins lowered his head, his next words delivered in a throaty whisper laced with regret; the pained mutterings of one who has ingested the ultimate sin for all of eternity without a shred of hope for possible extraction.

"Believe it: I live with that…tragedy every day, minute and moment of my existence. The guilt never…ever subsides."

"Hawk, I wasn't questioning…"

"If only I'd known, Doc. She…the girl was almost…feral. I had no time but do anything but react. I've relived it a million times in my mind through the years, and tried with all my might to forgive myself even as all the critics and society as a whole never would. Despite some weak moments when it just doesn't fly, I've mostly succeeded. It was…unavoidable. I know this to be true. Deep down in whatever tiny fragment of a soul I might still possess, of this much I *am* certain."

A brief silence ensued, during which time the two men locked eyes and exchanged a nod defined of mutual respect.

"I read…studied the file long ago, Hawk. No need to sell me."

Tate Hawkins' sad, shaky attempt at a smile was the ultimate frown turned upside down.

"I do appreciate it. And, speaking of said file, one clarification."

In lieu of a verbal reply, Zack cocked a brow.

"The authorities didn't so much apprehend me, but graciously accepted my willful surrender."

"I thought as much."

"After that debacle, that horrendous miscalculation, I found…well, I had no more malice to exorcise. It was an apt time to go quietly."

Yet another brief respite, eventually broken as Hawkins cleared his throat and resumed.

"Sincere apologies if I've misunderstood, but other than…that *other* set of skills I've honed through the years, developing a keen sense of where people stand on my actions has proved fairly accurate."

Alternating troubled glances from the waiting lagoon, where his spouse casually boarded their assigned ride, back to the man he was paid to both serve and incarcerate, Zack swallowed hard, as if fearing the prying ears of some covert, invisible presence.

"I'm a law enforcement officer above all else, sworn to uphold the written law. Therefore I can't...am unable to support such extreme meas—the *acts* you perpetrated in the name of justice."

Hawkins cocked a brow in obvious bemusement.

"As far as I know, my bodily crevices possess nary a single hidden recording device. Sincerely, it's just you and me, Doc."

In response, Gorman's perpetually buff, naturally stiffened frame deflated—his shoulders slumping, his normally jutting jaw dipping an iota, almost to the point of mimicking a semi-relaxed state.

"You didn't let me finish. Professional ethics aside, I was one of your biggest fans."

Hawkins' face instantly reddened a shade as he was temporarily forced to break eye contact. For want of reengaging the previous stare-down, he instead rechecked the deep blue heavens, the whole of which remained uneventful.

"Appreciate the candor, big guy. Proud to have proved myself correct. Just wish your partner felt the same."

"The old ball-and-chain there is, admittedly, a bit mule-headed. Just between us, it's one of the things I adore about her."

"Well, opposites do attract, they say."

"Yes indeed. She's a certified fireplug. Tough as titanium and stubborn as a blind mule. But you know, both our partnership and marriage would be boring as hell otherwise, so I don't mind a single iota. Well, maybe *one*."

"You're a lucky man."

"This I know," Zack replied after a moment's hesitation, as if contemplating the honest truth behind such an oft-uttered cliché.

"Well, someday I hope to be regaled with the tale of not only how you two came to meet and marry, but also came to make the same…rather odd career choice."

"Be my pleasure. It's definitely soap-opera worthy."

"Fascinating at the very *least*, I'm sure."

The two men nodded in near flawless synchronization as Zack turned toward the lagoon.

"Oh yeah, before I forget…" the Senior CO said without turning, "…those sleep issues you mentioned last time out. Left you a bottle of snooze-aid in the duffel, packed between the Suave hand lotion and Cool Breeze Crest. Over the counter crap, so it's mild, but it's the best I could do. Hope it helps."

"Excellent…appreciate the thought, big guy. Hey…'til next time…keep safe," Hawkins replied with a swooping wave fated to go unseen.

Two nights later, at precisely three-forty-one AM, he would stumble from the hut's economy-sized bedroom and into a similarly diminutive kitchen. Pulling a frosty bottled water from the mini-fridge, he proceeded to swallow down two of the aforementioned tablets in a single gulp. Within a half-hour of resuming a fetus-style pose atop a slightly bowed air mattress, Tate Hawkins fell into a deep, coma-like sleep and commenced to dream…deep, vividly and without diversion.

Two

Isle of the Wolf

"So what's the prognosis, Rimshaw? Is Tank-Girl there gonna survive or head off to the eternal Kingdom of Marxist Lezzies?"

As with the majority of her assigned bodyguard's baiting wisecracks, Rimshaw felt no need to respond, instead clearing her throat while tending to the slumped patient kneeling before her.

"Don't take no rocket surgeon to figure out the reason behind the big Russki's health woes."

"I think you mean rocket scientist…or perhaps brain surgeon…and she's…Miss Wolf is German, not Russian," the doctor corrected with less malice than exasperated resignation.

"Whatever. Nazis and Commies are fairly interchangeable as far as the history books see it. Scum is scum, regardless of bloodline, and it's damned obvious this here particular bottom-feeder is comin' down something fierce from a severe lack of human-growth hormone. DB's prognosis: Steroid withdrawal, plain and simple."

"Excuse me, Officer Barnes, but you're breaking my concentration. Please refrain from speak—"

"Shit. In her prime, I'd wager this big-ass dyke was probably bein' pumped with enough male hormones to supply an NFL locker room…"

"Officer Barnes, please. I need a moment here."

"…bet if you check 'neath those cut-offs, you apt to find the beginnings of some male-type plumbing takin' shape…"

"Mister Barnes, zip it please! If you must know, Miss Wolf's present condition is due to…*more than likely* due to complications from diabetes, compounded by a severe vitamin deficiency."

Dylan Barnes' mouth hung ajar, the edges of his comically bushy mustache trembling like squirming tendrils at the corners of his overly plump, slug-like lips. Before adhering to the doctor's rather sternly stated wish, he fired one final verbal folly.

"Hey, whatever you say, lady. Careful she don't lean up and take a chaw outta your chin. Chick might not be feeling a full bowl of oats, but guaranteed she's still one horny red devil after four months on this burg. Your age differences aside, I'm betting in her mind you're the next best thing to a Victoria's Secret model."

"Please leave us now, Officer Barnes. I can take it from here."

With that, he stormed from the hut's cramped living room and out the open entrance. Cut from the same sanitary mold as the similarly constructed hut designs, Bertha Wolf's assigned abode was the ultimate in generic living, due mostly to its inhabitant's lack of effort and/or interest in upgrading its ultra-bland interior. This, despite being allowed a surprisingly lengthy list of choices with which to decorate and create a sense of 'hominess.' Unlike several other, similarly housed individuals, Wolf apparently had no interest in establishing a sense of normalcy, either from a residential or behavioral standpoint. Hostile and uncooperative with staff from minute one, supply requests had been of the minimal sort; basically just the bare essentials required to survive.

"Just yell if ya want me..." came the muffled reply, "...or *scream bloody murder*, dependin' on the severity of the need."

Barnes shambled off the structure's narrow stone porch into the wet sand, patting the outer shell of his Taser's holster with the side of a clenched fist. Pure Texan to the bone in both attitude and drawl—to describe the man as merely stocky was the ultimate in understatements—his arms, chest and thighs shared a rock-solid thickness that was only partially offset by a pot gut of considerable girth. Glaring in the general direction of his assigned cutter, its glistening, dark blue bow barely visible floating between the sporadic partings of waist-high Laua'e ferns, his nostrils flared at the foul scent permeating from his own pores.

It's your own damn fault, bucket-mouth. Midwest sector is too damn cold, I bitched. Volunteer for duty in the tropics, I moaned. It'll be a new beginning, I spouted...a new challenge...new thrills. Break you outta your rut. Hell, if nothin' else, at least you won't spend ten months outta the year freezin' your gonads off.

A sudden gust temporarily drowned out not only his own muffled rant, but the doctor's sporadic mumblings. Though he seriously doubted any type of violent reaction forthcoming, he nonetheless closed the gap between himself and the open entrance with two swiftly-executed back-steps.

True enough...one outta three ain't too shabby, I reckon. From ice-crack, Wyoming straight into the fuckin' volcano belt as the aforementioned gonads shrink away in a never-ending pool of sweat.

Spewing forth an exasperated sigh, Barnes turned an ear toward the door and grimaced at the doctor's overly-sympathetic, cooing tone.

"Bertha...Miss Wolf, how's your breathing? Does...is the tightening *here*," Rimshaw said, pointing at her own breastbone with an emptied syringe while speaking deliberately as if addressing a small child, "is it...better now? Are you...can you catch your breath?"

The large woman sprawled before her hissed between bared teeth, her eyelids fluttering repeatedly without fully opening. Her buzz-cut matted in sweat, she was decked out in cut-offs and a skin-tight halter, the latter straining mightily to detain thick rolls of muscle and flab at her midsection and lower back. Her arms, thighs and calves held a similar shape and thickness, almost eerily so—as if as weirdly interchangeable as any Transformer figurine. The skin of her exposed face, neck, arms and legs went beyond merely pale—it was as if she wore a pasty cloak doused in cooking flour.

"It's...you'll be fine. Just breathe normally. Your airways are slowly opening and your pulse rate is normalizing as the insulin takes effect."

A tiny, slim-framed woman just past her sixtieth birthday, Charlotte Rimshaw had spent over thirty years on the government payroll, plying her trade at four of the U.S's most notorious federal prisons. Following the sudden passing of her husband of a heart attack a year previous, she'd come out of retirement if for no other reason than to occupy a portion of what had become an overabundance of free time.

"How's it goin' in there, Doc?" she heard Barnes bellow and flinched at its abruptness. "Is Fraulein Tank-Girl snappin' to or what? If not, I'll need to call in a life-flight."

She stood with knees popping.

"She's showing rapid improvement. Just needs to stabilize."

"Need a hand?"

"Um, yes, as a matter of fact. We need to move her to a softer resting space. Her bed perhaps."

His Taser drawn, Barnes stomped back in wearing a scowl.

"You won't be needing that, Officer. At this point, she's quite helpless."

Barnes eyed the patient with a cocked brow as Rimshaw tucked the used syringe into a small black purse.

"Hate to doubt your professionalism, Doc, but I'm of the belief that this one has never known a state of complete helplessness."

22

"I've read her file. Take my word that at this time she isn't capable of anything other than the involuntary release of bodily gases."

Having kneeled over and dug spindly yet sturdy arms beneath the trembling woman's shoulders. Rimshaw peered up toward her assigned guard through narrow slits.

"Officer Barnes, I cannot lift her on my own. I *could* try, but then you'd have two patients on your hands."

"Well, goes without sayin' this is against my better judgment," Barnes sighed, holstering the Taser, "but then, that's always been questionable at best. Alright then, but if we're gonna do the transport thing, I'm thinkin' I'd better be on the upper torso end, just in case the Dyke-Devil here comes to with a hankerin' to snap some federally-employed bones."

Rimshaw groaned while standing stiffly and side-stepping Barnes, her tiny, pug-like nose crinkled as if detecting a foul odor.

"Officer Barnes, please cease and desist with the homophobic slurs. I find them most troubling, not to mention *asinine* considering the present century."

"Point of order, Doc," he replied curtly, bending down to mimic her previous position. "I ain't the least bit *scared* of *her* kind, just thoroughly disgusted."

"Jurassic-period thinking duly noted. Let us commence then to relocate…*her* kind to the bedroom."

Just as Barnes leaned forward with upturned, splayed fingers to acquire a suitable grip beneath the patient's armpits, the woman's eyes flew open, wide and aware.

"*Verpiss dich*!" she howled, whitish foam spewing forth from between bared teeth, "*Fick dich*! *Fick dich*!"

"Jesus… she was playin' possum!" Barnes shrieked, jerking his hands free. "Back off, Doc! Back the hell off!"

The woman lunged in reverse, using the back of her skull as a battering ram and connecting with a resounding crunch, sending him pin-wheeling back with blood-soaked hands cupping his mangled nose.

23

Back-peddling, Rimshaw's left sneaker caught the edge of the black purse and tossed it onto its side, scattering its contents in all directions.

"*Assen Sie gehen von mir, Schwein!*" the larger woman bellowed, rising to her feet in a clumsy lurch before striking a classic defensive pose with feet spread wide and forearms crossed eye-level to ward off potential blows.

Barnes gargled, coughed and spat a deluge of dark maroon while rolling onto his right side and away from her in order to free the pinned Taser from its holster. The woman stormed toward him, looming overhead in a red-faced rage as the volume of her rant intensified.

"*Sie denken, dass ich das leicht begrenzt werde? Sie? Übertrieben selbstbewusster Sohn eines Weibchens!*"

Blinking madly through a haze of his own nasal spatter and his attacker's descending spittle, Barnes palmed the weapon while attempting to combat-roll to a semi-standing position. He'd barely managed to prop onto one knee and whip the Taser up and around before being pummeled as if mule-kicked, the trauma at his breast-bone immediately voiding his lungs of air. A split-second before impact, peering through drenched eyelids that threatened to stick shut, he'd been able to visualize the prominent backside, as if in flight mode. In retrospect, while pin-balling into the nearest wall and subsequently landing face-first sans the lost Taser, fuzzy logic dictated he'd been on the receiving end of a perfectly executed reverse kick, the big German's heel having supplied the proverbial hammer to his nail.

Gasping in a desperate attempt to regain the power to regulate oxygen, Barnes faded in and out of consciousness and thus was aware of only fragmented segments of surrounding sounds and movement. The German's intelligible spiel had apparently continued unabated even as badly blurred, perhaps even dramatically altered imagery revealed her leaning over the doctor's still, prone form. Barnes managed to roll onto his left side just as an initial rush of air successfully replenished a severely drained power supply. Using a

24

shirt-sleeve to clear semi-coagulated build-up from each eye, his initial visual confirmed those earlier, excessively bleary scenes, with one noted, rather grisly exception.

Less than three feet to his right, the German did indeed loom over Rimshaw's upper torso, her tucked knees pinning the doctor's scrawny chest to the floor, and although Barnes couldn't quite make out specifics due to both an awkward angle and less-than-perfect vision, it appeared as though the patient was, inexplicably, treating the physician. Even as she rocked gently to and fro atop Rimshaw's petite frame, her tone did not lose its bitter, angry edge.

"Sie sehen? Ich, werde ja nicht so leicht ausgerottet? Sehen Sie? Nein, ich denke nicht! Ich denke, dass Sie sehen, dass Tage, Schwein zu Ende sind!"

Barnes could only deduce she'd dismissed him as incapacitated and, upon scanning his surroundings, spotted the Taser leaning barrel-up against the same wall he'd previously used as a pinball machine flipper. Moving as deliberately—as stealth-like—as his battered condition would allow, he first rolled onto his back in hopes of completing a slow-motion spin that would bring him to within reaching distance of the weapon's blunt handle. Before he could complete the slow-motion roll, he heard yet another rage-fueled folly spew forth, the clarity of which left little doubt as to whom it was aimed.

"Oh, du bist nicht so leicht geschickt, nicht wahr? Nun, seien Sie versichert, Dämon...Ich bring dich so oft wie notwendig ist. Weißt du, meine Spezialität ist, ebenso wie Ihre eigenen..."

He finished the maneuver, gripping the Taser in a slick, sticky palm, at the sound of bounding footsteps, a veritable stampede, that jarred the floor beneath his sprawled frame like pre-quake tremors.

"Sterben Sie wieder, Dämon! Immer wieder sterben!" her voice shrieked so close he could practically smell her rancid breath, like aged cabbage and soured meat on the verge of turning. Flinching in anticipation of an impending blow, Barnes curled into a fetal position

with his eyes firmly clamped and the Taser held up and out like a protective cross. Once unclamped, several mysteries were solved within the perimeters of a single vision; not only why he'd heard and felt what had sounded like multiple sets of trampling feet, but more importantly by far, why he hadn't yet been fatally bludgeoned or at the very least, permanently crippled.

Though Bertha Wolf was far from petite in stature, the man who had essentially pinned her to a far wall practically engulfed her squirming form, having hoisted her airborne in a frontal bear-hug and planting her back against the cool, smooth stone.

"Break off, I've got her!" a piercing female voice, vague Asian accent intact, shrieked from just outside the hut entrance, a voice laced in a cool desperation, obviously frightened but not necessarily shaken to incapacity by said fear.

"Shove away, Zack! Break contact, damn it!"

As if somewhat hesitant to do so, the big man held firm for several ticks more before lunging back and immediately thrusting forward, executing a vicious combination chest-bump, double-arm shove.

Left grasping at thin air, Wolf flailed back with all four limbs, levitating as if experiencing zero gravity. With ample force to induce unconsciousness in the average *Homo sapien*, she thumped the wall with her upper back, bounding forward with equal momentum and directly toward the one responsible for her present trek. Mouth agape and foaming at the corners, wild, darting eyes pulled wide, arms held straight out in sleepwalker-mode and fingers curled like claws, Wolf drew to within reaching distance of her target before being instantaneously stood up and halted in her tracks as if impacting a field of impenetrable force. Crumping downward not all at once but in delayed segments, her arms went limp as both eyes rolled upward to show only the blood-streaked whites.

"Bingo," Zack Gorman huffed, taking a single, fluid step forward with his right arm cocked, "nice shot, Z. Now, just for safety's sake…allow me the *coup de grace*."

The arm shot down in a blur, accompanied by a faint electrical buzz, much like a downed wire sizzling atop moist pavement. As Wolf's upper torso had begun its inevitable descent at that precise moment, the blow's impact was minimized somewhat, though in landing at the upper portion of her skull, it did serve to flip her in cartwheel fashion onto her back. Upon making impact, the woman's lungs audibly emptied in a resounding huff—the milky whites of her eyes glowing like twin strobes—the tip of her tongue wedged securely between clamped teeth, having secreted a dime-sized bead that hung suspended in place like a crimson-shaded teardrop.

From there, it took less than a minute for the senior correctional officer to sheath his baton, remove a pair of carbon-steel, double-lock cuffs from the same utility belt, roll nearly one-hundred seventy-five pounds of dead weight onto her stomach and secure said restraints.

Procedure complete, he literally leapt up and backed away as if to QA his own handiwork.

"Shit, that electro-club action really necessary, big 'un?" Liza inquired, stepping gingerly into the hut's only semi-lit interior with the wireless Taser still draw and aimed, its squared barrel emitting a single, thin tendril of smoke. "The setting reads incapacitate for a reason. Overkill, anyone?"

"Tell you what," her partner retorted gruffly, having already discarded their comatose, well-secured target for the splayed form a few feet to their right, "stride on over here and check out this train-wreck and *then* bark to me about overkill."

Puffing a loose strand of hair from her line of sight, Liza glanced briefly toward Barnes, whose comically befuddled expression remained frozen in place while he was obviously still attempting to process the scene.

"You still alive and kicking over there, Barnes?"

"Ugh…y-yeah…where the h-hell did y….when you…did you guys get h-here?"

"Parked our ride next to yours less than three minutes ago. Regularly scheduled supply drop. Second of three on this fine, sun-drenched day, I'm told. Solid timing, right?" the senior officer answered, side-stepping over as to allow his spouse an eyeful at the opposite side of the room. In doing so, he accidentally kicked away several items of as-of-yet-unidentified medical paraphernalia.

"Fuckin' A, b-boss. Ugh, watch your st-step. Rimshaw's little b-black b-bag was the f-first casualty."

Zack treaded extra cautiously, gently shoving aside a wrapped package of gauze with the glistening toe of his left boot.

"I can see that. I keep stomping on the evidence. So tell me, how'd you end up with sentry duty? I thought Jimmy Weems was on shift."

"E-emergency leave. Wife's 'bout to pop…a-again."

Having holstered her Taser, Liza stooped down on one knee before openly gasping.

"Oh Jesus…who….is that… Rimshaw?"

Zack shrugged, snorting sourly.

"Took me a hard stare or two to make the ID, but yeah, it…was. Obviously past the saving stage."

Lying on her back with all four appendages splayed out as if to construct a snow angel, the semi-retired caregiver had long ceased breathing—not the least bit surprising considering the extent of the facial traumas on display. Her lower jaw had been crushed downward with such force it appeared partially unhinged, hanging askew and tucked snugly between the base of her neck and her upper chest. Several bloodied, broken teeth had been dislodged and lay scattered about her frail torso. Still, in terms of raw, unfiltered grisliness, such horrid mutilation couldn't hold a candle to the condition of her eyes, the pupils of each pierced with multiple syringes, the narrow, rounded plungers still protruding outward like grotesque flag markers.

Zack Gorman regarded the carnage one final time before spinning around on a heel, the pained grimace he wore a mask of exasperation.

"Talk to me, Barnes. What could possibly perpetrate such a thoroughly FUBARed scenario?"

Clearing his throat, Dylan Barnes struggled to stand upright, eventually able to prop himself against the room's long standing piece of furniture, that being a high-back wooden chair that squeaked its disapproval.

"Nobody m-more surprised th-than yours truly, boss," he croaked—so ragged and hoarse the tone it actually served to soften the extreme southern drawl—picking crusted specs of semi-dried fluids from each bloated nostril. "Atlantis re-received the EMA at oh-seven-sixteen. With Doc Jarvis on leave, Rimshaw t-there was…drew the duty as on-call sawbones. W-we popped outta the shoot at ar-around oh-eight-oh—"

His superior nodded, raising a hand palms-out.

"Didn't ask for a detailed write-up, Dylan. Rest assured, that request will come soon enough. How about fast-forwarding to explain the hockey game that broke out just before Liza and I arrived rink-side?"

"Oh…g-got'cha, b-boss," Barnes replied, scooting forward with a pronounced limp and sitting gingerly in the same chair that had previously doubled as his cane. "You gotta…give me a sec here to…reboot the ol' memory bank. Damn Nazi rug-muncher over th-there rung my bell but g-good."

Cocking a brow, the big man sneered even as, out of the corner of his right eye, he watched his partner rise silently and depart the hut in a stiff, purposeful gait.

"By all means, take your time. Gather your thoughts. Get your story straight."

Barnes regarded him with a severely creased brow, as if he were being addressed in a foreign dialect.

"Boss?"

Arms crossed defiantly, Zack backed up a step and a half, just enough to allow a clear visual to the sunlit beachhead, where Liza had already covered roughly half the distance to the waiting cutter.

"I'm just saying, those Incident Review Board boys are quite the sticklers even in the most routine cases. Toss in a staff fatality and we're talking full-blown, leave no pubic-hair unturned investigation, so I'd suggest you organize those blurry recollections to as close to perfect as you can get 'em. By the way, before you punch the rewind button, allow me a single query?"

Having unbuttoned the top three buttons of his dark gray uniform shirt to reveal a light brown protective vest beneath, Barnes' response was a weary expression of utter befuddlement, a look that was fast becoming commonplace.

"Where is your shock baton?"

Befuddlement instantly transformed, via drooping shoulders and broken eye-contact, into an expression wrought with guilt.

"Well, um…circumstances didn't…ugh…dictate the necessity..." he stammered, "...I mean, it *was* an EMA, and considerin' the...her vital readings, I didn't give armorin' up a second thought—"

As a precursor to verbally intervening, Zack Gorman cleared his throat nosily.

"Officer Barnes, do I really have to remind *you*, a corrections veteran of what, ten, twelve years? UNC regs dictate proper armament, no matter the situation, before ever taking that initial step onto restricted grounds, or in this particular case, the moistened sand."

"Zack…*boss*…first-shift chip readers reported her BP at sixty-five over forty-two and a pulse rate of fifty-one and falling. Chick didn't have the energy to pass gas by the time we pulled in. Found her sacked out here on the living room floor in a puddle of her own slobber."

Leaning forward with clenched hands tucked at his lower back, Zack nodded solemnly before shooting his subordinate a playful wink.

"Regs are regs, and you know as well as I that the board has 'em all memorized down to page number, paragraph and table. I would strongly advise that you *misremember* that little gem, if you catch my drift-a-rino."

30

Barnes nodded, nervously gnawing into his own mustache with bared lower teeth.

"Loud and crystal clear, boss, will do."

"And Dylan?"

"Yeah?"

"Do yourself a favor and trim that damn lip-caterpillar waaay back before the board convenes, yes?"

"Affirmative, boss...and...uh, I appreciate the well, that *other* advice."

Like a man twenty-plus years his senior, Barnes arose with Herculean effort.

"I mean, took me three years to secure this promotion. Much as I've grown to despise this damnable heat and humidity, I'd sure as hell hate to lose it on a technicality that wouldn't have mattered for beans anyhow."

"Forget it. By the way, any idea what Wolf was babbling about while she was wailing on you?"

Stepping gingerly forward—and obviously favoring his left hip and knee—Barnes reached to gently scrub beneath his federally-issued, dark-green ball-cap with the letters UNCA stenciled in black.

"Not as fluent as I should be, boss. Only thing I made out were the curse words, plentiful as they were."

Gorman leaned back and stared out the entranceway just in time to spot his spouse dismount the cutter and beginning a deliberate trudge back toward the hut.

"Caught a few of the more prominent profanities myself, but I also heard her blurt something about...devils or demons and not being so easily killed off by...their kind."

"Psychotic r-ramblings, boss. Nasty dyke was off in her own alternate universe for sure. Probably some Nazi-Germany wet dream where she was fightin' off Beelzebub for Papa Hitler's soul. Either that or she's been cultivatin' some seriously stout wacky weed somewhere on this sandy burg."

"I'd wager on something similar to the former, that is unless she's found a way to cop a buzz from snorting ground seashells," Gorman snickered. "As far as alternate motivations, you can never rule out an escape attempt."

"Ya-you think, boss? I mean, if that's the case I figure we're back to square one, that bein' the psychotic element. Why else would any of 'em risk climbin' aboard one of our rigs and bein' vaporized for the effort?"

The big man shrugged, shuffling his size thirteen boots leisurely from side to side until their highly glossed, sand-coated heels clicked.

"They...she might risk it for want of having nothing to lose. Hey..." he paused, raising a gloved finger airborne, "...Jerome Kirby, remember? Safe bet Riggins and Palmeroy weren't expecting that initial lunge—off-balance, wide-eyed with shock—no time to react 'til it was too little, too damn late."

Barnes nodded wordlessly, his complexion pasty—ghostly pale.

Kirby, a former low-rent pro grappler and mob muscle for hire with a talent for eradicating city officials and one of the sector's initial assignees, had used the element of surprise to murder both officers during a routine supply drop. Coroner's reports stated Riggins, the junior officer of the two, had died instantly from a broken neck, while Palmeroy hadn't been nearly as fortunate. Injuries were multiple and varied in severity—as in twenty-eight broken bones (mostly the feet and hands), a ruptured spleen, punctured lung and, second runner up for worst of the lot, an extracted eye (left) and several teeth said to have been removed by homemade pliers forged from metal tubing pulled from beneath the hut's bathroom sink and screws from the kitchen cabinet. All minor in comparison, one might logically deduce, to having one's left hand sawed off at the wrist with a clam shell.

"Little shock, given the Spanish Inquisition treatment, that Palmeroy had eventually revealed the bridge password sometime before Kirby had finished him off. Six numbers, two letters, two symbols."

"Yeah, but still...the last laugh was on him," Barnes said , his head bowed wearily, as if far too heavy to hold upright. "I mean, no way Palmeroy spilled about that main failsafe, right? If so, why would the crazy bastard have taken the risk?"

"I do believe we're back to the aforementioned nothing to lose scenario, DB."

"Oh yeah...there is that. Still, ya think he had a clue that stickin' that dead piece of meat against the palm reader was only half the equation or just didn't give a shit?"

"Reasonable enough to assume, considering the work it took to slice that hand free, that Jerome Kirby had no clue the reader required live flesh to authenticate, much less voice recognition to complete the deal. Otherwise, he would've kept Palmeroy alive long enough to drag 'im aboard and attempt to force the required ID scan."

Barnes raised his head just enough to shake it weakly from side to side.

"I heard there wasn't enough left of that rig to scrape on toast. Blew like a tin can full of nitro."

"Coroner's report listed the source of Kirby's ID as teeth fragments and assorted skin tags," Zack countered, leaning back with ankles crossed and his chin resting atop a clenched fist. "As for the cutter, *Black Swan* I think she'd been called, I heard the remains could've fit on a tablespoon."

"So, ya think she...the big lezzie there...was planning on a similar move? As in, yours truly beaten to a juicy pulp and missin' an appendage or two?"

"Hard to say, DB. We'll know more once she's been properly poked and probed. Personally, I'm still leaning toward some sort of temporary psychosis caused by a lack of proper meds. Regardless, count your blessings. I'd even consider taking up religion if you haven't already. The big guy upstairs was *definitely* looking out for your gnarly hide."

With that, each man sucked air greedily and exhaled in similarly fatigued fashion, the relatively short silence broken by Gorman's comically incensed intonation.

"Dylan, if you don't mind, one last tidbit of advice…"

Grinning sheepishly, his mustache and lower jaw still painted in specs of maroon, Barnes hung his head in mock shame.

"Oh, h-hell…"

"…bone up on the languages. *All* that apply to every regional sector, in case you're called upon for temporary duty outside your normal assignments…much like today. It is, after all, part of the job description, remember?"

"Yes, sir. I've been slackin' since my normal sector is mostly of the native tongue. Rest assured I'll be hittin' the books at first opp."

Gradually making his way toward that wonderfully illuminated opening like some crippled, nocturnal beast searching for a precious life-source of light from the bowels of a dark, dank cave, Barnes' mouth hung agape, his breathing raspy and strained. Just as he stepped near his superior's personal space, he stumbled forward and avoided taking a full header only via Gorman's reaching over to clasp each of his trembling shoulders.

"Steady as she goes. Just take it easy. Med chopper's on its way. Probably need to check you for a concussion."

Seconds later, he practically carried the smaller man outside and sat him on the edge of the hut's squared porch.

"Thanks, b-boss. For once, I just f-feel like I need some sun."

Zack applied a soft tap to his shoulder just as Liza approached, removing her wraparound Raybans in order to better wipe away a build-up of perspiration beneath. Though not yet noon, the building heat and humidity were nothing short of stifling.

"Medvac three is airborne. ETA is two, three minutes," she said wearily, "pulling double-duty as body-bag detail, as I understand it. Must be the cut-backs."

Her husband shrugged, reattaching his own pair of comically oversized sun-blockers.

"Payroll cuts, for sure. Not to mention less fuel to bankroll. Times we live in, Z."

"Whatever. Then they shouldn't be shocked when things go to shit on occasion—much like today. We out of here as soon as they dock, big 'un?"

"We'll call into HQ to confirm, but I wouldn't see why not. As of now, we're only five, six minutes off schedule."

Leaning down with an elbow propped on a bent kneecap, Liza eyed Barnes' curiously.

"You hanging in there, Barnes? I haven't seen you look this piqued since we found you drowning in a pool of your own colon acids at the New Year's Eve bash."

To that, Barnes could manage only the weakest of shrugs, accompanied by an equally pathetic smile.

"Boss, that better half of yours is a real card. Must keep you in constant s-stitches."

He then pointed a visibly shaking thumb toward the hut entrance at his back.

"So, Zack…they gonna haul the crazy kraut's ass back to HQ?"

"Affirmative. They'll schedule a full battery of physical tests, not to mention a little face time with Dean Graham to attempt a resetting of loose screws. Couch-time is mandatory whenever staff assault is involved. Needless to say, staff homicide qualifies as such."

Dylan Barnes laughed aloud, a pained, croaking giggle that induced an involuntary wince from the Junior Officer Gorman.

"Yep, figured as much. Ol' Doc Mind-screws will send 'er back more messed up than ever…if that's possible. Hell, with any luck he'll subscribe just enough anti-depressants for her to choke on."

"I wouldn't hee-haw too loud…" Liza chimed in, strolling listlessly past Barnes to pose at the hut entrance and stare inside as if to ensure their shackled, slumbering captive hadn't magically teleported away, "…you two might end up *sharing* couch space."

Barnes kneeled back onto his elbows with his legs splayed. He closed his eyes and, despite being fully clothed, appeared to be sunbathing. From the west came the faint whirring of an approaching chopper.

"Say w-what?"

"She's right," Zack confirmed, scanning the sky as to spot the incoming bird, "by regulation, any staff member who is a victim of assault must also sit through a few counseling sessions."

The humming grew louder just moments before a sleek, dark-blue shaded Sikorsky S-86 sailed directly overhead and past, flying low and at a surprisingly brisk clip before turning sharply and hovering just to the left of the parked cutters. It levitated forward and began a gradual descent, the cutters rocking with increased fervor in the background as a result of a sudden swell of chopper-blade windage-created waves. Despite the added roar, Dylan Barnes' exasperated response refused to go unheard.

"Ahhhh hell…this day just keeps gettin' better."

They stood elbow (Zack) to shoulder (Liza) as the EMT chopper sailed off in an easterly direction. At top speed it would reach Atlantis in just over twenty minutes—approximately ten less than it would take the cutter Proteus, also sailing atop the swirling, salty sea at full bore, to pull ashore at their current shift's third and next to last drop-off point.

As the copter faded to a pea-sized speck amid a light blue, cloudless sky, and following a check to ensure the hut's proper lockdown ('*The word is asinine'* Liza had complained, giving the lone entrance's metal nob one last, obligatory tug, *'who exactly are we expecting to burglarize the joint? Namor? Aquaman? Perhaps Charlie Freakin' Tuna?')* husband and wife correctional officers trudged slowly to the beachhead where their ride awaited.

"So as far as Barnes goes, you think he's looking at a one-way ticket back to the mainland?"

"Can't say. Depends on several factors. The man screwed up royally from a procedural stand-point. Then again, he's a hardcore vet with ten-plus years in service."

"Yowsa. Stop the presses," she exclaimed with a loud clap. "Sounds as though you're giving him a pass. Iron-Jaw Gorman? Bypassing a clear reg violation? Say it isn't so!"

"Wolf's an animal," he countered stoically, "A rep well-earned. She was...seemed incapacitated according to the medical professional on scene. Still, he entered the danger zone void of required weaponry."

"So, I'd venture to say, Iron-Jaw, that the statements we provide to the board might go a long way in deciding the fate of one Dylan Barnes, agreed?"

He nodded sternly without reply as they neared the parked cutter.

"Fascinating. You never cease to amaze, Zackary Cain Gorman. Right when I think I have your white-bread, tight-ass ways pigeon-holed, you flip the script. Unsettling as it is, I just can't help but loath ...whoops... I mean... *love* you for it."

The mandatory boarding and departure checklist was completed in a comfortable, familiar silence; the building dread of what had come to be their most trying drop-off all but forgotten in the troubling haze of what had come before.

Three

The Isle of Hyde

"You two are the definition of reliability. As usual, yours truly is left wanting for absolutely nothing. Rest assured I'll be filling out yet another positive critique on your behalves. I do hope your superiors appreciate what a pair of fine, dedicated professionals they have in you two."

"Yes, Mister Barton, um, Jed, I'm sure they do."

"How many times do I have to remind you, Officer Dorman, its J.B. to you *and* that fetching wife of yours."

He considered, ever-so-briefly, correcting him again concerning the continual butchering of his family name, the irritation level of which was compounded by the man's thick, deliberate southern drawl, but thought better of it. The skies had darkened substantially since their arrival and, after nearly a full calendar year of witnessing regular cloudbursts, Zack could predict with relative ease when a downpour was imminent.

"Yes, sir. Will do. Tell you what, you check present inventory and I'll assist my partner in hauling in the rest."

Possessing the thick, squat frame of a retired gridiron vet gone slightly to pot, the perpetually grinning man with the shoulder-length, fire-red hair streaked in gray nodded enthusiastically, submerging stubby hands—attached to grotesquely long, spindly fingers—into the last of three cardboard boxes that had been laid onto the dining room table.

"With pleasure, good sir," he barked with a level of loopy, wild-eyed joy normally associated with either the chemically dependent or clinically insane, his severely pock-marked cheeks glowing rosy red. "You just go right ahead, now. I don't want to hold you two up, no siree. I can imagine you have quite the cram-packed schedule to slog your way through."

Relived to be free of the man's sickeningly jovial company, Zack met Liza roughly halfway between the cutter and the hut amid a light sprinkle. Knowing her as he did, Zack wished he could've magically rewound his choice of an initial greeting. Still, in light of her muted ways—a true rarity no matter the situation—and the pale mask of indifference she'd donned since departing Wolf isle, he was helpless not to inquire.

"So, how you holding up?"

In light of such a direct query, her curt, tight-lipped response came as little surprise.

"Never better. Should I be otherwise?"

"Well, being that you haven't strung three words together since we pushed ou—"

Speeding up, she pushed ahead a few steps—a common practice within her vast array of emotional reactions in the face of extreme stress—a purely defensive measure defined mainly of sullen avoidance, the 'push ahead and persevere' method that he knew would eventually lead to a massive blow-up.

"Just mulling."

"Care to share?"

"The usual. Nothing new. Nothing original. Same old silly-ass retread. Such thoughts only seem to pop up whenever I eyeball a fresh, mutilated corpse."

Three wide strides saw Zack grow even.

"Oh, *that* mull. Know it well."

"Really? I have my doubts you have a blessed clue."

"Seriously? You think I've never doubted the sanity of choosing this particular line of work? Think again, Warrior Princess."

"A fleeting uncertainty, I'm sure. Patriotic, big-boned, gruff-voiced specimen like you was born to rehabilitate. Me, I'm just a meek follower in *those* colossal boot-steps. Besides, this is what, your second, maybe *third* career? At least you can draw from those memories. This demeaning monkey-shit of a job is all I know, well, other than canning tuna for five pesos an hour in that slave-shop in Cebu."

"Best damn tuna-stuffer in the biz. Don't think for a second I don't know the fortune you sacrificed in the name of love," he chided straight-faced.

"Square-jawed, flat-footed jackass that you are, what girl could possibly resist?"

As the hut neared, he reached over with a gloved, clenched paw and delivered the lightest of jabs to her left shoulder. It was easily, despite the circumstances, the lightest trading of banter between them in days, perhaps weeks.

"*Damn* but your mastery of the English language is now complete. Years in the making, but worth every penny and shred of effort."

Forced to leap clumsily away as she whipped her left leg over and out in a playful, slow-motion sweep, Zack barely avoided taking a header into a nearby patch of Marram grass.

"Just…excuse my funk for the time being. Bottle of gin, bowl full of olives and a good roll in the hay and I'll be my old cantankerous self."

"First two are easy enough…" he replied upon regaining his balance with a swooping wave of the arms and a brisk double-time march, "…can't make any promises on that 'good' portion of the third. That the gist?" he continued, nodding toward the bloated duffel propped atop her left shoulder.

"And nothing but the gist," she replied, the corners of her mouth gradually upturning to display the wryest of smiles. "Sooooo, I take it by that pale, drawn look that our biggest fan has yet to flip the MPD switch?"

With a grace and agility that belied his considerable bulk, he stepped behind her and propped the duffel's bottom-half atop his own shoulder, the drastic differences in their heights forcing her to dramatically adjust positioning or risk being hoisted airborne.

"Good as gold so far."

"Kind ol' Jed offer to brew us up some tea, did he?"

"Didn't give 'im the chance. I say we get the lead out and see if we can avoid the inevitable."

"Big boy, I second that motion. Last month it took three cleanings to get the stench of Hyde's spittle out of my shirt."

"Alters more than just his attitude. It's like his stink glands kick into overdrive. Locomotive breath could peel the copper off a rusty penny and sweat pits that reek like an open sewer."

"Ahhh yuk!," Liza winced between barely refrained giggles. "I can almost smell the love."

As if on cue, they simultaneously double-timed toward the hut, a strong sea breeze at their backs serving as a natural turbo-boost.

It took approximately a half-minute to forty-five seconds to cover the remaining sand, pull the hut entrance ajar and shuffle inside. Their respective nostrils flaring wildly, they dropped the duffel and groaned in almost perfect unison.

"Well shit, so much for avoidance," Zack whispered harshly while pulling the shock cane free from its electronically secured sheath. In turn, the younger, smaller, lower-ranking Gorman freed her Taser while instinctively sweeping the confined space.

"God, smells like peeled onions marinating in aged gym socks," came the nasal reply, the forefinger and thumb of her free hand briefly clamping her nostrils.

"Smells more like rented *pork* to me, Sunshine. Roastin' rent-a-cop whose lone skill, quite the stretch that, is collectin' whatever meager crumbs that cock-knocker Warden tosses their way."

As always, the accent modification, with origins from well below the Mason-Dixon line to its present incarnation, that being hardcore East Coast (think inner-city Boston by way of the Jersey Shore) was nothing short of jarring—perhaps even more so than the horrid stench that normally accompanied same.

As per protocol, the senior officer took point, striking a defensive posture in front of his junior partner and facing the source of the dialogue, that being in the general direction of the hut's dimly lit kitchen. With his free hand, he removed a palm-sized iPad and placed it gently atop the top shelf of an otherwise empty combination magazine/book rack. The sharp smack of billiard balls impacting precluded Zack's by-the-numbers command, delivered with minimal sincerity.

"All right, drop the cue stick and show yourself, Jessie. No time for games, be it straight or bank pool. Supply order is complete. You know the drill. We require an item check and your initials on the supply e-form."

A brief silence ensued, followed by the muffled sound of bare feet slapping tile from the adjoining playroom and finally, a squeaky fart and subsequent giggle.

"Oh, and what if I refuse, *Os-ci-pher*? What's the King Prick and Queen Cunt gonna do in the face of such blatant disrespect to their authority?"

"Not a problem, Jes," Liza spat, slapping the side of a nearby box with the open palm of her free hand, "we simply reload all the goodies and let you fend for yourself 'til next drop."

"Completely up to you," Zack chimed in, though noticeably calmer in both tone and deportment, "but from the inventory sheet I just skimmed, I'm thinking a few of these items, one in particular labeled Preparation H, wasn't requested on a whim."

"Ya know, big fella, for such a buff, macho lookin' dude, sometimes you surely have a way with the pretty words. Tell the truth, slant-eye, does big papa there deliver in the sack or have ya caught 'im tryin' on your undies on more than one occasion?"

Reaching over with an extended elbow, she playfully tapped her spouse's left triceps.

"Um, afraid that one's allllll yours, big 'un."

Apparently not amused, Zack took a half-step forward while cocking the baton near his right ear.

"You got exactly thirty seconds before we sail away and you can spend the next two weeks wiping your ass with palm-fronds. Your call, tough guy."

Nearly a full minute passed, during which time the silence was pierced solely by a short, wet-sounding fart and follow-up giggle from the general direction of their unseen client. Eventually, Zack stepped back while silently signaling Liza to follow suit.

"Fine and dandy then. Good luck with that raging case of hemorrhoids, buddy-boy. I've heard sitz baths can shrink 'em down at least to grapefruit-size."

"Awww, hold your horses already," came a raspy reply, accompanied by an angry huff and the dragging of feet. "Is it mandatory in the corrections field *not* to possess a workin' sense of humor? Geeez…"

As if limping forth from the cloudy vapors of a recently unearthed time capsule, Jessie Barton shambled from semi-darkness into the light, appearing as if he'd aged a full decade.

His left eye drooped dramatically, like the victim of a major stroke; his left foot tilting slightly upward and lagging behind its stalwart, healthier twin. His arms hung limply, the hands curled as if cloaking separate, menacing secrets.

"Just hand me the pad, lunkhead," he groaned, reaching out and exposing the flat palm of his right hand, which noticeably trembled, "then do us *all* a favor and get the fuck off my island. That is…" he paused to regard Liza with a wide, predatory smile made all the more malevolent by the freakish sagging of his left cheek and eye, instantly bringing to mind the infamous 'Two-Face' super-villain of Batman fame, "…unless slant-eye over there wants to hang out for a quickie."

"Believe I'll pass, Egor," she replied morosely, maintaining a steady aim with the Taser, "bestiality just ain't my bag."

Having retrieved the iPad from the shelf top, he glared at Zack with a full, warped sneer still fully intact.

"Don't know what you're missin', Slope. The big fella here is gettin' on in years…way past his trim-pumpin' prime, yeah? Hot young chink like yourself craves the high, hard one almost daily, am I right?"

Stone-faced and wearing a mask of bland indifference, Zack maintained a wholly defensive posture with the baton's positioning unchanged.

"Check off the items and type in your initials at the bottom."

The man did so, ever-so-deliberately, before gently replacing the pad atop the shelf.

"Still no tequila, I see."

"No can do. Santa said you've been a bad boy," Liza retorted sourly, garnering a stern glance from her better half.

Ignoring the obvious dig, Jessie cocked a brow and spoke directly to the senior sfficer.

"Worse still, the pesticides I ordered are nowhere to be seen. Still under board review, I take it?"

"Yes, Barton, and for the umpteenth time, if a requested item is not out for delivery, it's still under consideration."

The man's perpetual scowl intensified to the point of grotesque parody—a Halloween mask stretched and contorted like partially melted rubber.

"Horseshit. Stiff-shirt flesh-pipe lickers ain't got the guts to just tell me to fuck off, once and for all?"

"Personally, I'd revel in the opportunity to do so," Liza murmured, playfully rotating the Taser's front site from the man's groin region and then back to the center of his frowning mug.

"Or maybe the big man here is void the required gonads to pass on said message."

"Not my call," Zack replied calmly, refusing to take the bait and even lowering the baton to sit loosely atop his shoulder. As if following his lead, his wife loosened her death grip on the Taser's squared handle, which had grown slick with palm-sweat.

The stocky man suddenly lunged forward a single step, raising clenched, shaking fists to chest-level. In turn, both Gormans fell back with weapons repositioned in full strike mode.

"Who's call then, ya chicken-shit grunt? Get me the asshole in charge!"

"Back down, Barton. Back away. Back down," Zack commanded with controlled iciness.

"Or don't," Liza added, malevolent smirk intact. "*Bak'la.*"

Keeping with tradition, her verbal volley sailed overhead as the intended target's concentration remained fixed solely on the higher ranked of the two.

"I ain't screwin' around here, Gorman. There are rats the size of spaniels roamin' this burg, not to mention some of the ugliest damn insects this side of a H.G. Wells paperback. At the very least, I gotta be able to set up and maintain a protective shell around the hut. If not, it's only a matter of time 'fore I wake up to find a large chunk of my rear end either chewed away or sportin' a volcano-shaped boil."

"Rest assured I'll pass on these concerns, Barton, as I have several times already. Now, chill out, take a breath and wind down."

"Yeah, you do that," Jessie Barton murmured, dropping his hands to his sides and taking not one but several steps back—deflating like a pierced bladder—eventually collapsing onto one knee. "Tell 'em if they doubt the...validity of this boy's claims, they're more than welcome to camp out in his assigned digs for a few nights or at the very *least* provide some security cameras for video proof that these little beasties really do exist."

Despite the smaller man's apparent surrender, the two Gormans maintained their respective poses.

"You have my word," Zack said, "I'll see what I can do. However, to be fair, there are...the board does have valid concerns. I mean, a man of your special skillset and poisons of any type can be a volatile mix...um...pardon the expression."

"Hey, don't lay that steaming turd at my feet, pal. Ol' smarty-pants is the cocktail expert, remember? I'm just the hired muscle. The Hulk to his Banner. Bug-eyed little weasel would probably try to keep the rats as pets and toss the spiders in Mason jars for studyin' purposes. I just want 'em croaked, period...end of sentence. Professor pencil-dick be damned, I need some peace of mind here, man. This is, after all, be it ever so fuckin' humble, my home."

Liza's nostrils flared in anger as she bit into her lower lip.

"*Kantot*...what the—...ugh, in case it's slipped that cracked, demented mind, *Monsieur* Hyde, this isn't some swanky island resort and we're not your personal wait staff. The word of the day is...*incarceration.* Learn it, live it, love it or take a long, leisurely swim. My superior's valued opinion notwithstanding, I'm kinda rooting for the latter. Oh, and just a reminder, you *do* share the same genitalia as Professor Pencil-Dick. Just saying."

His worn visage sagging like a woozy bloodhound, Barton appeared to fight off a yawn glaring indifferently from the junior Gorman to the senior.

"Poisonin' my…wait staff would only make sense if it aided in some hare-brained escape attempt. Since no such option exists, what the hell are you…is everybody so damned antsy about? Please push 'em to do the right thing, big fella. I'd…me *and* my egg-headed associate would appreciate it. Now, if you don't mind, I'm suddenly feelin' severely bushed."

"You got it, Jessie," Zack said, tucking the iPad beneath one arm before turning to Liza and gesturing toward the door. "Good luck with the…those issues down below."

Liza backed out cautiously, though maintaining the firing pose.

"Touching. A real heart-tugger. Let's book."

As if not to awaken a slumbering resident, Zack closed the hut entrance with extra care before taking off in a wild sprint in order to catch up to his trail-blazing better-half, thick tuffs of sand spewed airborne from the heels of his boots.

The screeching voice reverberated at almost the precise moment he'd pulled even and the cutter swam into view just over a pear-shaped dune.

"Hey! It Isn't like you two to leave without a proper, police send-off!"

"Shit…do we *have* to?" Liza inquired, never breaking stride.

Reaching over to acquire a gentle hold on her left forearm, Zack slowly applied the brakes.

"Liza, that's not nice," he grinned. "He's the one wearing the white hat, remember?"

"Blood-spattered white hat," she blurted between giggles, somehow managing to transform back to stone-face mode immediately upon turning about.

He stood at the edge of the hut's stony porch, his right hand raised high and waving frantically.

"I just put on a fresh pot of tea if you're game!"

"Afraid the schedule simply won't permit it, Jed," Zack bellowed between cupped hands. "Appreciate the offer. Maybe next time, okay?"

"I've heard *that one* before, Zackary Gorman. One of these days I'm gonna hold ya to it!"

"Scout's honor, Jed!"

"You make sure he keeps that promise, Miss Liza!"

She waved in response, flashing a wide, utterly faux smile and whispering between clenched teeth.

"Only if *we* supply the tea bags, cups and water, you psychotic son of a bitch…"

Briefly breaking character, her usually stoic spouse guffawed aloud before regaining a semblance of self-control.

"Take care of each other, you two!"

"Will do, Jed!" he barked with a final wave as the pair executed a textbook about-face and in the process, digging twin protractor-perfect semi-circles into the sandy, well-worn trail.

Steering the cutter toward open sea through a light rain and a buildup of foreboding black clouds hovering above, Liza stood just to Zack's left with a flat palm resting atop his massive left shoulder.

"You really need to work on your professionalism, Z," he chided, square-jawed and utterly without humor. "Personal opinions aside, our job isn't just security but to serve these people's needs, not to judge, bait, piss off or ridicule at every opportunity."

In response, she jerked her hand away as if from a red-hot cooking eye.

"You're professional enough for the both of us, Captain Square-jaw. I'll perform my duties as outlined in the regulations we're bound to follow, which, correct me if I'm wrong, as you surely will, does *not* include a chapter on ass-smooching the likes of those…sadistic nut-jobs."

"Sure, sure, blah, blah, blah," he retorted curtly, though quick to lighten his tone while wisely changing the subject. "Well, better buck up, lady. *You-know-who* looms as the final stop of this here workday, and his suave ways and natural charms have rarely improved your mood."

As if to act as precursor for what was to come, a loud chap of thunder cracked overhead, soon to be followed by a blinding squall that, although mercifully brief in duration, made it appear the cutter was being steered directly into the swirling black eye of a ravenous typhoon.

Four

The Isle of Flames

The slim, gangly young black man stood at the edge of the porch, his heels resting upon the smooth stone surface even as fidgety toes dug ten separate grooves into wet sand. Decked out in a dark purple, sleeveless cut-off tee with the words '*Tupac Lives*' scrawled across the narrow chest in bright yellow, his bald head glistened with a fresh layer of sweat, which he sporadically attempted to wipe free with alternating palms. The right side of his otherwise baby-butt smooth cheek was riddled in a thick patch of purple scarring, protruding like a bloated trauma injury that, when viewed from a side angle, appeared pasted on like multiple layers of semi-dried liquid nails. Baggy shorts, the kind made popular in urban settings of questionable integrity, hung nearly halfway down his stringy shins.

"How 'bout the discs, Moose? Hopin' you ain't baggin' me," he said as Zack approached, bear-hugging a sizeable cardboard box with a smaller one balanced atop its loosely taped lid.

"Dig in and see for yourself, MC Shammer."

50

His smooth, scar-free cheek wrinkleless despite wearing a deep, scornful frown, the young man performed a lazy variation of a matador's bow as Zack tromped by. The two had briefly stood eye-to-eye—equals in height but extreme opposites in girth—the dramatic variations in both their age and size not lost on Liza, who eyed the odd-couple teaming from perhaps a dozen yards away. An overstuffed duffel propped atop her right shoulder, she couldn't help but think that, from such a distance, her behemoth of a husband appeared comically gigantic—like a mythical giant addressing a dark, fleshy bean-pole.

"You're 'bout a wishy-washy cracker, ain't ya, Moose? Don't ever wanna give a nigger the straight scoop. Always with the silent gig, always with the non-verbal diss, like my kind ain't worth wastin' your breath."

"We don't pull or pack them, Marquez," a stern reply echoed from the hut's interior. "We just deliver the goods and acquire the necessary signature."

"Lazy-ass white folk I'm used to, but this one here," the young man whined, gesturing toward Liza as she grew closer, "I gotta say…I'm trippin'. Your *kind* is supposed to be hard-workin', dependable. I mean, all you gooks suffered the same kinda treatment as my people, right? Yo, maybe not whips and chains, but slavery is slavery, right?"

Liza stopped in her tracks at the porch's edge, playfully tossing the duffel through the hut entrance before peering up with a dramatically cocked brow at the freakishly slinky entity.

"Did you just….Yo? Seriously, *yo*? What exactly have you been using as an urban reference, What's Happening?"

Tilting his head with both eyes rolling back as in deep thought, Chandler's mouth hung agape in obvious confusion. Once dialogue did emerge—a fumbling, mumbling stutter—both the tone and accent had mutated in dramatic fashion, the former several octaves deeper and the latter from North American inner-city thug to Aussie bloke straight from the vast, desolate outback.

"What's happening...when? I don't...please clarify, lil' G."

"Late seventies American sitcom," Zack chimed in, leaning out and flashing a wry grin. "Forget it, Z. Wrong continent, unless Rodge, Rerun and the boys played in some seriously long-distance syndication. Give it another shot, please. I'm entranced..."

"I stand corrected," she conceded, hands on hips. "Um...how about...*In Living Color*...no! I'll say...old Eddie Murphy concert vids?"

"In-live colors is a definite no. Eddie Murphy is...wasn't he the *Beverly Hobbs Cop* guy?"

"That's Beverly Hills Cop, and yeah, that is...was the dude. You hip to his rant?"

Chandler nodded, self-consciously palming his scar.

"Hip to hi....um, nope. Don't be spewin', Lil' G, and I'm not meanin' to be a whacker, but we seem to be speakin' different tongues altogether."

She nodded knowingly, stealing a quick glance at her leering spouse.

"Don't we, though. Reminds me of the first six months I spent with big G there. Constant western slang and pop-culture references were a killer to comprehend, as in daily migraines. So where *did* you pick up the act?"

"Why, here I always took you for something of a conch, Missy."

Liza reached down and began to gently pat the Taser's outer holster.

"Say wha...*cunch*? That better not mean what I'm thinking, Crocodile Dundee."

Raising both hands in mock surrender, Chandler exposed bare palms.

"Whoa, mate, hold off on the voltage-meter. Means a bookworm...a *studier*. I'm just saying I figured one as conscientious as yourself would've done their homework. No need to spit the dummy."

The dramatic tilting of her head and a distorted frown that screamed perplexity compelled him to continue.

"Translation: *no need to get so upset*. I just figured my past being an open book was part of your training."

"So, it was a sort of…on-the-job training type situation?"

"Once the majority of employment was obtained stateside, yes. Fortunately, my line of work does tend to favor the silent type, as in the man of few words. In a pinch, though, I found a variety of personalities from which to choose: the dag, the dill, even a complete dipstick, if need be."

"Da…" she paused, open-mouthed, and waved him off. "I'll take your word for it. Zackary, I take it from this prolonged silence we're good to go for a lengthy stay or have you detected a whiff of smoke in there?"

"Odorless, colorless, flame-free as far as I can determine," the reply echoed from deep within the hut's squared confines. "Bring the rest inside."

Chandler rolled his eyes as Liza reached down and scooped up the duffel in one fluid movement before waddling through the entranceway with it planted firmly against her left side.

"Not to complain, but why are such measures even necessary, mates? It isn't as if fire by constriction is even remotely possible on this damnable sandbar and even if it was, I couldn't exactly conceal its presence in my sock drawer, now could I? Similarly, one cannot ignite a random explosion simply by *wishing it so*. There has to be a catalyst, a fuse, an igniter. Salt air, sand, palm trees, shell-rock. None of these can go boom merely by proxy."

Zack and Liza stood side by side, the former removing items from the first of two open boxes and the latter with both arms submerged deep into the duffel.

"Hey, whine all you feel is necessary, Marquez. To bitch and moan is a guaranteed right," Zack said, hugging a six-pack of toilet paper to his chest before placing it on a nearby glass coffee table with several similar toiletries.

"And besides, Slim, what are they gonna do? Add to your sentence?" Liza added morosely, cupping a can of unlabeled veggies in one hand and a two-liter Sprite with the other.

"Oh, that's a beaut, that is," Chandler chortled, again running the back of one hand over his scar and sporadically wincing in the aftermath. "Spoken like a true fruit loop."

Briefly pausing her inventory, Liza stared at him icily.

"I'll take that as a compliment, though with serious reservations."

"All I'm saying is, a pyro ain't a pyro without the tools of the trade, much like your master carpenter, cabinet maker, doctor…cat burglar. Why, even you two—without the weaponry—mortal as any common bloke, right?"

"Not quite accurate, Slim," Liza retorted with a gloved finger raised airborne. "All artillery aside, the big lug here and myself are well-trained, professional officers of the correctional trade and thus well-versed in hand-to-hand techniques designed to cripple, maim, or, as a last resort, disable with extreme prejudice."

Chandler hung his head and nodded slowly.

"Yeah, well, if we're going all technical, I've been known to periodically release a toxic air biscuit in mixed company—enough to drive one out of the room with bleeding eyes and pinched nostrils. You've missed my point, mate."

"Afraid you can count me among the confused," Zack injected without looking up from the tabletop, where he'd piled assorted food products pulled from a small igloo cooler from which thick plums of frosty air flowed.

The spindly, gaunt man tucked his hands to the small of his back and commenced to pace, first out to the porch and then back inside, repeating the trek numerous times at a fairly brisk pace and executing a textbook about-face maneuver whenever a change of direction became necessary.

"Simplicity in itself, mates. Not only have I been stripped of my power, a la Superman dipped in a tub full of kryptonite, even if provided the items necessary to ply said trade, *how* and *why* would I bother to do so? What possible motivation could exist? Blasting this stony coffin into rock fragments would only serve to leave me homeless, right? Similarly, torching the furniture would serve no purpose save to leave me without a place to park my lazy caboose. I have no agenda—no reason to blow off steam as you blokes say—my fate has long been accepted. What would be the harm of providing a stove of some sort—a single electric eye would do—or a low wattage microwave, for shit's sake? Tropical temps or no, my inner craving for a hot cup of Joe is beyond severe at this point.

"Don't misunderstand, however, I don't exactly crack a fat at the notion of spending my remaining days holed up like a sand-crab, but when one's options are exactly zilch, resignation comes relatively easily."

Lining up a trio of generically labeled cans on the table's opposite side, Liza abruptly stepped back and snapped the fingers of both hands, the effect somewhat muffled by their leather-glove covering.

"Ugh, *crack a fat*? Lemme guess…a reference to marijuana use—as in a fat doobie from which to toke?"

"Swing and a miss, lil' G. It means, um, *obtain an erection.*"

Zack snickered aloud while sealing the tiny cooler's hard-plastic top and thus eradicating the stream of frosty emissions.

"Make that…*big* swing and a miss, Z."

"Regardless," Chandler continued, "all these damn precautions are, without a doubt, the height of absurdity."

"Long-winded whine duly noted, bean-pole," Liza exclaimed, pecking away with a stiffened forefinger at the palm-sized iPad she'd procured from an inner-vest pocket. "Doesn't change shit, but duly noted nonetheless. Now, wanna see something really cool? No pun intended."

The frenzied pacing having ground to a slumping halt, Chandler collapsed onto the living room couch with a resounding groan.

"If it concerns that assortment of either overly chilled or sickeningly lukewarm consumables lining my dining table, I'll take a rain check. I'm a bit stuffed, ugh, *tired* from proper lack of snooze."

Liza stepped back, regarded her husband with a raised brow and performed a mini-curtsy before gesturing toward the couch with the casual wave of an arm.

"Senior Officer Gorman, care to intercede? The *thin man* there is obviously tuning me out."

"My pleasure," he replied, clearing his throat while filling each hand with a canned food item. "Marquez, your continued request, four at last count I believe, for a means to heat daily meals has been addressed and, as of today's delivery, granted. Check it out."

Holding out oversized mitts that engulfed all but the can's silver, circular tops, he appeared to be squeezing in an attempt to literally pop them open. Chandler fronted him cautiously, striking a rigid, defensive pose.

"Don't be shy, big fella. I've got a can opener in the other room."

Zack shook him off as Liza silently took up position at her husband's side, arms casually folded and ankles crossed.

"Patience, Slim, just give it a few seconds," she said, gesturing toward the cloaked containers and the thick, callused fingers curled around them.

"Yep, that ought to do it. Here you go," the senior Gorman exclaimed, releasing all but the tip of the cans, where respective forefingers remained loosely attached. In reply, Chandler reached tentatively out with splayed digits as if to touch live, squirming electrical wires.

"Ought to what? I don't get…"

Liza groaned in mock exasperation.

"Just take 'em already, bean-pole, before the effect wears off."

Gripping the cans from the bottom, Chandler took their possession with obvious trepidation, prompting a giggle from the junior officer.

"Amazing. Now there's one of your great ironies, big 'un."

"How so?"

"Think about it. The mad bomber there handling those tin containers like they were filled with nitro."

Her spouse nodded in agreement without verbal reply just as the subject of their exchange burst out in a wide, toothy smile, his normally dull, lifeless eyes gleaming.

"Well, I'll be…how cool is that? Um, so to speak."

"It's not like the technology is old in theory… heating elements ignited by one's own body warmth, but these bad boys are right off the assembly line from the Tokyo labs. Haven't even lined store shelves yet, at least not in North America—difference being that it only takes forty-five seconds to a minute of flesh-time to heat the inner product to a max temp of one-fifty-plus Fahrenheit—therefore eliminating the need for stovetops or ovens; electric, gas or microwave."

Chandler hugged the cans to his bony bosom and sighed, ear-to-ear grin still intact.

"Damn, it ain't quite boiling point, but close enough for someone used to either room temperature or downright chilled," he blurted in a high-pitched wail before abruptly switching both accents and decibel level, the former in comically overheated ghetto-styling, the latter bottoming out in the tradition of Barry White at his velvet-voiced best.

"For a po-po wannabe, you are the slammin' H-bomb, mutha-fucka! The knees to my mutha-fukkin' bees, yo!"

"Uhhhh, you're…welcome?" Liza inquired with a befuddled glance toward her equally perplexed spouse.

"Complimentary I'm sure..." he nodded straight-faced, "...except perhaps that twice-repeated, bluntly profane reference to my mother."

Putting the cans aside, Chandler instantly reverted back to his native tongue, sans the earlier enthusiasm.

"Dead-set, uh, very much so, mate. Now, to show my appreciation, I feel a tradeoff is in order."

Simultaneously, both officers cocked a quizzical brow.

"It's only fair, right? Otherwise I'm going to feel like quite the swagman...uh, hobo. I mean, last month it was the cricket equipment, and now hot meals. This deuced Aussie pride dictates I reply...*repay*...in kind."

"Truth be told, Slim, we're a little bushed," Liza said wearily, the accompanying shrug equally weak. "It's truly, truly been one of those days, right big un'?"

"What *she* said," Zack agreed with a nod her way. "Maybe next time we can book a longer layover."

Waving them off, Chandler sprinted past in three lengthy bounds through the open entrance.

"*Aces!* C'mon...won't take but a blink. Promise."

Moments later, their sweat-moistened flesh gradually drying amid a semi-cool sea breeze blowing off the ocean's calm surface, they circled a small, granite picnic table at the rear of the hut.

"So, what's in the box, Marquez?" Zack inquired sourly, arms crossed and squinting down at the square cardboard, its short ends riddled with circular, pen-sized holes.

"For your sake, I sincerely hope we're not talking contraband. Hate to see you lose privileges over possession of some...illegal concoction."

Leaping back a step while simultaneously freeing the Taser from its holster, Liza alternated her aim from the box to Chandler and back again.

"Z, what the hell?" Zack barked, taking an instinctive step back while gracefully freeing the shock-cane from his utility belt.

"Don't look now," Liza whispered calmly, "but that box is jittering."

"Jittering?"

"It's alive, boss."

"Whoa, whoa now, stand down, you two," Chandler intervened with raised hands, stepping between the box and its erstwhile attackers even as it visibly trembled in the background. "Cool those naturally aggressive jets for a sec, what say? Word of honor, mates, there's no element of danger involved. Allow me to demonstrate…"

Grinning all the while, he carefully peeled back the box's top panels before reaching inside and retrieving the inner contents. Chandler stepped back, gently holding the squirming cargo between cupped palms.

"Officers Gorman, meet Blaze."

Announcement and accompanying comically menace-free reveal aside, neither relaxed their respective stance.

Its plump, black-backed frame visibly shook beneath his firm grip—its sizeable beak, bright yellow with a scarlet tip, pecked and jabbed at open air.

"A…gull? You've been keeping a pet bird?" Liza queried as Chandler strolled purposely past and in the direction of his personally requested soccer field, complete with matching nets set twenty yards apart atop a wide, squared patch of light blue artificial turf.

Zack shrugged in light of his wife's searing glare.

"Well, the local animal population doesn't come under the heading of actual contraband."

Standing at the midpoint between the two metal-framed nets, Chandler turned and held the bird high overhead, its thin, orange-tinted legs pumping frantically beneath his grip.

"Tell me, you two mates enjoy the occasional magic trick?"

"Seriously, Slim, the sun is dipping low…" Liza replied, holstering the Taser while assuming a parade-rest pose just to Zack's right, "…so if you must mimic Marvin the Magnificent, make it snappy."

"Merlin," Zack whispered behind a raised palm.

"Huh?" she sneered.

"*Merlin* the Magnificent. Still, I'm damn impressed at the reference, however mangled."

"Whatever. I can practically feel myself turning to dust. We should've been on-board and cruising a half-hour ago, being that it'll take us another half-shift just to fill out incident reports. Or have you already forgotten that little fiasco on Wolf Isle?"

"Oh shit," he frowned, rubbing the underside of his squared jaw with the same open palm, "Yeah, we're looking at a few hours of OT at lea—"

Chandler's overly-campy, circus barker act shattered their respective trains of thought.

"Behold then, Officers Gorman, the spectacular, *singular* flight of Blaze, the queen Phoenix of the south seas!"

He released the bird with just a slight upswing of his arms as if to boost its takeoff amid a flutter of wings and brief, high-pitched squawk. Chandler stepped back, eyes pulled wide, mouth agape and arms still upraised as if signaling touchdown.

"Soooo, am I missing the magical, mystical part?" Liza asked, playfully nudging her husband while watching the gull flutter clumsily and almost make landfall before finally gaining enough control to ascend to a higher altitude. "Nothing real earthshaking about a bird *flying*, right big 'un?"

"Wait for it, mates…" Chandler beamed, "…just wait…for…it."

Arms crossed, Zack squinted as the bird's winding trajectory caused it to temporarily vanish when lined directly with the setting sun.

"Give the man a break. Such utter isolation could break even the stoutest of psyches."

Liza nodded, peaking underneath a flat, outstretched palm while using her free hand to retrieve the wraparound Raybans hitched to her utility belt.

"Uh-huh, and toss in the fact he was quite the cracked egg upon arrival, you get this sad visual...the Birdman of Alcatraz, Federal Inmate edition. Tsk tsk tsk..."

Shockingly, neither even flinched when the bird exploded in a bright flash of yellow to equal its vaporized beak, the only immediate movement the almost perfectly synchronized dropping of their lower jaws.

"Oh my. My, oh my oh my..." Chandler chanted, falling to his knees while being showered in smoking flakes of charred feather, "...that truly went well. Beyond all earthly expectation."

Only when a section of the gull's foot bounced from her left shoulder onto the sand, the blackened flesh still partially aflame, was Liza able to graduate from nonsensical babble to a semi-comprehendible dialogue, though she'd briefly, inadvertently reverted back to her native tongue.

"*H-Hala*? Th-the h-hell? The...that bi-bird went...b-boom."

"Chandler..." Zack bellowed, storming toward the kneeling man with the shock-cane freed and clutched tightly in his left hand, "...you'd damn well better have a plausible explanation for such bat-shit behavior."

Eyes glazed and arms outspread with the palms exposed, Marquez appeared utterly oblivious, his bald head and shoulders riddled with flecks of feathered shrapnel.

"Wasn't that the shit, though? I...I had hopes but without a proper test run, it was the ultimate flying blind scenario. I just never...never, *ever* dreamed of such perfection in both the timing and execution." The sound of static—a hissing sizzle like raw meat tossed atop hot coals—Chandler tensed, eyes rolling back to reveal the bloodshot whites, before jerking forward and then back with a final, violent thrust that left him lying on his back with both legs kicking frantically and each arm slapping wildly with fingers digging frantically into the soft turf.

Zack kneeled to within reaching distance of the man's wriggling frame, peering over one shoulder at his wife as if she were a complete stranger.

"Jesus, was that really necessary? Was a threat being posed that I was utterly clueless to spot?"

Holstering the Taser, its squared barrel emitting a pencil-thin stream of black vapor, Liza stood with feet shoulder-length apart with hands placed firmly on hips. It was, Zack instantly recognized, her 'stand your ground' pose, a spunky trait—dog stubborn and defiant in the face of criticism—that on countless past occasions he'd found quite cute, not to mention sexy as hell. This, however, was *not* one of those occasions.

"Hey, for all we knew, Pyro there might well have pulled another gull-grenade out of his ass and lobbed it our way. Wasn't about to take that chance."

Confident enough time had elapsed that an accidental transference of electrical charge was highly unlikely past a mild shock, Zack curled one hand behind the smaller man's head while tucking the other beneath his right armpit. Gradually he raised Chandler into a sitting position, the man blinking madly even as thick streams of frothy drool leaked from each corner of his mouth. He made low grunting sounds while releasing the sporadic fart, obviously having lost control of his inner faculties in the charges' aftermath. Zack wore a mask of disgust, matching his tone perfectly.

"Load of garbage and you know it. You were just looking for an excuse to pull that damn zap-gun. Been looking to unload on somebody...*anybody,* since Wolf Isle."

Stomping forward and kicking a pound's worth of sand onto the otherwise spotless turf in the process, Liza's voice crackled with a building rage. Zack realized she was mere moments from total hysteria—screaming, tears, arms fluttering about—a less than enjoyable sight for certain, though to consider backing down was not an option, lest she not only sense his weakness, but worse yet, deduce his backing off as a sign of approval.

"Looking to unlo—listen up, Sergeant High, Tight and Mighty, I'm no less a professional than you. Time in service and time in grade bullshit aside…past military heroics aside…the never broke or even bent a regulation in my entire fucking life horseshit aside…I'm no less a trained professional."

"It was an unnecessary use of force and you damn well know it. Skinny little shrimp posed no threat to us," he interrupted gruffly, "Now, what say we drop the subject, resuscitate your victim and ask him straight up what that bird-bomb thing was really all about."

Mouth agape and lips trembling, Liza pumped out her chest as if to reply but instead held her tongue and stepped back, obviously deflated.

"Let's get him inside. We'll need to stick around 'til he comes to."

"Mental stability?" she blurted, tossing gloved hands airborne.

"Hate to go all logical, big 'un, but I'm of the *logical* belief he blew that notion the minute the sky was filled with barbecued gull-guts."

Zack leaned the smaller man's head back and used a pen-light to check his eyes, both of which lolled about like loose marbles.

"Regardless, departure will only occur if and *when* he can string together a coherent sentence or two and isn't pissing blood."

"Oh, for shit's sake, Zackary, it was a quick jolt of stun juice, not a triple-shot of termination rays."

His jaw muscles visibly tensing, Zack pocketed the pen-lite before allowing Chandler to lean back again.

"Regardless, procedure is procedure, and your trigger-happy ways just cost us another half-hour to an hour."

His spouse grunted, stormed away a half-dozen steps and sighed heavily before reversing field and taking up an apathetic stance directly behind her kneeling better-half.

"Grab his feet, Z. The sunlight is turning him green."

His left eye blinking wildly in a fitful tick, Chandler continued to mumble and grunt a nonstop, incomprehensible rant as they carried him, human-crutch style, back into the hut's lone bedroom and laid him atop a padded cot. After instructing Liza to retrieve the first-aid kit from the cutter, Zack pulled a small plastic pouch from his belt and commenced to tear it open with clenched teeth.

"Wh-wha-zat? Wha-wha t-tha do?" Chandler inquired as the syringe was plunged into his inner right forearm, his formerly spasmodic eye appearing fully dilated and stuck open as if the lid was glued into place.

Having fully engaged the plunger and extracted the needle, Zack rolled the works back into the plastic cover from which it came and shoved the package in one of his camo pants' roomy side pockets.

"Just relax, Marquez," he replied calmly, carefully folding Chandler's shaking hands one atop the other and gently patting them with the caring professionalism of a veteran healthcare worker, "Breathe deep and exhale slowly. It'll help smooth out the shock to your central nervous system."

"Wh-what wuz....it?" Chandler croaked, his right eye aflutter even as the left appeared to marbleize with fear.

"Whoa…ease down, sport. We're talking a non-lethal mix of B-12, mega potassium and complex Neurontins—basically an anti-shock martini created specifically to offset the effects of a Taser blast. Now, just settle in and find a happy place for a few minutes. Oh, here…" he paused, removing a trio of similarly pre-loaded syringes and carefully stuffing them between the cot pad and its coiled metal frame "…leaving you three more of these. Hope you're not needle-shy. One load a day, preferably at night before beddy-bye. Oh, and don't mention this to Li—to the wife. Totally against regs, and the old ball and chain is a stickler for such...formalities."

Chandler's smile was sickly. He swallowed hard as if to refrain from vomiting.

"T-thanks, big g-guy. J-just a lovely w-wanker, you are."

"Oh, speaking of which, your would-be assassin, pardon the expression, is on her way with some concentrated pain meds that'll help complete the healing."

As if instantly reassured, Chandler shut both eyes while simultaneously folding lean, slender arms over an equally skeletal chest.

Zack exited to the kitchen, returning moments later with a bottle of water that he proceeded to hold to his patient's trembling lips.

"What the hell, Marquez? Was that moronic little exhibition meant to impress or enrage? Either way, I need to know *how* it was accomplished. As for *why*, well, given that checkered past of yours, that answer is fairly obvious."

Leaning up and coughing into an open palm, Chandler's only reply entailed a severely cocked brow.

"Hey, you know I have to report it," Gorman shrugged, "No choice or it's my ass in the proverbial sling the next time you decide to blow up or torch the local wildlife in front of witnesses. In the aftermath, there will undoubtedly be consequences, as in, a possible severe loss of privileges."

"Oh b-bugger that," Chandler mumbled between lazy wipes of a bare forearm over drool-lathered lips.

"I…it was d-done specially t-to…for you and y-your w-wife as a k-kind of personal t-thank you."

The big man cracked a wry smile, having parked his square jaw atop a clenched fist.

"Wait, you figured this…*that* rain of flaming feathers as some sort of tribute to the relationship of hired sentinels to convicted inmate?"

"Yeah, well…it's just that you blokes have been s-so accommodating c-compared to…well, every other swinging donga….um, di-dick in this particular correctional sex…sector."

"Nice, sweet, real touching. Now, how'd you do it, Marquez?"

The thin man's eyes gleamed with sudden delirium—the unbridled joy of a young child explaining the complexities of a new toy—the fingers of each hand dancing and gyrating like electrified spider-legs. Just as his euphoric rant began, Liza entered through the kitchen with a double-palm-full of generically labeled pill bottles. Zack quickly turned and flashed a 'shush' gesture—a forefinger tucked firmly against pursed lips. With that, Marquez Chandler's voice, ragged and hoarse and cracking with emotion, rang out with unabashed glee.

"The incendiary device is…was quite th-the bizarre m-mix, b-big guy. No n-need to spe-…confuse y-you with d-details. Let's just say it involved ingredients both man and n-nature-made, t-though if I do say so m-myself, for b-being so s-severely limited in available tra-triggers, the result was quiet…quit…quite s-satisfactory.

"As for the f –flight of my br-brave, sacrificial cre-creature, truly, it w-was the timing thing th-that was, as you Yanks say, the b-bear sha-shatting in the w-woods. It c-could've easily gone off the moment I tugged it from its box. As it was, I…it was damn near perfect, yes? Bloody hell! A bona fide ripper! Beautiful beyond a-all I could have ever imagined. I had…had hoped for a more…for a more positive response, but then, blokes in your line of work ha-have an image to preserve, yes?"

"Posi-…" Liza stammered, her hands resting atop her lesser half's wide shoulders, the fingers of each tapping nervously, "What exactly did you expect, bean-pole, a standing O? Generous monetary tips? Or maybe you figured I'd whip off my bra and shower you with it?"

At the sight and sound of her scathing rebuttal, Chandler merely stared slack-jawed and blank-eyed, held upright by spindly, quivering arms that gripped the side of the cot in twin death grips, as if hanging on the jagged edge of a narrow cliff wall.

"Hardly, on all counts. Oh, you're in a world of hurt, Slim. You consider this *present* set-up an inconvenience? As you Aussie gents are apt to say…*fiddlesticks*…"

Zack reached back and gently tapped the top of her right hand.

"Z, we've….I've already covered this particular ground."

"…better buck up and prepare to start wiping your privates with palm fronds, bud…"

Zack tapped a bit firmer.

"Liza, there's no need to speculate."

"…or topping the ol' toothbrush with beads of wet sand…"

Wrapping his own massive hand atop her own comparatively diminutive one, Zack executed a gentle squeeze.

"Officer Gorman, he's hip to the potential punishment."

"…and say bye-bye to that newly awarded food-heating perk; 'course a resourceful beach-chef such as yourself probably prefers *extremely* grilled squib, am I right? Maybe you can torch a few land-crabs or sizzle a school of Red-eyed Tetra…"

"Liza, *enough* already!" he shouted, intensifying his grip until she openly winced. "I've advised him of…similar actions being taken. Besides, the object of this passion-fueled, undeniably impressive rant isn't exactly in an absorbing frame of mind at the moment."

"Who gives a sh—say what?" she asked, frowning and pulling her hand free with a jerk.

Smiling, Zack arose with a strained grunt even as she stepped past and leaned over the cot with a cautious glare.

"Take a closer look. He may be *up* in a physical sense, but mentally he is definitely *out*."

Head bowed, eyes fluttering and a single droplet of drool hanging from his lower lip, Chandler miraculously remained propped upright via severely locked elbows.

"Hey! Hey! Firebug! Snap to! No way you're getting off that easy," Liza spat, snapping glove-free fingers mere inches from her comatose target's downturned eyes.

"Give it up, Z. He'd down for the count. Here…"

Zack moved past her and freed the man's surprisingly stout grip on either side of the cot and assisting in allowing Chandler's own dead weight to descend with a series of mild creaks.

Frowning sourly, Liza loomed over the sleeping man like a stalking vulture.

"Hmmph, probably faking it."

"Really, Z? How soon we forget. Remember the mandatory zapping at the Academy? The norm in regaining *full* use of one's faculties is twenty-four to thirty-six hours, and that was a stun setting."

She walked back toward the kitchen, hands on hips.

"Not me, big boy. Hot shower, cold brew and a power bar, and this girl was back on her regular cycle in three, four hours tops."

"Uh-huh. Sure you were," he replied with a weary sigh, rising and striking a guarded pose not dissimilar from his spouse just seconds earlier.

"Alas, us ordinary mortals aren't nearly as tough as your average Filipina storm-trooper. You ready to shove off and head for Atlantis?"

"Affirmative. Skies have cleared, at least. Seas are calm. Should be a relatively smooth sail."

Following a final glance Chandler's way—the slumbering Aussie's open snores comically nasal—Zack soon joined her on the hut's stony porch.

"Meaning we should give her the gun, yes?"

Suppressing a yawn, Liza donned her shades and stretched out her arms while staring up into a cloudless sea of light blue that successfully mimicked its oceanic twin below.

"Well, we do have numerous reports to dictate."

"Indeed we do," he replied, shutting the door gently so as not to wake the lone inhabitant. "It has been one helluva shift."

"And speaking of which…" he continued, pausing to clear his throat, "…I could set up a quick chat with Doc Graham once we dock.

I'm sure he could spare us a few minutes of his professional time." She quickly waved him off.

"Nope. I'm good."

"You sure? It's no sweat. One quick phone call and he'll clear the couch."

"Don't you mean the court? Thanks but no thanks. All I need to clear my head is: A, a nice, sweat-soaked torture session in the gym, followed by B, a rigorous roll in the rack. Of course, I'm depending on some manly cooperation on number two."

Zack chuckled, reaching over and down to deliver a light pinch to her upper left shoulder.

"Only if you work in a shower between said sessions, my dear, and I think you meant roll in the *hay*. That *rack* thing is more in line with torture."

"Whatever," she groaned, playfully planting the same shoulder into his right elbow.

"As long as the roll in question is executed to my satisfaction. God knows the memory fails on the last time that particular wish was fulfilled."

"Ouch. Low blow, so to speak," he grinned.

They walked side by side within the well-grooved path leading away from the hut, a Hallmark card in every aspect missing only the obligatory hand-holding.

"So, you…sure you're okay not talking this out with a pro? I know Dean's methods aren't exactly textbook, but he's one hell of an advisor on all things trauma."

Tossing her arms in the air, she huffed aloud, pouting seductively in the aftermath.

"Would you stop worrying? I've witnessed death before. This was…just so damn unexpected and…it had been a long stretch between fatalities. Oh, and another thing…"

The softness and sense of reason left her tone, instantaneously expunged and replaced by the icy-cool, barely restrained maniacal rage of an evil twin.

"Pull that hand-squeezing shit on me again, regardless of scenario, and you'll be wearing your balls around your neck..." she grinned devilishly, "...courtesy of the steel-toed boot of my choice."

Sliding to a stop, Zack watched her, slack-jawed, motor slowly forward without a hitch, as if the open, shockingly graphic threat to his family jewels had sufficiently closed the subject.

"Hey, I wasn't trying to *hurt* you, but you wouldn't clam up."

Sighing, he trudged on with shoulders slumped in dismay.

"Geez, thought you were made of sterner stuff."

Once it was obvious no reply was forthcoming, they trudged on in an uncomfortable silence, the junior officer speaking up only when their assigned cutter floated into view between swirling patches of sea-grass.

"You know big 'un, I can find many things to complain of concerning this line of work, but *monotony* is definitely not one of them."

This time, it was the senior of the Gormans who offered no verbal follow-up while struggling to properly digest and possibly decipher his spouse's latest, inexplicable personality transference.

Roughly three and a quarter hours later, Marquez Chandler awoke with a start, wincing at a sharp pain emanating from the tip of his right forefinger. Pulling the adjoined hand from beneath the cot's narrow mattress and the cool, metal coils of its frame, he was forced to study the plastic covered syringe for several moments before successfully identifying its unlabeled content. Laying it, fully wrapped, atop his bony chest, he leaned back and immediately relapsed into a deep, dreamless slumber.

Five

Home Base Therapies

United Nations Pacific Correctional Outpost D, codename Atlantis, home base for thirty-six full-time and two dozen part-time corrections employees, is located atop the largest of forty-eight nearby islands; a three-mile wide by two and a quarter mile long, L-shaped beachhead once officially labeled *Federation island* on all nautical maps—that is until its purchase by a conglomerate of governments and thereby wiped from said directional instructs and declared off-limits to all foolish enough to seek it out atop constantly patrolled international waters.

Within weeks of its initial construction, a typhoon of moderate strength had essentially leveled the island, prompting the building of a twelve-foot high stone flood wall encircling the entire perimeter.

Less than six months after a second ground-breaking, a trio of buildings, all conveniently connected by globe-shaped, reinforced glass walkways, were completed and christened, obviously without fanfare of any type, and dubbed the Hearts of Atlantis. All three: the Admin (also containing the medical wing), Communications (motor pool, generator room) and Housing (employee barracks, gymnasium, dining facility) units, held an identical makeup (reinforced steel and glass, lead-coated aluminum)—cookie-cutter in every way but where it mattered, that being to withstand the meanest, cruelest storm Mother Nature could concoct while providing a service deemed necessary as the millennium's newest and most humane method of infinite incarceration. Separate landing pads, the larger utilized for the more bulky supply choppers and the smaller for the sleeker, slimmer medevacs, bookmarked the island on the north and south, respectively, while on its eastern edge, tucked inside the crook of its letter-shaped borders lay the marina, a glass and steel box that contained a dozen individual docks. Parked within her stringently guarded walls were the cutters, six of which were taken out daily and rotated whenever maintenance needs dictated.

As far as personnel, patrol COs, self-nicknamed Sentinels-of-the-Sea, were permanently assigned, a la remote military tours, each tasked a rotating six-month-on, two-month-off work schedule, during which time they were assigned specific supply and observation routes. An average workday entailed twelve- to thirteen-hour shifts, six days a week, during which they were housed in old-school, G.I. barrack-type conditions. Once the one-hundred-eighty day assignment was complete came a welcome trip back to the mainland for rest, relaxation and mental rehabilitation.

Support personnel, the majority supply, dining hall or admin workers, shipped in and out on a weekly basis, normally pulling no more than a ten-hour shift, Monday through Friday, unless workload dictated a weekend's OT was required (a rare occurrence).

The medical staff was skeletal at best, with usually a lone doctor-nurse team on-site, though an on-call physician and trio of caregivers were merely an hour's flight away on the mainland if the need arose.

As was the case in such a stressful line of work, the mental health of both the employees and those they were paid to guard were deemed the highest of priorities. Thus, the services of an on-site psychiatric professional were offered on a first call, first treat basis.

Atop the relatively smooth, sandy, vegetation-free terrain of Correctional Outpost D, codename Atlantis, Doctor Dean Graham held, on average, a dozen or more daily sessions of what he referred to as 'noggin purges' with both employees and permanent residents, more than a few of whom would be labeled *unofficial* due to his admittedly woeful lack of organization skills—that and recent budget cuts that eliminated a part-time secretary position within the tiny office from which he held court—the location of said sessions as unpredictable as the local weather forecasts.

"I'd heard you rarely use your office for these…little chats, Doc," Dylan Barnes commented off-handedly, hoisting his water-wrinkled fingers into the air and instantly appearing entranced by the assorted tendrils of steam that arose from each splayed digit.

"Got to admit, this beats the hell outta some musty old couch."

"Setting warm enough for you?"

"Oh yeah, perfec-to. Already doin' a world of good to these battered old bones. Great idea, Doc. I'd heard your particular brand of head-shrinkin' wasn't exactly by the book."

"Well, unlike most in my profession, I consider distraction a good thing."

"Sorry I couldn't join in on the whole…Olympic swim meet thing. 'Fraid I just ain't up to the strain just yet. Plus which, I ain't exactly sure I even remember how to tread water."

"Understood, Dylan. Right now your priority is to heal, both physically and mentally."

Standing outside the squared hot tub decked only in snug, dark blue swim shorts, Dean Graham's slender, meticulously chiseled ebony physique was an underwear model ad come to life, complete with washboard abs, carved pecs and sufficiently chiseled but not overly bloated appendages. In his mid-forties with just a spattering of gray hair at the temples and encircling each ear, he could easily pass for a decade-plus younger. Following a brief, intense, stretching session involving arms, shoulders and neck, he laid a small brown pouch atop the tub's flat, squared outer rim.

Barnes lay one tub over with all but his head and upper shoulders submerged in the churning water.

"Doc, you ever think about workin' out? Seriously, dude..." he chuckled, adding a few extra bubbles with the free release of previously built-up gas, "...you moonlightin' as a biathlete?"

Gripping the singular unit on both sides, Graham practically levitated inside and yelped cheerily at the sudden intrusion of soothing heat.

"Perhaps in retirement, though in truth I was once a regular on the iron-man circuit in Hawaii."

"Good grief," Barnes replied wearily, ascending to prop himself upon extended elbows, his normally snow-white neck and chest noticeably reddened. "I was just funnin'. The Iron-Man circuit. Wow. If nothin' else, just sharing space with you should inspire regular trips to the site gym. I've been neglectin' the ol' physique of late, as if you couldn't tell."

"Solid biceps, deltoids, *latissimus dorsi.* Admittedly, midsection could use some work."

"No joke, Doc, soon as this blasted soreness eases up, you can call me *Captain Crunch,* sans the bowl full'a milk, o'course."

To that, Graham cracked a brief smile that dissipated as quickly as it had appeared.

"Good to hear. Now Dylan, I believe there is the matter of a rather grisly death to discuss. A rather violent, woefully untimely demise involving a colleague of mine that you bore ...unfortunate witness to."

The sauna room contained six such tubs, all encircling a larger, oval-shaped unit built for multiple bodies. Having been pre-booked for the session at hand, it was otherwise deserted and, if not for the humming of the tubs' respective motors, encased in tranquil, soothing silence.

"Yeah, well, witness and involuntary *participant*, Doc," Barnes replied, his usually pale features practically glowing red, his caterpillar-thick mustache matted with wetness and thus laying comically askew. "You nailed the grisly part, through and through, though I wasn't privy to the backstory. Things went kinda hazy, you understand. Big-ass kraut would've surely left me in a similar state of fucked up if not for the Gormans ridin' to the rescue. Oh uh, pardon my butchered French."

Graham gestured with an open palm, inadvertently splashing his own eyes and thus rubbing them vigorously in the aftermath.

"Don't hold back on my part. Trust me, I've heard them all, and in at least a dozen separate languages."

"Well, you know the gist, I'm guessin'. Rimshaw and I arrived on an emergency med callout. She began treatment, somethin' about Wolf's diabetes and lack of Flintstone's chewables as bein' behind the collapse. At one point, well, I guess I got overly lippy in the crude sense and the doc booted me outside. I rushed back in just as the muggin' commenced. Can't honestly say if the doc bit the dust before or after Wolf kicked me around like a rented mule."

"Yes, I have indeed perused both Zackary and Liza Gorman's written reports. Gone over each several times, in fact," Graham replied sheepishly, reaching over to retrieve a palm-sized reader from the unzipped pouch and flicking a forefinger across its glass surface with the grace and dexterity of an expert swipe and searcher. "The facts detailed in each are an exact blow by blow match to your own. There is, honestly, nothing more to be gained from rehashing the whos or whats. It's the *why* that intrigues, as in why she…why Bertha Wolf snapped the way she did."

Even as he continued to swipe the miniscule iPad, the doctor paused periodically to peek over at his patient's pale, sweat-soaked visage, as if to ensure suitable attention was being paid.

"My task at this point is to attempt to find an answer so as to avoid similar outbursts from...the clientele. Being as they all share similar behavioral issues, the trick is to prevent future occurrences via a form of telepathy. In other words, to be able to detect early warning signals *before* the inevitable comes to light. Perhaps there was simply no saving Charlotte Rimshaw from an act of completely random violence, but if even the vaguest of clues to the attack were somehow overlooked, well, all possibly avenues of prevention must be thoroughly investigated.

Tell me, how much did you know of Bertha Wolf's past before this...temporary assignment outside of your normal sector?"

Barnes openly coughed, what had been faint lines beneath each sagging eye growing increasingly bloated and pronounced as moments passed.

"Not a hell of a lot, Doc. I read the synopsis, as was required, but honestly, it was a quick skim before I'd even had the chance to gulp down that morning's first cup of Joe."

The doctor's finger continued to dance across the tiny screen, a streaking blur between periodic pauses.

"Of course, duty dictated *I* make as intensive study as possible into her past—predictably checkered as it may be. Not surprisingly, her resume includes a three-year stint in the German Army's infantry, where she'd reached the rank of *Stabsgefreiter*, equivalent to a sergeant in the U.S. ranks. She separated abruptly before her stint was officially up—for reasons unspecified in her file other than the per functionary *disciplinary action* remark. Several years after, she was tied to an extremist militant group and eventually taken into custody for terroristic threats against several government officials near Hamburg."

"Neo-Nazis?" Dylan inquired, wringing the sop from his mustache with a thumb and forefinger.

"Doesn't specify."

"She owns the look and same pit bull temperament. Dealt with similar supremacist nut-jobs in and around Fort Worth during my badge and IDA days."

"Patrol or detective?"

"Never owned a suit, Doc. I was a street enforcer all the way. Worked on gang detail for several years, a good portion of that undercover hangin' with pimply-faced skinheads and Hitler-worshipin' SS-wannabes. Let's just say I had a knack for...speakin' their language."

"Interesting. Well, in taking in what little information provided concerning Wolf's childhood, it's obvious she shares at least one trait common to those of her ilk. Abused and abandoned as a child and raised in squalor, thus the lack of a suitable authority figure. The army hitch was, I'm quite positive, her initial introduction to both stability and discipline. Still, according to her personnel file, she was in and out of trouble for the duration of the stint, and more than likely sidestepped early termination of duty due solely to her...special soldiering skills.

"There are...subtle hints, at least in some of the training she received, that her true calling involved government-sanctioned assassinations and that she'd taken it upon herself to...perform said duties above and *far* beyond the call of duty."

"She went rogue."

"In so many words. Mere speculation, you understand, but it would explain a lot."

"Yep, and there's no way in hell it was simple coincidence that two of her former infantry commanders were found murdered just before those other, more publicized killings commenced."

"I agree, Dylan, whole-heartedly."

"Like I said, Doc," Barnes grinned, tapping the side of his semi-bald noggin with the tip of a finger from which thin tendrils of vapor arose, "I never was no clue-sniffin' suit, but that don't mean common sense ain't stocked in abundance. That chick was eradicatin' her past as to better cover her future tracks."

"Well, It certainly appears that way, to include…eliminating—with extreme prejudice—the aforementioned COs' families as well. Wives, children, even grandchildren. Miss Wolf possesses the single characteristic all in her line of work require, that being a complete lack of conscience."

"I'll say. Big Lezzie ain't gonna garner no awards for compassion or mercy. Then again, as far as rating job performance, hard to argue with that work history. She's damn good at what she does. Don't mean to come off as admirin' the sick bitch's accomplishments, but you've gotta admit, the word predictable can be tossed out with the bathwater."

Tilting his head quizzically, Graham cocked a brow, temporarily discounting the iPad.

"How so?"

"You've studied her methods, right?"

"Indeed."

"Ya notice she never, not even once, chewed her cabbage twice?"

"Chewed her cab—"

"Every…*each* kill was a totally different beast. It's a damn wonder she was ever caught."

"Indeed, yes."

For the first time since entering the sweltering tub, Barnes' eyes lit, gleaming with newfound vigor even as both water-wrinkled hands arose from the churn to point, gesture and gyrate.

"Impressive as hell, really, how she pulled off those last two murders, I mean considerin' the distance between victims and the time-line involved."

"Ah yes, you refer to the chancellor and the foreign minister."

Barnes clapped enthusiastically, a thin mist firing out in all directions from the impact.

"Yeah, that's the pair. Wasn't that fucking amazin'? Must confess, it's the only part of her bio I recall with crystal clarity, I guess for obvious reasons. Kinda like a great real-life crime documentary, as ruthless and cruel as it was, there is that *slow down and craned the neck to check out the car-crash* fascination-thing, right?"

"There is that," Graham nodded, his ever-tapping, ever-swiping digit working overtime "Pardon me a moment while I call up that specific file, ripped from the headlines, as it were. If only my German weren't so rusty. Still, I *can* make out the gist." Once his finger arose from the slick, fog and water-proof glass, Graham reached with his free hand for the case, from which he produced a pair of narrow-lensed reading glasses. As he proceeded to openly read from the archived text, Dylan Barnes felt the drowsiness depart his battered psyche like an exorcised spirit, his interest piqued despite having read (an English-translated version) of the same report just days earlier.

~ * ~

Chancellor Jorg Adler belched into his wife's diagramed napkin before tipping the ice-filled glass and gulping down the last of his orange juice in three lengthy swallows.

Checking his watch, a Laco Pilot that had been a recent anniversary gift from his faithful spouse of twenty-five years, he noted the lateness of the morning and groaned in disgust while pushing away from the dining table. At six minutes past seven AM, the two-story estate was cloaked in silence save for the ancient grandfather clock ticking away in the living room and the nasal whistling of his wife's pet pug, Maynard, parked as usual at his loafer-covered feet. Pushing the OJ glass aside, he took a final bite of a generously buttered blueberry bagel before departing the kitchen in stocking feet for the connecting utility room, where he regularly left his shoes, overcoat and if necessary, a sturdy umbrella—purposely as not to wake his slumbering better-half, whose nightly meds normally kept her in bed until well past nine AM—and concluded the morning dress.

A quick trip to the downstairs half-bath to brush his teeth and ensure his daily comb-over was sprayed down to satisfaction to withstand the day's predictably stout winds, and the recently re-elected Judge to the Regensburg Chancellery court walked briskly to the front door with the handle of a slightly scarred black briefcase curled into his left fist.

A daily occurrence, sans weekends and holidays, was the familiar, utterly devoted presence of Maynard jogging alongside to, at least in Jorg's way of thinking, wish his master a pleasant and resourceful workday. Ritual dictated that Master reach down and deliver a light pat to his dutiful companion's rounded, fur-coated noggin and receiving a soft whine and vigorously wagging tail in return.

Similarly, tradition dictated that Maynard back away as his master gripped the door knob and tugged inward. In that faithful moment, together as Master and companion, a sinking, inexplicably feeling that something was horribly amiss was both shared and duly vocalized via Maynard's fearful cries and Chancellor Adler's barely audible whisper.

"Was zur Hölle? ("What the hell?") he croaked, suddenly dry-mouthed and strangely apprehensive yet pulling ever harder at the mysterious resistance coming from the thick oak's opposite side, as if it were frozen in place—highly improbable considering temperatures in the mid-fifties—or perhaps, equally mystifying, somehow jammed.

Oblivious to Maynard's having already abandoned ship, scampering away with tail tucked tightly between frantically pumping paws, Jorg Adler ignored a fearful, deep-down gnawing at his gut—a gnawing that screamed flight in a similar fashion as the now absent pug—and instead increased the forcefulness of both his grip and subsequent yank. As the door finally released and pulled inward, Jorg had time but for a single, choked gasp.

A barely audible click, followed by a nova-like flare of light, and Regensburg would soon be forced to appoint a chancellor by proxy until such time a new election could be organized.

80

~ * ~

"Plastic explosive, German-made type Sprengkorper DM12, and triggered by reverse resistance. According to her own confession, Wolf had applied the device, no bigger than a quarter, mind you, a full four hours before implosion, at just past three AM."

"DM12. I hear tell that shit's like C-4 on 'roids. Amazin', right? Said she'd been casin' his home for two full weeks so she'd have his schedule down pat. His wife was a well-known pill-head who slept in regularly, and their kids were long grown and out of the house. Still, she took one hell of a chance that only ol' Jorg would take the bait. Gutsy. Say the wife sleepwalks and decides on a little night-stroll or a cat-burglar chooses that specific night for a break-in? The chancellor would've immediately gone into protective hidin' and her chances for a second hit vanishes."

His gestures still comically animated, Barnes leaned forward as he spoke, his bulky arms hooked over the tub's squared edge, as if prepping to crawl out head first.

"Very true. Some might deem it foolish or highly overconfident, but the end result speaks for itself. The woman was, by this point, quite the professional."

"No denials. Said they found the top of the dude's skull lodged in the kitchen's back wall, and assorted other parts, crispy as pork rinds and black as freshly laid tar, scattered all around what was left of the living room. Even vaporized the man's dog, and it was hiding a room away. You know what really blows my mind, Doc? Even more than the amount of damage that coin-sized bomb incurred or the charred human and doggy remains?"

Graham shrugged wordlessly, removing his glasses and waving them around in an attempt to clear a thick, foggy build-up.

"They said the wife never woke up...never even stirred. Half the first floor gutted and torched by that flaming, pliable cannonball, blown to everlasting hell and back, and the woman snores away like it had been nothin' more than a covered sneeze."

The doctor replaced his glasses and reclaimed the iPad. Barnes, meanwhile, shifted his position to the back of the tub and rested his head on its cylinder-shaped edge.

"Well, it goes without saying The Wolf of Brunswick had counted on the little missus' habitual over-medicating not to interfere. Later that very same day, just as Chancellor Adler was being…"

"Spooned into evidence bags?"

Barnes' attempt at humor, admittedly lame even by his own standards, fell predictably flat as Graham's naturally stoic expression remained unaltered.

"Yes, well, I was going to say, " he continued, following a brief throat-clearing, "Just as his untimely demise was being discovered by local authorities, hours away in the sprawling, northern-Ostesfalen-Lippe township of Bielefeld, yet another public official was meeting a similar fate."

"Lemme guess, Doc," Barnes interrupted, hands tucked restfully behind a thoroughly sweat-saturated head, "at one time or another during your college days, you majored in drama."

Graham gestured with a raised hand as to salute his client's sharp-witted observation.

"Indeed, Dylan. At one point, I fancied myself quite the future thespian. Luckily, I had a brutally honest instructor who saw much less potential than I and rightly pointed me in a different direction. Regardless, at just past noon that same fall afternoon, The Wolf was on the hunt again, only this time, her chosen method of eradication seemed a bit more, well, personal…"

~ * ~

"beschleunigen Sie …. Ihr Mittagessen wird kalt wachsen."
(Please hurry…your dinner will grow cold).
"Zwanzig Minuten, lieb. Dreißig am Anfang. Ich verspreche."
(Twenty minutes, dear. Thirty at the outset. I promise).

Moments following this oft-repeated exchanged with his fiancèe and soon to be wife—thirty years his junior and the fourth marriage in his sixty-seven years—Steffen Gernot, retired federal judge, mounted a recently purchased Italian racing bike and sped from the opened garage onto the smooth, cement drive.

A flat, narrow stretch of perhaps seventy-five yards ensued, followed by a trio of looping curves centered by separate rock gardens and perfectly coifed shrubbery. Soon after, pavement transformed to loose gravel as wide open spaces gave way to assorted trees and foliage stripped nearly bare by autumn chill. Blinking through a light mist that just hours earlier had soaked the terrain in the form of a torrential downpour, Gernot—lanky and lean at six-three and one-hundred seventy-five pounds—picked up the pace as a sizable grade approached, his breathing as unstrained as his pulse rate was normalized.

Five minutes into his morning ride and he'd hardly broken a sweat. Nothing unusual, as it usually wasn't normally until he'd covered approximately seventy percent of the manmade trail, the middle section of which was riddled with multiple U-turns, low-hanging branches and hills of various steepness, that the initial signs of strain appeared.

Having purchased the seventy acre estate over twenty years previous, he'd ridden the same winding trail almost daily—excluding some weekends and the majority of the winter months, when he would make the logical switch to an indoor treadmill—for the last fifteen-plus. Being that the nearest neighbor was located two-and-a-half miles to the north of his less-than-modest five-bedroom, three-and-a-half bath, four-thousand square foot abode, Gernot ensured his cell accompanied him in case of an unexpected crash, packed securely into a well-padded fanny-pack tucked at his lap.

Just past the halfway point, roughly three and a half miles in length, the rain had ceased as he'd braked at the highest point on the trail. A convenient break between gargantuan oaks overlooked a deep, lush valley from which a winding, narrow creek ran a beeline directly toward his two-story home. Steffen would, without alteration, pause daily to sip from a chilled bottled water and catch his breath—a brief respite, normally no more than a full minute—that he'd secretly thought of as his own personal 'moment with nature.'

He'd only just reattached the mostly emptied bottle to its strap-on Velcro holder between slender but remarkably strong handlebars when a strange hissing noise reverberated from his immediate left. By the time he'd twisted his head around to the source, it had been replaced by an altogether different sound that was all too easily identifiable.

The arrow pierced his right, upper thigh with a muffled thud, much like a heavy, blunt object striking a pliable substance—a cement block tossed onto a wide, deep patch of mud for example—its silver, multi-bladed tip protruding several inches from the inner portion while its spotless, feathered tail-section, light blue and spotless, stuck out from the opposite side in equal measure from its pointy, blood-drenched twin.

"Guter Gott .. welcher ... der ... w-was?" (Good Lord...h-how...w-hat? he whispered, remarkably calm while casually lifting his uninjured leg and sweeping it gracefully over the bike seat. Limping to one side, he allowed the Italian racer to tip noisily over onto the gravel shoulder.

"Welcher Wahnsinn ...dieser ...ist?" (What madness... is...this?) he mumbled, grimacing as the initial numbness of the wound slowly gave way to a raw, stinging throb that quickly intensified while spreading from hip to toes. Whirling about, he scanned the bare, surrounding forest through vision which grew increasingly spotty and found nary a clue to a possible suspect.

The second penetrated his left triceps—the attached hand, strangely steady and unshaking considering the circumstances—had curled loosely around the base of the first from the rear and yanked, revealing a dime-sized tunnel before exiting cleanly from the upper bicep.

"Oh Gott ...w- wie ist das ...E-Ereignis?" (Oh god ... what is...happening?)

Stumbling in the loose gravel, the tip of the first arrow jabbing his previously unwounded left leg with each lurching step, he soon stood over that second projectile, buried nearly to the hilt in a soft patch of terrain directly between a pair of grapefruit-sized stones. His mind raced as full-blown panic set in, the question of who might logically be responsible (a near-sighted hunter perhaps?) to the quickest, most effective way to stop the torrential bleeding spewing forth from several newly created orifices. A rumble of distant thunder echoed, soon followed by a steady downpour that only served to enhance an overall sense of impending doom.

Gernot's breath hitched as he hopped back as if tiptoeing through a live minefield, his designer, bright yellow riding shirt drenched in dark maroon leakage, the matching long-short, previously light blue, equally saturated and color-altered.

"Haben Sie zu ...b-bekommen Hilfe ...A-Aufruf... Hilfe..." (Have to...get help...call for...help...) he babbled, frantically digging into the fanny pack for his cell as still another clap of thunder boomed, this time noticeably closer.

Despite a hand wracked with tremors and fingers numb from shock, he'd managed to flip the device's cover free and peruse a lengthy list of contacts, eventually able to levitate a shaking forefinger over his wife's number, said digit descending downward just as his right ear detected the faint echoes of a sickeningly familiar hiss.

~ * ~

"Correct me if I'm wrong, Doc, but didn't the kill-shot brake at the poor bastard's skull? *In one ear and out the other*, ya might say?"

"Correct on all counts, Dylan."

"Thought so," Barnes barked loudly, snapping a finger in self-adoration.

"Damn. Kinda like an earwig made up of steel, wood and feathers. Didn't the coroner's notes say it entered one canal and exited the other?"

Graham nodded, studying his patient's obvious glee with grim fascination.

"It did indeed."

"Never would've thought such a thing possible, unless she'd been standing a foot away. Ugly-ass Kraut is one helluva marksman with a crossbow. Two to one she ain't half bad with her firearm of choice."

"No bet. Not to mention the...artistic flare she displayed in the homicide's aftermath, yes?"

In true Boston Blackie fashion, the veteran flashed a devilish grin while twirling the corners of his mustache.

"Oh, that was some wicked shit, Doc. I can still see those snapshots the forensics team took at the scene."

The doctor cocked a brow.

"I'm looking at them as we speak. Undeniably a grisly work of maniacal art."

"You got 'em there?" Barnes inquired giddily, wide-eyed and reaching over with wet palm exposed, the bone-white flesh severely wrinkled from the constant moisture.

"Ya mind? Promise I'll keep 'er above the waterline."

Graham casually laid it in his palm.

"Not an issue. They're all waterproof these days."

"Oh yeah? Wouldn't know, Doc. Old school dude like me? Still peckin' away on a laptop."

"Laptop? Talk about a collector's item. There are words for people who flat refuse to surrender to modern technology, Dylan."

Having initially appeared perplexed on how to properly scan the tiny screen, Barnes soon found a groove and began flipping freely.

"Yeah, I know, fossil comes to mind, right? No sweat, Doc, I get called worse several times a day by the old ball 'n chai....HOLY

86

SHEEEEEET!" he blurted suddenly, holding the pad mere inches from tightly squinted eyes, "I haven't seen but a few of these. You must have one hell of a security clearance, Doc."

"Limitations are few. Eye-opening, yes?"

"Damn near *blinding*, Doc. Still blows my mind. I mean, you'd figure it would've taken her three, four hours to string 'im up like that, but the ME's report said that from the time he'd biked from his own drive to when they found his corpse hangin' from that tree was just over an hour, seventy minutes max, and he'd spent the first fifteen of that ridin' the trail. How the hell is that even possible? That barbwire, wound tight as a drum...multiple layers around his wrists, ankles, and neck, and how did she manage to hoist 'im eight feet off the ground to begin with? Dude was slim but still no shrimp, and she was haulin' dead weight. A team of assassins maybe, but not a single individual. Wolf's skills, for want of another word, are quite remarkable."

"Fuc...freakin' mutant is what she is. In retrospect, I'm definitely beholdin' to the man upstairs for Zack and Liza showin' up when they did. Otherwise..." Barnes paused to sigh heavily while handing the pad back over, "...she, Wolf might...would have surely caved my skull and proceeded with a similar mutilation as the doc...as Rimshaw. Who knows? They might've found us both trussed up and swinging from the nearest palm tree."

"The perfect segue, Dylan, for the inquiry I'm duty-bound to ask."

"I'm braced."

"All these many days later, do you consider yourself fit to rejoin the ranks of Atlantis's finest?"

Dylan Barnes stood with an eye-squinting, teeth-gnashing wince, messaging his prominent gut with both hands as he cautiously backed and took a seat atop the tub's rear edge.

"Honestly, Doc, I won't know 'til I hop back in the saddle just how screwed up I truly am. Physically, I'm just about there. Brain-pan wise, well, your professional guess is as good as mine."

"Appreciate the honesty, Dylan. Quite refreshing. I'll take that, officially, as a yes and recommend you be returned to duty at the first opportunity."

"Thanks. I have been gettin' kinda antsy about that first shift back. Don't get me wrong, Doc, I've witnessed my share of penal carnage in the past," he paused, his forehead crinkled in thought. "Damn if that didn't sound queer, pardon the slur."

Graham smiled beneath a clocking palm and gestured for Barnes to continue with the other hand.

"Anyhow, breakin' up melees or arrivin' after the fact ain't quite the same as facin' your own mortality. Wolf had me dead to rights, so to speak, and that's one colossal boot to the mid-section, psyche-wise, if you can dig it."

"I can only imagine. I'm of the belief, though, that you are made of sterner stuff. No need to ponder a career-change at this juncture."

"Here's hopin' you're as good a judge a character as ya are a noggin evaluator. Um, speakin' of big Bertha, how'd her, ugh, counselin' session go?"

Virtually expressionless, the doctor crossed his arms and stared down into the churning bubbles.

"Let's just say it was...quite the ordeal."

Barnes crawled from the tub, rubbings his arms from the sudden chill of exposure, before taking a seat on the tub's outer edge.

"I'll bet. You sure don't look no worse for wear, at least physically. Hell, strappin' Iron-Man like yourself might even be able to take her in a fair scrap."

"Fortunately, it never got physical."

"So, just between the two of us, what was the...your diagnosis, Doc? She completely off her SS rocker or what?"

"I'm not at liberty to say, Dylan, as you well know. Suffice to say Miss Wolf's troubles were examined, evaluated and subsequently treated."

"She's back roamin' Wolf Isle then? Frothin' jaws, rollin' eyes and all?"

"Atlantis does not possess a mental health ward, temporary or otherwise. We can only provide the appropriate medications, pat them on the head and send them back on their merry way."

"Spoken like a true company man," Barnes quipped sourly, switching to a lighter tone almost immediately upon viewing the doctor's grim visage.

"Just yankin' your chain, Doc. But..." he paused, leaning forward with hands clasped in prayer, "...don'cha think I'm due at least an explanation on why she went so unexpectedly ballistic?"

The doctor's hesitation spoke volumes.

"Sincerely, two more seconds and she'd have romper stomped my ass into oblivion. I got a right. C'mon, you must have a clue, right?"

"Fine. As long as you understand this goes strictly against regulations."

Barnes winked, raising a hand palms up as if taking a sacred oath.

"Mum's the word."

"I *mean* it. If divulged to anyone at any *time* in the future, our rears would share the same sling."

Practically genuflecting, Barnes stiffened his hand's pose before finally dropping it swiftly to his side.

"Wolf could only recall coming to and seeing both you and Doctor Rimshaw as appearing very familiar to her as...former hits."

"Hits...ya mean she thought —"

"Targets she'd previously eradicated, yes."

"Geez, so she thought we were— damn. Didn't know wild mushrooms could flourish in sand."

"Well, those we serve are not exactly the most stable of individuals."

"Goes without sayin', Doc. So basically she just went bananas?"

"Nothing found in her system save her daily meds, though if not for the treatment Rimshaw provided just before her *own* death, Wolf might've gone into diabetic shock."

Reaching up with a clawed right hand, Barnes rolled his eyes while groping and grasping at his left breast.

"My heart bleeds."

The doctor exited with a graceful leap and equally smooth landing, his bare feet slapping the moist tile with a resounding clap.

"During our session, I sensed no deception. I'm convinced her...Wolf's attack wasn't personal."

"Whatever," Barnes shrugged. "You'll have to excuse my natural skepticism."

Pausing to pat himself dry with a towel decorated in patches of red, white and blue, the doctor was unaware of his client's intense glare.

"Duly noted and understood, Officer Barnes. I will then recommend you be returned to active duty, with the single stipulation that a certain sector be avoided at all costs. Sound reasonable?"

Barnes flashed a double-thumbs up.

"A-okay. Thanks for the tub-time. Heck, it's already done wonders for the lower back."

The two shook hands firmly, each wrapped in patriotic-themed towels that cloaked them from the upper waist to the ankles.

"My pleasure, Dylan, and good luck back in the salt mines."

"Ditto, Doc. Say hey to Zack and Liz for me, ya hear?"

The doctor cocked a brow.

"I'll...do that."

"I just figured they were...due a little couch-time as well."

"Indeed they are. Within the next several days, in fact. Not much gets past you, does it, Officer Barnes?"

"Sharper than I look, Doc. 'Course, I realize that ain't sayin' much."

They departed the site gym at separate internals, no more than five minutes apart—in stark contrast both from a fashion-sense and outer deportment: the doctor decked out in a sleek, dark blue Italian blazer, matching slacks and gleaming black boots, his patient in a plain green tee, blue jeans, and mud-stained high-top Reeboks. The doctor, his lean, muscular physique moving forward with piston-efficiency, strolled purposely, shoulders pulled back and long, gangly gait utterly without flaw; his patient slightly bowed and nursing a noticeable limp.

While the former's thoughts raced steadily forward, focusing solely on sessions to come, the latter's remained stuck in a perpetual state of nostalgic flux; a permanent, incessant rewind, gnawing without mercy on his battered subconscious, as it had every waking moment since that horrifying moment, lying prone and helpless as his life flashed before him and a convicted killer lunged.

It wasn't simply a matter of being caught in the lingering grip of past fears—the 'what might have beens' that curled his gut into knotted steel—more a bothersome, never-ending itch at the back of his skull that screamed conspiracy, that something unknown and potentially fatal about the attack had yet to scratch the surface.

Bertha Wolf had *not*, Dylan Barnes' inner voice chimed without pause, murdered Charlotte Rimshaw and subsequently bludgeoned him into a quivering mass of uselessness merely due to some diabetic haze—whether or not the German-born assassin had visualized them as former victims was debatable—the brutal assault had instead been perpetrated by outside forces; outside forces that lurked closer than anyone could possibly imagine.

Six

Wolf Isle Revisited

Upon waking, she realized she wasn't alone, regardless of an utter lack of evidence it was so. Less than six days since her return from Atlantis, it came as no surprise. There was nil in the way of shock value, as she'd been half-expecting such a visit, be it midday, bathed in blinding sunlight, or of the nocturnal variety. Being as the digital clock at her bedside read two-sixteen AM, it seemed obvious her mystery guest had preferred the latter shift.

Engulfed in deafening silence, she tumbled from the padded cot with a cotton sheet still wound around her hips, her knee landing atop the hardwood with a mild thump.

She temporarily froze on all fours, dressed only in a sports bra and panties, before freeing herself from the sheet with a forceful tug. She then crawled to the inner edge of the bedroom entrance and halted, squatting with her upper back planted firmly against the wall.

"Grüße dort. Ich bin Kielwasser wach, Sie feig Ficker. There'll, kein Kriecher sein, greifen an, wie ich sicher bin, dass Sie geplant hatten

(Greetings out there. I'm wide awake, you cowardly fucker. There'll be no sneak attack as I'm sure you'd planned)," she barked hoarsely, already in the process of regulating her breathing and thus her pulse rate for maximum effect, the muscles in her neck, shoulders and arms flexing in time with each inhale and subsequent exhale.

"Wenn Sie die Bälle haben, um mir ins Gesicht zu sehen, haben Sie vor, die Chance zu bekommen, aber gewarnt werden, wenn Sie hier kamen denkend, dass Sie nichts hatten, um zu verlieren, meine Situation und ...in Betracht zu ziehen, Sie würden am besten diese Positur nachprüfen (If you have the balls to face me, you're about to get the chance, but be warned, if you came here thinking you had nothing to lose, take into account my situation and, well, you'd best reconsider that stance).

Stilted silence was the lone reply; that and the mild hiss of her own breathing. Just as she twisted around and prepped to charge through the opening, a cool breeze struck the bare flesh of her neck, upper chest and arms. As her eyes were still adjusting to pitch blackness, she couldn't yet visualize but could easily deduce the source; that being that the hut door had been left standing ajar.

Perhaps they are waiting outside the hut, on the beach, she thought, having struck a slightly crouched, defensive pose with a foot positioned half-in/half-out of the bedroom, *preferring wide open space to cramped quarters for the confrontation.*

Abruptly, she delivered a firm, open-palmed slap to her own right cheek, shaking her head vigorously from side to side in the stinging blow's aftermath.

I know what I saw. I know what I'm feeling now is just as real. This is not, as the federation's hired monkey was paid to advise, an illness-induced hallucination. They came before to settle a debt, just as this one is doing. That they came from beyond the grave is beside the point.

Bertha Wolf took a tentative step forward...then another, a slight trickle of blood streaming from the left corner of her mouth.

"*Es gibt kein Bedürfnis nach der Scheuheit wie? Sie sind hier für die Vergeltung ... für die Entschlossenheit...* (There is no need for shyness, eh? You are here for retribution...for resolution)" she bellowed, her vision completely adjusted and thus able to ascertain no shifting of the living room's sparse furnishings. *"lassen Sie uns treffen und dann wie grüßen? Verstehen Sie diese jugendliche Schreckenstaktik ist nicht notwendig...* (Let us meet and greet then, eh? Understand, these juvenile scare tactics are not necessary.)"

She crouched while moving gradually toward the entrance, which not surprisingly did stand wide open, its outer edge gently tapping the inner wall, thanks to a slight ocean breeze.

Briefly turning to give the hut's darkened inner sanctum a final, forlorn glance, she inhaled deeply before facing front and exhaling in measured increments. Her shoulders, arms and chest, noticeably bulky from an almost constant state of tension, trembled in perfect synchronization even as a wide, toothy grin literally enveloped her otherwise stoic mug.

"*Fein dann! Wusste nicht, dass es sogar möglich war, dass rachsüchtige Gespenster auf einer blutdürstigen Mission der Rache auch den Titel des Kätzchens halten konnten! Bereit oder nicht, Ficker, hier komme ich* (Fine then! Didn't know it was even possible that vengeful phantoms on a bloodthirsty mission of revenge could also hold the title of yellow-streaked pussy! Ready or not, fucker, here I come!)!"

Blasting through the opening in a slight lean with crossed, strategically placed forearms leading the way, Wolf leaped from the porch onto the beach, executing a combat roll that concluded a full ten yards from the hut entrance.

Poised on one knee with a blocking stance firmly intact, she scanned her shadowy surroundings and spotted nary a single enemy, vengeful phantom or otherwise.

"Was zum Teufel? Methinks kann ich von meinem Rocker schließlich sein," (What the hell? Methinks I may be off my rocker after all...)

Wolf peered up and over her left shoulder into a clear, crescent moon and visibly relaxed, though far from dropping her guard completely; standing erect only following another visual check of the grounds. Tranquility, stillness, and silence appeared to reign supreme— not at all uncommon—the occasional whistle of a stray wind current sporadically breaking the mold.

She managed but a single, shuffling step toward the hut before halting abruptly as a faint echo, strangely familiar, whisked past her right ear from the direction of the lagoon.

For a full minute, she stood motionless, statuesque, golem-like, save her head, which twisted and swiveled and spun like a top in the chance there'd be an encore performance. Sighing wearily when this did not occur, she'd only begun to pivot away when a sequel of sorts sounded off—a sparse few notes just audible enough to be considered genuine.

"Oh, dieser..., dass Scheiße nicht echt sein kann (Oh, this... that shit can't be real),"* she mumbled, the level of self-denial clearly not strong enough to dissuade her from following the phantom beacon; stepping lively onto the well-worn path toward the open beach.

"Ahhh, yes...this ist gerade, was ich zu relax...and brauche vielleicht schließlich einen sleep... yes einer guten Nacht bekomme, ist das vollkommen. Musik under...the stars...sand zwischen meinen Zehen (Ahhh, yes…this is just what I need to relax…and maybe, finally, get a good night's sleep…yes, this is perfect. Music under… the stars… sand between my toes)."

Thick, muscular arms hanging limp at her sides, Wolf traipsed on, zombie-like, cresting a steep dune as the spectral beacon droned on, no longer in spastic, static-filled blurts, but an incessant, relentless hum that pushed her forward in a hypnotic state, her movements robotic, her expression a pale, blank slate.

She braked before ascending the hill's opposite side, even gripping handfuls of brittle yet still surprisingly firm ammophila on either side of the trail to slow her downward momentum.

Standing at the dune's oval-shaped peak, the partial moon glistening off a calm sea serving to better illuminate the beach below, Wolf felt the mystery, the enigmatic puzzle of possibilities melt away as origins were clearly revealed.

"Neunundneunzig Entscheidungsstraße ... neunundneunzig Klosterkirchen trifft sich... (Ninety-nine Decision Street... ninety-nine minister's meet)," she crooned softly, a single drop of drool coating her lower lip.

"Um sich zu sorgen, sich zu sorgen, ruft Superhasten ...die eiligen Truppen heraus... (To worry, worry, super scurry... call the troops out in a hurry)."

They stood shoulder to shoulder; or in the case of children next to adult, shoulder to waist, the waves brushing the backs of their bare heels. The music that had served as hypnotic beacon droned on in the background, ever clearer and without pause—no matter a noticeable lack of origin to do so—serving as a most poetic theme for the uber-surreal scenario at hand.

Slowly loosening her grip on either side, the sun-dried sea-grass flayed apart and tore free between her splayed fingers until liberation was complete and she was released to drift down the dune in a staggering lurch. The foursome nary twitched, their pasty, peeling flesh aglow despite the miniscule light.

"Neunundneunzig rote Ballons (Ninety-nine red balloons)...*"* Wolf continued to sing, keeping with the music, Nena's massive crossover hit and U.S. top-forty entry from three-plus decades earlier, though the mangled vocals were strained and woefully off-key. Having joined her guests atop the board-flat beachhead, she scooted to a halt with less than a dozen feet separating them, *"...das Schwimmen im Sommerhimmel* (floating in the summer sky)."

Despite hollowed-out eyes—equivalent to blackened pits—from which behind eternal darkness lurked, tattered clothing so ancient and ashen it seemed on the verge of literally flaking away and features either grotesque bloated (the adults) or severely malnourished and rail-thin (the children), recognition had been instantaneous.

They were, had been, the Huber family. Harmand, the father and patriarch: a twenty-plus year veteran of the Dresden Bundespolizei (BPOL) Federal Police force, retiring from a supervisory position and taking a lead administration role at Aachen Prison near North Rhine-Westphalia. A tall, lanky man with squared shoulders, pointy nose, and jug-like ears who had made a living from utilization of a fierce, intimidating stare and accompanying sneer.

His wife of twenty-six and a half years, Gretel, the definition of homely (complete with severe overbite, weak chin and a lazy right eye), perpetually pudgy homemaker and mother of two, those being: Eli, their coltish, blonde-haired, eleven-year old daughter and Tobias, the once chubby-cheeked, slightly cock-eyed son of seven winters. Despite four years having passed since their first and last meeting, Wolf held little surprise that the children appeared to have not aged a single day.

The music halted abruptly, though despite its absence Bertha managed a final, croaking refrain.

"...und ist hier ein roter Ballon... Ich denke an Sie und lasse es ...' *gehen* (...and here is a red balloon... I think of you and let it go).

Harmand was the first to initiate movement, spring to life, albeit a tad stiffly, as soon as the tune had stopped, as if on cue—programmed to resurrect—a lifeless marionette whose puppet-master remained a mystery. Raising both arms straight out, mummy-like, he took a single step forward and was accompanied by what began as a faint yawning sound that would soon escalate to full-blown, anguish-fueled moan. The left arm dipped slightly at the midpoint of the forearm, obviously shattered beneath a thick, wool shirtsleeve inundated from wrist to shoulder in assorted blood spatters. It wasn't until the walking husk had shuffled forward and they stood within reaching distance that Wolf was able to fully visualize the level of carnage; carnage that, despite the time passage between infliction, appeared shockingly familiar.

"Zurück für mehr, wie, Harmand? Ich muss sagen, Sie blicken zum Kampf nicht auf (Back for more, eh, Harmand? I must say, you don't look up to the fight)," Wolf said, having already, instinctively, struck a sideways defensive pose with one arm raised in block mode and the other cocked at her side with fist clenched.

The husk once renowned as a merciless, head-cracking law enforcement officer and ruthless penal administrator did not respond other than a slight parting of its slug-like lips, a bloated black bug of unidentifiable origin crawling free, dropping into the sand and scurrying away. Harmand the husk continued to display his hands, the yawning wail instantly growing in both intensity and volume. Wolf, perhaps to break his former mark's lifeless stare, briefly regarded the remaining Hubers, who seemed to levitate forward until they stood directly behind their beloved patriarch.

"Das Aussehen der Familie ein bisschen schlechter für das Tragen muss ich sagen. Komisch nahm ich nie die Frau und Kinder als der Typ, um einen Groll zu halten (The family's looking a bit worse for wear, I must say. Funny, I never took the wife and kids as the type to hold a grudge. You, on the other hand)," she turned back to Harmand, pointing directly at the dead man as to deliver a forceful finger-poke that fell just short of impact, *"Sie, andererseits, verstehe ich völlig den Drang für ein kleines ...Auge für die Augenhandlung wie* (but you ...I completely understand the urge for a little ...eye for eye action, eh?)"

Harmand the husk shook the hands in an increasingly animated gesture, flashing the backs of each hand mere inches from the top of Wolf's flaring nostrils in a clear attempt to draw attention to the accessories adorning each.

"*A, Harmand, ich bekomme es... Ich bekomme es! Sie sehen identisch aus. Sehr eindrucksvoll, wenn nicht allzu dramatisch* (Yes, Harmand, I get it ...I get it! They look identical. Very impressive, if not overly dramatic).

The husk dropped his left, whirling it back and around with a slight bow in an obvious gesture toward his family.

In taking in their respective displays—each individual object showcased like some recently awarded prize—Wolf giggled manically as her tattered subconscious was flooded with memories long repressed.

~ * ~

The client had requested a specific type death for Herr Harmand Huber. Paid extra to see it carried out by such vile means, in fact. The request, a rarity within the trade in the age of modern eradication techniques, was that the former federal officer be literally beaten to death...a slow but efficiently fatal bludgeoning that would leave him a bruised, broken, utterly unrecognizable pile of quivering flesh, all the while inflicting as much conscious pain as was humanly possible. Never one to question a paying client's motives, Wolf could only deduce a man of Huber's past held many enemies, at least one of which refused to forgive past transgressions.

Nearly forty-hours of surveillance outside the Huber home seemed to verify earlier reports of his wife and children being out of town visiting relatives, as there had been no sign of anyone inside or outside the spacious, conveniently remote countryside abode save the intended mark.

Wolf had slipped silently from the thick camouflage of the silver fur from which she'd perched, having chosen it for both its cloaking and location advantages, as it had stood atop a nearby hill no more than fifty yards from the Huber home's front entrance. It was just past four on a chilly, pre-fall afternoon and Harmand had been tending to the grounds, first mowing a patch of overgrown vegetation at the east side of the home, then raking a patch of dried leaves into separate piles on the opposite end.

Wolf, armed with only a pearl-handled serrated blade strapped to her outer left thigh and a set of solid-steel, gold-plated brass knuckles attached to each clenched fist, had watched him walk around to the back of the house, where he'd apparently planned on burning the leaves following transportation via a trio of large black garbage bags.

Harmand had just completed pouring out the contents of bag two when Wolf purposely cleared her throat noisily. She had taken a stance perhaps ten feet to his rear, her thick, bared arms crossed over her chest and her knees slightly buckled with one leg poised slightly behind the other.

Upon turning and first laying eyes on the thick-bodied, pasty-fleshed woman decked out in only in camo pants, black boots and a halter-style white tee, Harmand had flinched back with a surprisingly feminine yowl, barely avoiding tipping over backward into the dune-like leaf pile.

Before Harmand could even begin to inquire of her sudden presence, Wolf lurched forward and landed a solid left hook to the area of his right kidney, the metallic knuckles aiding greatly in the instant snapping of two ribs in the process. A follow-up right purged the air from his lungs and sent him sprawling onto and effectively transforming the hill of collected leaves into a flattened mound marked at all corners by his flailing appendages. With the mark down and all but out—wheezing and groaning and grasping his damaged side—Wolf removed a palm-sized device from a front pants pocket and quickly snapped off several photographs. Re-pocketing the camera and resetting the knuckles, she proceeded over the next several minutes a deliberate but deadly efficient pounding, striking at specific regions upon the man's quivering frame and being careful not to exude an over-abundance of force. She would pause between bludgeonings to take pictures, later handing over a digital catalog to the client, per contract, that showcased the gradual punishment inflicted.

By the time Wolf pulled a small tin of lighter fluid from a side pants pocket and drenched Harmand's motionless frame, the man's pulse was faint and fading, a result of numerous broken ribs, shattered jaw, both eyes swollen shut, grotesquely warped and bloodied nose and assorted fractures along his neck and spine.

She kicked several small piles of the crusty leaves onto his fluid-spattered face, chest and legs before stepping back and tossing a lit match into the mix.

Clicking off a few final shots of Harmand's fiery frame, Wolf then strolled casually around toward the front of the house as black smoke rose in thick plumes over its gabled rooftop.

She spotted the back end of the black, four-door BWM sitting in the paved drive just as she turned the corner; its female driver and two small passengers a split-second later as they halted at the Victorian-styled domicile's colossal front door. One of the children, a young girl of perhaps ten with flowing blonde locks that hung well past her thin shoulders, turned on a heel just as Wolf had prepared to dart behind a circular, red-brick water-well at the eastern edge of the property. She'd planned on waiting until the trio had entered the home before escaping into a nearby patch of forest, figuring on at least a five to ten minute window before Harmand's remains would be stumbled upon and subsequent, panic-driven actions taken in the aftermath.

Slouched behind the rock barrier, Wolf heard the child's shrieking confirmation that she had indeed been spotted, followed by the mother's frantic, hitch-pitched command to both of her offspring to move quickly into the immediate safety of the home's interior. This of course, Wolf knew to mean the woman had also caught an adequate glimpse. Perhaps not clear enough for a positive identification, but then again, perhaps so, and such risks were never an allowable convenience.

The sturdy oak door caved surprisingly easy with the third kick to its midsection. Barely two minutes had passed before Wolf was successful able to track and thereby corner Harmand Huber's better-half to a second floor bedroom, one of three similarly sized and decorated upstairs sleeping quarters. Gretel was crouched inside a wide, walk-in closet, sobbing uncontrollably while jabbing a shaky forefinger into a bare palm, from which the faint chirping of a cell phone's keypad echoed. Wolf figured she'd taken at least the first one-and-a-half minutes of freedom hiding the children—no doubt stuffed inside a nearby closet or tucked beneath a bed—and thus had only just begun attempting to contact authorities concerning the malevolent stranger roaming the Huber estate grounds.

Strange, the eradicator would later ponder, how her very presence had initiated full-blown hysterics from Harmand's spouse, a bug-eyed, run-for-your-life mentality when so few facts had been known. Why couldn't she simply have been a lost traveler? How was it so abruptly assumed that the Reaper had arrived in their midst? Guilty consciences perhaps? One of your tried and true 'face the music' presumptions. No matter, she'd eventually conclude, a job was a job and as such tasks went, the Huber sanction was the best-paying of her relatively young career.

At the very moment when clawed hands reached for her throat, Gretel Huber, a woman long-fancied amongst her peers as truly one of the good ones—kind, gentle, compassionate, understanding to a tee—dug deep and had apparently located the survivor gene within, her inner tiger. Proof positive to said discovery arrived courtesy a rod-iron fire-poker, the hooked top of which grazed Wolf's chin, breaking the skin and opening a narrow, bloodless cleft.

Gretel Huber would soon perish amid a series of guttural growls and snarls—the protective mother to the very end—her left eye popped like a grape and the right side of her skull caved in like a deflated soccer ball. Wolf tucked the poker in her belt like a captured enemy sword, its sharpened end coated in a combination of blood, gore and reddish locks, and commenced the search for the Huber's missing offspring, having first ensured Mama Huber's attempt at an emergency call-out had been interrupted in time.

Eli and Tobias were located within the home's laundry/utility room, hunkered like hibernating cubs inside a cramped wooden cabinet utilized by their recently deceased parents as a coat rack.

Wolf had passed through a spotless, spacious kitchen, following the children's faint whimpering to the space their late mother had deemed the best of hiding places, stopping just long enough to retrieve a black-handled, serrated steak knife from one of a dozen perused pullout drawers.

She slit their throats with great care and, if such a thing is possible during the act of cold-blooded murder, a rare showing of sensitivity, having procured a pair of Harmand's neckties from the coat rack and blindfolding each before completing the acts.

Both Harmand and Gretel were soon relocated to the kitchen and piled next to their equally expired heirs, Papa Guber's corpse a blackened, glutinous mass that left behind a gooey, ash-coated slug-trail in its semi-cooked wake.

Fearing she'd left a sizeable amount of assorted DNA evidence behind in wake of such unplanned carnage, Wolf cranked the stove's gas nozzle to full blast, paused for a cool sip of tap water and departed out a side entrance while whistling a lively rendition of The Beatsteaks' pop hit 'Demons Galore.'

Soon after, a flaming arrow crashed through a kitchen window, effectively igniting the entire first floor of the Huber estate in a yellow cloudburst of billowing flame. From a nearby hillside, Wolf knelt with her backpack in place and watched the rest of the home gradually swallowed up and greedily consumed.

The late-night news would report the incident, local police and fire officials listing the fire as 'suspicious' in nature. Several hours *distance from the burn site at a most inconspicuous motel, Bertha Wolf viewed this breaking news through a bland, lifeless gaze. Tucked snugly within a thick, cotton robe, her buzz-cut coif still moist from a recent shower, she would soon mute the telly and go about the business of sharing digital photos to those who would subsequently fatten her wallet for a job perhaps more overdone then merely well-done.*

By the dawn of the following morn, Bertha Wolf's one-track, steel-trap of a mindset would've already turned to future missions, the ghosts of past eradications instantly exorcised without benefit of divine intervention, but a woeful lack of human conscience.

~ * ~

Currently, a foursome of such ghosts of that highly-checkered past; slightly charred, certainly soulless and entrenched in the putrid scent of decomposition, stood within arm's reach of their personal Angel of Death. Be they real or imaginary, their semi-entranced host and creator could do little but invite their haunting intrusion with open arms and mouth hanging ajar.

"Was Sie sich fühlen, ist dann ...notwendig gerade erwarten eine Scheißentschuldigung richtig nicht (Do what you feel is necessary then, just don't expect a fucking apology, right)?" Wolf stated defiantly, chest and jaw equally jutted forward, *"Ich werde eine Entschuldigung dafür nie ausgeben, meinen Job zu tun, egal das Niveau der Folter mich in der Hölle erwartet* (I'll never issue an apology for doing my job, no matter how many of these hellish tortures await me on the other side)."

Physically submissive despite the harshness of her words, Wolf attempted not even the slightest counter assault, standing statuesque even as Eli slid the serrated blade into and through the soft tendon just below her kneecap. The assassin collapsed onto her uninjured knee, groaning softly through tightly gritted teeth and watching through tear-filled eyes as little sister calmly handed the cutlery, its once gleaming edges tarnished in rust the color of crusted blood, over to her little brother. Shuffling past Wolf's mutilated leg, which she held out stiffly to one side, little Tobias moved directly to the opposite appendage and with surprising skill reached down and neatly severed the Achilles heel. Wolf lurched back with an anguished cry that she managed to cut off in mid-cry, biting into her own tongue while falling onto her back as precious bodily fluids spewed from separate, gaping wounds, staining the beach in a torrent of blackish maroon.

Her vision badly blurred from a massive pooling of hot tears, Wolf could only make out the outline of the adult Hubers as they hovered overhead like circling vultures. Harmand's first blow, not at all ironic considering the history of his own demise, landed with a muted crunch just above her right kidney. In the aftermath of impact, one of Germany's most feared and notorious eradicators, coughed out her last, a garbled "*Das ...alles Sie ...D-Dämonen k-kam?* (That... all you... d-demons... g-got?)' just moments before brass knuckles removed the majority of her upper plate and the hooked-end of an eerily familiar fire-poker tore away a bloody strip of scalp. The Huber clan's charred, misshapen nostrils flared as if savoring the salty vapors of a sudden ocean gust, a faint hum spewing forth from deep down within their damned souls—hardly recognizable as the backing vocals from Nena's iconic chart-topper.

As they fell upon her as one, Bertha Wolf's hellish screams reverberated like a shrieking banshee lamenting its own anguish-filled demise.

Seven

Skullduggery

"You know, Zack, for such a sizeable presence, you sure play soft on the inside. That is, errr, if you don't mind me saying so."

"Oh yeah? Tell you what there, Doctor J, saunter on down the lane at full tilt just one more time and I'm liable to alter that perception."

"You're on, big fella. But hey, no flagrant-type fouls now. It's a good four hour chopper ride to the nearest mainland dentist."

"Oh, for the love of Peter, Paul *and* Mary Lou, cut the macho malarkey and play already. My high-tops are sprouting mold out here."

True to his word, Dean Graham drove from the top of the key, past the foul line and directly down the center lane, turning his back to the goal as he was being met half-way by Zackary Gorman, huffing and groaning like an overtaxed freight with his massive, bared chest puffed out and both bulky arms hiked overhead in a slightly askew 'touchdown' gesture.

Liza stood near half-court, hands on hips and hair tied snugly atop her scalp in a tight, tar-black ball, her services not required until her lesser-half obtained possession. Unlike her bare-chested male counterparts, both of whom donned long—well past the knee—baggy shorts and high-topped sneakers, she preferred sweats, low-top Reeboks and an official NBA 'LA Clippers' jersey with *L.Gorman* stitched across its back in bright gold lettering.

The gym was predictably deserted at ten AM on a Wednesday, its tinted glass dome ceiling inundated with a rash of dime-sized droplets from an early morning deluge.

As was normally the case when such a challenge arose, this being their third such counseling session in the past year, it was Doctor Graham versus the Gormans in a two-on-one round-ball skirmish, first to twenty—one point per basket—victory awarded only with a spread of two or more points. To even odds somewhat, Liza would not be allowed to play defense at all and only occupy the offensive side from beyond the foul line.

Currently, as Graham's attempt at a skyhook bounced from the front of the rim directly into Gorman's enormous mitts, the good doctor was on the cusp of defeat while staring down a nineteen to fourteen deficit, due mostly to a combination of Zack's pinpoint accuracy within ten feet and Liza's sharpshooting antics past fifteen. Superior athleticism aside—the good doctor appeared to have barely broken a sweat while Zack looked to have just exited a wading pool—the Gormans' double-teaming was nigh on impossible to slow, must less stop if one or the other had the hot hand.

Firing the ball to his better half, Zack immediately took up a prime rebounding position as Graham shuffled frantically back and forth between them, unable and/or unwilling to oblige.

Given free rein to fire away, Liza stepped just inside the top of the key circle and let fly with a relatively spin-less line-drive that managed to bank neatly in despite the overabundance of force applied.

"Game!" she shrieked gleefully, pumping a fist skyward.

"Ohhhh man, that's just *not* right!" Graham groaned, throwing his lean, muscular arms airborne in comic exasperation while collapsing onto one knee, "Island rules say it doesn't count unless you call it beforehand!"

Striding by, wearing a toothy grin, Zack applied a light slap to the doctor's left shoulder.

"Island rules, Doc? Really? *Ghetto* rules maybe."

Tucking the ball beneath one arm, Graham sauntered between and then past the husband/wife team on his way toward the side exit.

"Fine, okay, but I don't want to hear any more fairy tales about that wife of yours having never picked up a basketball in her homeland."

"Cross my heart," Liza countered, gesturing accordingly.

"Soccer is king on Cebu isle, right Zackary?"

Her husband—sweat dripping freely from his chin and tip of his nose and bent over with hands atop knees—regarded Graham with a playful wink.

"No lie, Doc. I laid eyes on maybe two, three basketball goals in all my time in the PI, and if memory serves, that was in and around Manila. They love their boxing and baseball gets its due, but logic dictates a male population whose average height is around five-three couldn't give a rat's rear about hoops."

"Uh-huh, uh-huh. I hear the respective gums flapping but I'm not, repeat, *not* buying the bush-wah they spout."

Stepping through the exit, Graham waved forward with his free arm as if to blaze an unknown trail.

"Step lively, you two. This workout is just warming up, so to speak."

With the good doctor out of both sight and sound, Zack and Liza briefly locked eyes, the former nodding weakly while flashing a tiny smile that quickly faded in face of the latter's bland, utter indifference.

The workout room was equally vacant; a windowless, dimly-lit, two-thousand-plus square foot, fully-mirrored enclosure containing multiple tons of both free weights and state of the art Nautilus, NordicTrack, and Valor fitness equipment.

As Zack strolled toward the nearest weight bench, joining Dean Graham as he slowly affixed forty-five pound discs to either side of a heavy-duty bar, Liza paused at the entrance.

"Off to the little girls' room. Careful not to sprout hernias in my absence."

Graham lay back and slid beneath the gleaming, solid-steel shaft before obtaining a purposely wide grip.

"Really, Doc? Two-oh-five for a warm-up set? Damn showoff. Hey, you snap a rib, don't come bitching to me."

The doctor paused to secure his grip.

"So, Zackary, how go the retirement plans?"

The big man groaned, shoulders visibly slumped.

"Same old story. All plot, not a hell of a lot of action. I've got... some irons in the fire though."

"Oh? Those investments you mentioned last time we jawed?"

"Affirmative. With a few breaks, I'm looking at hanging out the 'Gone Fishing' shingle in two, maybe three years."

"More power to you. I take it Liza won't fight the change."

"She's got some bags packed already, Doc... just in case certain prayers are answered."

The doctor inhaled and exhaled noisily as if on the verge of beginning the set but paused again.

"So, Senior Officer Gorman, just between us, come clean. Is she *really* doing all right? I mean, other than that brash, *brave-is-as-brave does* outer persona?"

Taking up prime spotting position, Zack stretched out his arms and levitated bare palms over the bar's cool, shiny surface.

"Oh, a small portion is still bluster, but yeah, she's swept away the worst of it."

Graham paused before a labored, extended exhale.

"Swept away? As in, beneath that plush, shag carpet of her subconscious?"

"You're the master."

He heaved the bar upward and lowered it onto his chest with great care, the veins in his neck and forehead standing out in thick cords.

Three mostly unstrained reps later, he replaced the bar and pulled himself upright with a resounding huff.

"In other words, she's buried it."

"Partially."

"Not healthy. Certainly not recommended."

"Like I always say, Doc, those multiple diplomas hanging on your wall were neither forged nor pulled from assorted cereal boxes, no sir."

"Seriously, Zack," he said as the two men commenced to swap places, "this isn't exactly a ringing endorsement in terms of my decision to return you...return *her* to active duty."

Leaning back clumsily, Zack's buzz-cut scalp barely avoided scraping the bar.

"She's ready, Doc. Believe me, the biggest danger to *both* of our sanities is another week assigned to that damn supply room. Hey, um, do me a favor and pull a ten from each side, will you?"

Graham did so with a mild smirk.

"Hernia paranoia, I presume. How exactly does big, bad *and* wimpy fit into the same colossal package?"

"Just gimme a set or two to warm up, smart-ass," Zack replied, acquiring a suitable grip.

"Now about that recertification thing..."

"Fine. I'll take your word that she's ready to dive back in."

Five relatively easy reps later, the two men stood side-by-side while prepping to swap positions yet again.

"Just between us, it can only a positive for both of us."

"Really? Why so?"

"Oh, same old garbage, Doc," Zack replied after a short pause and turn of the head to ensure Liza's continued absence. "We've been kind of scuffling lately as far as the warm and fuzzies are concerned."

"I see. The gambling thing, I presume?"

"Well, there's that for sure, but…well, there's something else. She just seems…"

The big man hesitated, checking the weight entrance again and only resuming in a strained whisper, "…I don't know, distracted and increasingly irritable. She…we argued about this particular choice of assignments and I get the distinct feeling I'm to blame for her building disdain."

Graham's eyes widened in comic shock.

"*Disdain*? Hey, impressive. Pardon me while I surf the web for a proper definition."

"Gnaw excrement, Egghead," Zack replied through a wide grin.

"I'll save you the time: She hates this place, plain and simple, and being the one who convinced her to sign on the dotted line, I'm the logical target of sporadic bitch-sessions that can become quite heated."

Upon fully absorbing Graham's curt, tight-lipped response, it was Zack's eyes that briefly grew saucer-wide.

"Not to worry. This too shall pass, that is as long as you're taking care of business in the sack."

"Geez, guess I should just go ahead and turn to *Penthouse* forum with any future marital glitches, huh?"

"Penthou—good lord man, you are *indeed* the modern-day Neanderthal …a walking, talking fossil. Well then, if given access to an operational time machine, then by all means."

Abrupt, muffled laughter from both men was quickly followed by a simultaneous throat clearing.

"So, what rotation number you up to, Zack? I mean, once I do give you two the green light?"

"I'd have to check the logs, but being that we've been riding the bench for a full week tomorrow..." the big man paused, squinting and scratching his head while leaning onto an incline bench opposite the flat model one they were currently using, "...I'd guesstimate somewhere between sectors forty and fifty, that is if the subs have kept pace."

"And how many sectors you two cover these days?"

"Seventy-two, boss. Six more than this time last year."

Graham nodded, contemplating with hands on hips and eyes turned briefly skyward.

"So, being that you cover what? Five or six drops a day..."

"Six. I know what you're digging at, Doc. Once back on active duty, we'd revisit Wolf Isle in four, five days from today."

"And... well..."

"How do I *feel* about that?"

Dime-sized sweat droplets coating his sleek, ebony frame, Graham shrugged while hapless to fight off a widening smile.

"Well, yes. That exactly."

"Doc, surely by now you know my resume inside, out and sideways. I worked Riker's. I worked Joliette. Long before that, wearing a different uniform, I frequented some rather unsavory areas in the Middle East and South America."

"This I indeed *know*, Zackary." "Might sound like a bad Hollyweird cliché, but I've shared ample face time with the Reaper."

"And Liza?"

Her voice echoed within the brief moment of silence.

"What about Liza?"

Head titled, she quick-stepped toward them, pumping her arms exaggeratingly.

"My profession dictates I inquire of you the same as your lesser half, Mrs. Gorman," Graham replied while loading twin forty-fives onto either side of the bar.

"Stage is all yours, muscles," Zack whispered, turning to spot, only to be nudged roughly to the side by a series of playful hip-nudges delivered to his upper thigh.

"Back off, big 'un…I got this," Liza exclaimed, taking up a similar position as she hovered over the good doctor's prone form and making it her mission to lock eyes with same.

"So I take it our reinstatement depends on the condition of my presumed battered psyche?"

"Reinstatement is but a formality at this point. I just…need to know that your next scheduled visit with Brenda Wolf won't end with either a retribution-fueled confrontation or… perhaps even worse, an underlying sense of apathy."

Before an answer was forthcoming, the doctor shoved the bar upward and, between timed huffs, completed a barely strained set of six reps. Liza assisted in securing the bar before concluding in a tone rife with bitterness.

"Really, Hercules? *That's* the burning question? I'm doubting the same query was aimed at the Gorman possessing a penis."

"Easy, Z," Zack began, only to be waved off as Graham arose and began removing the same iron plates he'd previously added. Shooting his wife a stern glance, Zack quickly shifted to the other side to assist.

"Fair question. Actually, I did indeed quiz Zack similarly."

With that, Liza took a step back and sighed, visibly deflated.

"Fine then. Simple and to the point, Doctor; I will not attack the client in the name of revenge nor will I feel the need to half-ass my assigned duties while in her presence. I didn't know…had never *met* Rims—Wolf's victim. Maybe that has something to do with how I was able…so *quickly* able to cope."

Graham shrugged, stepping over to a nearby squat rack and ducking beneath a heavy bar already pre-loaded with ninety pounds' worth of plates on either side. His purposely winded reply was delivered between labored huffs while aligning the bar behind his neck and atop each shoulder.

"Explanation accepted. No further questions, Counselor. I'll see to it you two are cleared within the next twenty-four hours."

"Hallelujah," exclaimed the husband a split-second before pumping the bar airborne and levitating it at eye level. The four reps that would soon materialize were completed with noticeably increased vigor.

"Yeah, yippity-dippity do," echoed his wife, the words dripping with a copious helping of unrestrained sarcasm.

The doctor concluded his fifth and final rep with a resounding grunt, practically sprinting over to apply a playful, simultaneous clap atop the couple's respective shoulders.

"More than happy to accommodate, good people. Just don't make me regret it."

While Liza's only reply was an exasperated roll of the eyes, her husband did manage a verbal folly that effectively closed the subject and cleared the way for what remained a relatively conversation *and* stress-free workout.

"Sure, Dad, sure."

~ * ~

An hour or so after entering the weight room and citing a vital errand to run, the Gormans departed with separate but equally appreciative shakes of Dean Graham's outstretched hand, leaving the good doctor to several additional sets of barbell curls.

"Had me worried for a second back there," Zack had chided good-naturedly as the two exited the gym's massive double-door entrance and directly into the mid-afternoon heat, strolling briskly atop a smooth stone walkway.

His wife's lone reply was a severely cocked brow.

"Just how close were you to cold-cocking the doc?"

"Huh?" she asked, the crease in her forehead unwavering.

"I mean, you never were too keen on anyone questioning your mental stability, much less devotion to duty. Graham's strong as a bull and quick as a feline, but in close quarters, my money is squarely on you, babe."

"No hard feelings. The man was…is just doing his job," she replied sourly, staring straight ahead and unblinking. "You know, I could've lied…easily, and played up the whole shaken and stirred bit."

Zack's smile quickly wilted in the face of her cool, icy tone.

"Shaken… and stirred?" he replied timidly while inwardly dreading her response.

"*Ohhh, Doctor,*" she wailed, face scrunched in *faux* misery as her arms flailed about wildly, "*I just d-don't think I can t-t-take it anymore… the danger… the death… the horror of it all!*"

Having donned a mask of contorted rage, she twisted about and simultaneously lunged forward, the impromptu head-butt brushing the bridge of Zack's nose as he reeled back just in time to avoid full impact.

"But you see, I just don't have it in me to fake a non-existent mental disorder in order to shirk a sworn, paid duty, no matter how tempting such an act might be."

As Zack struggled to regain his balance—stumbling off the concrete path into the boiling sand—his spouse and partner seamlessly reversed fields and stormed off with a final volley delivered entirely in her native tongue, its profanity-laced message not fully lost on its intended target.

~ * ~

The winding, narrow hall leading from the personnel and finance offices to the command center reeked—a surreal mix of antiseptic and stale cigars—as if they were treading ever nearer either a hospital/clinic or enclosed poker-game setting.

"Not even a hunch? Nothing?"

"If I were going to guess, I'd say something to do with our reinstatement. If so, it's a new wrinkle to the process."

"Wouldn't surprise me. Soon we'll need to wipe our butts in triplicate just to prove we took a dump on company time."

Crinkling his nose at both the hall's pungent scent and his spouse's crude reference to government red-tape, Zack dropped his voice several octaves as they strode through a final curve and the first of three admin offices came into view. Following the previous day's blow-up, Liza had, predictably, cooled off overnight, though Zack was finding it increasingly troubling to be forced to constantly tread atop eggs with the thinnest in outer shells.

"Charming, Z. Such sugary, honey-dew sweet comments remind me of just why I love you so."

"Sorry, can't help it," Liza whispered in reply. "Carmichael at close quarters always makes me uneasy."

"Why's that again?" he inquired, reveling in chiding her so when the forthcoming answer was far from a mystery.

"One; that damn in-grown mustache he sports. I swear when the old perv flares his nostrils the individual hairs swim around like floating seaweed. Two; he is constantly staring down my rack like a starving *bata*...um, infant drooling at mama's bare tit. You never noticed that, chief?"

They passed the first office to the right, the words *LT J.GARCIA – SCHEDULING OIC* stenciled in black lettering over stained glass, its darkened, silent interior coming as no surprise to either as the good lieutenant was prone to spending his on-duty hours hounding the communications troops.

"Point of order, Z; that 'old perv' is only two or three winters this man's senior. Besides, I can't fault the man for ogling," Zack grinned, "those *are* some heavenly tatas, even strapped down so. I mean, give 'im a break; I hear he's been on his own since he and wife number four called it quits, and that's been maybe two, two and a half years."

"Five."

"Five?"

"Wife number five, and it's barely been eighteen months."

Door two, approximately two dozen further down and to their left exclaimed, *MAJ D.WEEMS – PLANNING & TECHNOLOGY OIC* with similar decorative style.

"Got'cha, dear. Any idea what the man had for breakfast?"

Liza frowned, landing a lightly tossed elbow into the lower portion of his left ribcage, to which the big man flinched and snorted laughter, barely avoiding dislodging a nearby pastoral painting from the wall with a flailing arm. *Amazing*, he mulled, the drastic shifts of mood. One minute a teeth-gnashing, claws-fully-extended hellion on wheels—the next an exotic, charming, playful sexpot. Amazing… and at the same time, damn *scary*.

Clearing their throats as one, they soon stood behind the third and final office at the end of the hall, adorned with letters just a size larger and noticeably bolder that read *CAPT V. CARMICHAEL – INSTALLATION COMMANDER.*

Husband and wife exchanged a knowing glance at the muffled sound of conversation beyond the solid pine and glass barrier. Zack cleared his throat a second time and raised a hand. A light rapping of knuckles followed and the aforementioned conversation instantly halted, replaced by the shuffling of papers.

"Enter," a gruff, familiar voice rang out.

Moments later, they fronted matching cloth chairs pushed to the rear of the surprisingly cramped space, facing the clutter-ravaged, U-shaped desk of their commanding officer, who had moved around to the front to lean on the smooth marble edge with arms crossed. The office smelled of Old Spice and the aforementioned stogies, its otherwise drab walls brought to life somewhat by a matched set of paintings that displayed wintery conditions—picturesque, snow-encrusted mountain peaks and winding steams layered in ice—the subject matter hardly surprising considering the chief's Montana upbringing.

To Liza's immediate left sat a noticeably twitchy Dylan Barnes, decked out in full duty garb and toking on a vaporized fag as if

TERRY LLOYD VINSON

awaiting his own execution. His shaved dome shining brightly beneath harsh fluorescent lighting, Captain Vance Carmichael greeted the two newest arrivals with separate nods.

A thirty-year vet of corrections and nearing, at least as rumor had it, retirement at the hardly ripe age of fifty-four, Carmichael was that rare breed that commanded respect despite plain features and a slight, less-than-intimidating physical presence. Perhaps it was the unwavering, steely stare that, if directed one's way, birthed an instant wave of unease, as if his ocean-blue orbs held the power to peel back all layers of insincerity and spot the truth like some magical subconscious CT Scan. Perhaps it was the voice; a throaty croak that brought to mind pea-gravel being slid over tempered glass. Perhaps it was a temper, rarely viewed, so overtly vicious and razor-sharp in its psyche-shredding effectiveness, legend had it that none unfortunate enough to incur its wrath had survived further employment.

"Zackary, Liza. Punctual as usual. Appreciate it, as always. I believe you two know Officer Barnes."

The trio executed a rather awkward group nod before quickly refocusing on the chief.

"What's up, boss?" Zack inquired calmly, having instinctively struck a parade-rest pose. "I guess you know Liza and I just left the company of Doctor Graham."

The captain nodded, resting his chin atop a clenched fist while occasionally gnawing the lower edges of his thick, grayish/brown mustache.

"Ah yes, Dean's infamous *sweat while you spill your guts* routine. All went well, I take it?"

"Yes, sir. He's going to advise immediate reinstatement."

"Fine, fine. I had no doubts. Have a seat then, Officers Gorman. Take a load off."

They did so, Liza taking the middle chair next to Barnes, whose haggard, pale appearance seemed to indicate impending bad news of a sort. Barnes flashed a brief, rather pathetic attempt at a smile before resuming puffing duties on the electronic smoke, the whole of his face soon engulfed in billowy vapors.

Sighing deeply, Carmichael reached up to vigorously rub both eyes before stepping slowly back around to his own chair, a black leather recliner, and literally collapsing into its slick, padded folds.

"Dylan and I started without you, I'm afraid. He's also looking at resuming duties once we get word from the Mainland. As he and I were discussing, there's been an incident that I felt it only fair to share before you heard it through the CO grapevine."

"Got word of a SE early this AM. Your sub team, Garner and Jacobs, arrived on scene at just past eight. It was their first blessed drop of the day at that. In some ways I guess that's best. Rest of the shift had to be a downhill slide in comparison."

Liza had somehow known…almost instantly. Intuition perhaps, but she didn't need Carmichael's officially announcement to confirm what she had already deduced.

When pulling duty in the islands, SE was CO jargon for 'Self-Eradication,' meaning suicide.

As if sensing a thick aura of impatience with such formalities as breaking the news slowly and with great sensitivity, Carmichael quickly cut to the chase.

"As of eight-forty-seven AM this date, Wolf Island is officially uninhabited."

The Gormans exchanged a brief glance, the male representative cocking an inquisitive brow while the female cracked a wicked smile, before turning their respective glares to Barnes, who merely nodded blandly between tokes.

"Pardon my butchered French, Cap, but good fucking riddance," Liza blurted with such unrestrained glee her lesser half was tempted to reel her in with a firm sock to the shoulder.

"Not that I don't understand such a response, Officer Gorman, at least as far as knee-jerk reactions go," Carmichael replied, arms again crossed and his tone increasingly authoritative, "but I'll remind you of the code we are bound to uphold as wards of not one but several governments."

Staring down at her booted feet, which shuffled nervously from side to side, Liza cleared her throat and inhaled deeply before responding, no doubt feeling the searing heat of not just her commanding officer's stare but her husband's as well.

"My apologies, Chief. It's just that, well, I saw… recently witnessed the woman's work up close and personal and, well, in knowing the past that brought her here, it's very, *extremely* difficult to feign pity."

Pacing the limited space between himself and his charges, both the captain's demeanor and tone instantly softened. Zack Gorman was then reminded why such a man, sleight in build and thus possessing nary a single watt of power from which to intimidate, still commanded such a high level of respect from his subordinates.

"Well said. I do appreciate honesty, even when delivered in such sledgehammer terms. Liza, in my three-plus years as CO in charge of this facility, this is the twenty-eighth such episode of self-extermination—that's right at ten per year on average. Of those, I can honesty state not the faintest twinge of sympathy surfaced. Still…" he paused, back turned to them with his hands tucked at his lower back, "…there is always a feeling of failure, a sense of dereliction, when forced with the fact that yet another SE occurred on my watch. I would hope all those with the Atlantis PCS patch sewed onto their shirts felt at least a twinge of the same. Again…" he turned, facing Liza and gently placing a flat palm atop her left shoulder "…I can't blame you for a lack of sensitivity in the fate of such a vile entity, but I would also challenge you and every other officer assigned to these islands to take a good look in the mirror and reevaluate exactly *why* they chose to accept an assignment that is clearly an acquired taste in the corrections game.

Like it or not, and damned if I always do, we're not here to rehabilitate those in our care. We're here to serve."

"Yes, sir. Understood. Again, I …it won't, um, affect the way I, ugh…" Liza stammered, mercifully interrupted by a raised palm and stern yet clearly sympathetic nod. In the aftermath of her superior officer's query concerning choice of assignments, she fired her spouse an angry, squinty-eyed glare that quickly dissipated.

"It's all right, Liza. Sermon's over. Besides, I truly detest chewing my cabbage twice and well, since I covered similar ground with Dylan just moments before you and Zack's arrival, I have to confess to a degree of counseling fatigue."

Barnes chortled aloud, snorting narrow tendrils of vapor from each nostril in the aftermath.

"I'd say you were a might easier on Gorman than you were me, Cap. As it is, I'm gonna have to regrow a butt-cheek just to be able to sit without leaning."

To this, Carmichael remained characteristically poker-faced.

"This might well be, Officer Barnes, due to Officer Gorman *not* utilizing the phrase, feel free to correct if I misspeak, 'here's hoping she rates Hell's hottest vat of boiling demon-barf and that the ugly-ass dyke-devil stews in her own rotten juices' upon first hearing the news of Bertha Wolf's passing."

"Well, sir," Barnes cracked, the left side of his mustached comically warped as he prepared to inhale yet another lungful of tar and nicotine-free fumes, "if you're gonna get nitpicky."

"*Demon-barf*, Dylan? Really?" Zack chided playfully, though Liza somehow remained stone-faced.

Releasing yet another double-barrel stream of smoke from each flaring nostril, Barnes shrugged but remained silent as the captain retook his chair behind the clutter-swamped desk.

"So, bottom line is this, folks; whatever trepidation you might've felt about revisiting the company of Miss Wolf is now, obviously, a non-issue. I just felt it right you heard it here first."

"Cap? Um, any word on just how she went about it? I mean, the deed itself?" Zack inquired, breaking a brief but awkward silence, "That is, unless we're talking a strictly need to know basis."

The captain scoffed, leaning back with both hands cradling the back of his neck.

"Like that would really matter. As remote sites like this one go, barracks scuttlebutt beats the hell outta need-to-know without breaking a sweat."

Apparently in complete agreement, his subordinates all nodded silently as one.

"Glad we're all in agreement. Sooo, the details are a little sketchy until the body-baggers forward along the digital pics, but from Officers' Grimes and Prater's initial audio report, the Wolf left quite the mess. A three-AM monitor check showed her vitals pancaking. Not a gradual phase-out either. Chip readings revealed it was a matter of minutes, no doubt as she started to bleed out.

They found a discus-sized sea-shell clutched in one hand and she'd apparently carved herself up pretty good, finally slashing herself a second mouth just below the first....ear to ear...damn near decapitated herself."

As before, the trio of correctional officers exchanged individual glances, all but Liza's glowering smirk appropriately grim.

The final five or so minutes of their meeting consisted mostly of might, might nots, as in the trio *might or might not* be called upon to testify during the mandatory inquest into Wolf's death. Similarly, there *might or might not* be procedural changes in wake of what was fast beginning an epidemic of such expirations.

In a concluding statement, Carmichael offered up his infamous 'the times they are a'changing' speech, a semi-regular, ritualistic bemoaning of the drastic changes in the correctional universe over the previous decade.

"I'm hearing there are plans to expand the region to over two hundred sectors within the next five to seven years. It isn't as if there's a shortage of available islands. More fact than fiction considering the list of institutional closings scheduled in the next twelve months is as long as it is depressing. For now it's just the worst *death row* has to offer being handed one-way tickets to their very own private beach solitary. Ten, twenty years from now, who the hell knows? Since the powers that be have so foolishly legalized so many of the same drugs we used to bust the masses for, not to mention treating muggers and rapists like they were habitual jaywalkers, it's only a matter of time before the few surviving federal and state prisons are turned into Goodwills. Times we live in, folks. Here's hoping we're all living off well-earned pensions before that full load of feces hits the proverbial fan."

In departing first their CO's office and then the admin building itself, the trio of correctional officers did so without speaking. It wasn't until they'd covered roughly half the one-hundred yards distance to employee housing that Liza broke the silence beneath a blazing afternoon sun whose ferocity was magnified two-fold by a complete lack of breeze.

"Wonder why Graham didn't mention Wolf kicking off? I mean, why bother questioning our stability when she wasn't going to be around to deal with?"

Zack shrugged, staring up into the glare through mirrored, retro-style Devos. Decked out in a black muscle tee, baggy cargos and high-tops with a small gym bag tossed over one shoulder, he appeared the stereotypical Muscle Beach-bum, albeit an extremely well-groomed version.

"Simple, Z. Dean obviously hadn't heard the news."

"You think?"

"Only explanation. Otherwise that little counseling session *slash* gymnasium gauntlet would've never happened, and if so, with drastically different subject matter."

"I'm with you, big fella," Barnes added, leaving a trail of vapor in his wake, the e-cigarette hanging loosely between the thumb and forefinger of his left hand. "From what I've seen, Graham ain't one to mince words or falsify. No reason to fib to the likes of us peons, right?"

Breaking formation in a wild sprint, Liza split the two men and quickly closed distance between herself and the approaching structure.

"Personally, I think the man gets his jollies playing mind-games."

If anything, the men slowed in wake of her sudden burst of energy, watching silently as she pulled ajar both sides of the glass double-door and practically skipped inside.

"Real firecracker ya got there, big guy. Stock up on Viagra much?" Barnes asked blandly, having eyed Liza's shapely rear end hardly bounce beneath a pair of tattered short-shorts.

"You sir..." Zack replied blandly, "...are a crude, uncouth prick."

The smaller man hardly broke stride, replying between vigorous inhales.

"No argument."

"And to answer your question," the senior CO concluded with no less banality, "I do indeed maintain quite the secret stash."

Eight

The Hawk's Descent

Beneath dark, swirling clouds, his slender, nude frame (all save a pair of knee-length boxer-style shorts) bathed in a fine mist that was equal parts perspiration and precipitation from a light but steady rain, Tate Hawkins bombarded the hard-bag with a vicious combination of jabs, hooks, and even the occasional reverse-forearm.

Though positioned beneath a wide-reaching overhang, both puncher and punching bag were slick with moisture from windblown droplets, the former huffing and groaning with each connecting blow as if enduring the punishment of the latter.

Standing just inside the hut's back door, Zack Gorman studied his client through a tight squint birthed not from a non-existent glare but a heavy dose of bewilderment. Since he and Liza's arrival atop Hawk Isle some thirty-five minutes earlier, the man they'd come to resupply with life's necessities had barely acknowledged their presence. Such behavior was in direct contrast to previous visits, wherein Zack could hardly get a word in edgewise upon the spastic, nonstop verbal barrage usually endured.

As it was, Hawkins had greeted them with a limp, lifeless wave before retreating to the back of the hut to commence battering both the hard and speed bags, impending storm be damned.

"Um, excuse me there, Mister Balboa, you got a second?" Zack blurted playfully between cupped hands, his curiosity, not to mention a building impatience, finally getting the best of him.

"Earth to Tate Hawkins! Hey man, we're almost done here. Gonna need a John Hancock and do the twenty questions thing before shoving off!"

Turning from the hard bag to that of the speed variety, Hawkins lone response was in briefly raising a glove airborne and exposing its padded palm Zack's way.

"What's up his butt?" Liza's voice echoed from the living room, where she'd offloaded the last of a trio of large cardboard boxes. "And what's with the peeled dome?"

The senior Gorman shrugged, shoulders slumped and arms crossed.

"Not a clue on either count."

"Maybe he decided it was time to look the part."

"Meaning?"

"Hmmm, let's see now: shaved head...check. Fu Manchu with matching goatee...check. A ruddy, pasty as powder complexion despite residing in the tropics, meaning he's either anemic or he's holing himself up inside that hut like a mole. Appears he's surviving on sunflower seeds and peach-pits. Either he's applying to pose for a *Psycho's 'R Us* centerfold, or there's a biiiig problem brewing beneath that bald, dementia-filled cranium."

"Answer me this," Zack replied while maintaining a careful watch on their client, who continued to batter and bludgeon away, though at a noticeably slower pace.

"Why is it you seem to save the majority of your hatefulness for Hawkins when, of the sixty convicted murderers we serve on a monthly basis, there are so many more ...deserving of your anger and disgust?"

"Because in my eyes, that one..." she paused, entering the kitchen while gesturing in the general direction of Tate Hawkins, "...is not only a child murdering bastard, but a blatant phony who constantly proclaims a crippling guilt for his sin at every opportunity. A *self-proclaimed* guilt I, for one, do not buy. Yeah, there are definitely worst resumes out there, but at least they clearly accept *what* they are and *why* they'll spend the rest of their waking days as human sand-crabs. That one craves sympathy and understanding as some kind of people's vigilante. To me an assassin is an assassin, and he needs to own up and cease the martyr act. I understand you disagree, but I'm won't apologize for my opinion, so how about dropping it?"

Temporarily shifting focus onto his spouse, Zack's grim visage appeared haggard and drawn in the sparse light pushing through the opened door. He considered, seriously considered, either changing the subject as advised or simply remaining utterly silent. When sufficiently perturbed to rant, the most effective way to calm the woman he loved was to remain mum and simply agree with her point of view, no matter how false the admission. It was a *bad* sign that her piney accent was quickly growing in prominence, a *sure* sign the train was fast derailing and needed an immediate switch of tracks. Regardless, as was wont to happen now and again, anger easily outpaced common sense.

"Duly noted. However, as for *my* way of thinking, just for the record, I do buy it. I truly buy into the fact that the man did not treat that unfortunate child as some sort of collateral damage."

"He never owned it, Zack," she countered sharply, slapping an open palm atop a nearby countertop and accidentally overturning a plastic drinking cup which tumbled into the sink atop a jumbled pile of assorted, unwashed dishes that appeared permanently stored in said condition.

"In my book, he's a notch *below* the run-of-the-mill eradicator."

"How so?" he replied sourly, turning his steely squint back toward Hawkins, who had begun to pummel the hard-bag with front and side kicks even as the light shower slowly intensified into a steady downpour.

"He's as much a conniving, convicted liar as he is a killer. Think about the others we so proudly serve in the commencement of our weekly duties—Jorgensen: confessed serial rapist and murderer of elderly women…kicked off his career as a high school sophomore and snuffed one victim a year for the next decade-plus. Like paying his taxes, he said. When asked, the sick, sawed-off little bastard will tell you that if he hadn't got caught, he'd still be out there picking them off the grounds of the local senior living facility. See, *he* owned it."

"So we're comparing the stench of those who may still possess human conscience and those who do not or possibly never did?" he shot back abruptly in the realization she'd paused only to reload woefully deflated lungs.

Much to his regret and chagrin, she'd begun to pace the room from corner to corner—arms failing spastically—their assigned iPad tucked snugly into her left hand.

"Or how about Brother Jerome? Slaughtered eight of his own flock over a thirteen year assignment to a tiny, remote church out in the sticks somewhere in urban Mississippi."

"Georgia. *Rural* Georgia."

"Whatever. Old Brother J targeted, charmed and eventually croaked all those trusting parishioners without raising a single eyebrow 'til the feds finally got curious and eventually found what was left of them bottled in jelly jars and stashed in his wine cellar.

"Now, did Jerome put the blame or *God*? Did he say the *devil* made him do it? Hell no, he did not. Preacher-man Jerome Jarvis Johansson said none of those things, no sir. Said he poisoned them, chopped and sliced their god-fearing hides into strips and bottled them like pickled eggs because he regarded them as closet-atheist phonies who attended his services under false pretenses. He too *owned* it. No excuses. No remorse, fake or otherwise."

From the corner of one eye, he could see her pace slow and hear the coarseness of her tone ease a bit. Mercifully.

"Truthfully Zackary, if asked to choose the worst of two evils, even Bertha 'The Beast' Wolf gets my vote over Mister 'Woe is Me' out there. She didn't give two shits about those two kids she murdered in cold blood and tossed onto the fire, and would've surely told you so with no qualms whatsoever."

"He's on the verge of collapsing," Zack said matter-of-factly, no longer in the mood to argue or attempt to budge or even slightly alter his wife's opinion. Hawkins had fallen to one knee, reaching up to punch the hard-bag with a jab so weak it hardly moved. His head had fallen back, his mouth ajar and overflowing from the constant downpour.

Eyes squinting floss-thin and brow severely creased, Liza busied herself studying the iPad's well-lit screen and briskly checking off the drop-ship inventory sheet.

"Poor baby."

"I'm serious," he replied sternly, half-stepping past the entrance threshold and receiving a misty facial for the effort.

"You really want to go through all that post-death report garbage again? Well, not me, sister…"

"Big-hearted pussy," she mumbled only semi-coherently, the rubber end of a rainbow-colored Stylus pen held firmly between gritted teeth.

A full five minutes later, Senior CO and convicted serial killer sat across from one another at the dining table, the former unconsciously mimicking the classic pose of 'The Thinker' while the latter slumped forward with splayed elbows taking the brunt of the considerable dead weight involved. The drop-ship form approved and duly signed in electronic form by its intended recipient, Liza had long since departed for the cutter, refusing even the most perfunctory in goodbyes.

"You look like hell," Zack had remarked initially and without a trace of humor. He'd been forced to lug the smaller man inside and practically position him upright, standing by for several seconds to prevent a possible tumble to the rainwater slickened tile. As the back door remained partially ajar and relatively blues skies and bright sunlight had replaced the earlier downpour, the interior was sporadically infiltrated by a gust of oppressively humid air.

"Mind I if click on the A/C, Hawk? I'm practically vaporizing in here."

Receiving no immediate response, Zack pushed away from the table and took the liberty of securing the door with a gentle shove. By the time he'd retaken his seat, Hawkins had raised his head from the tabletop, apparently utilizing Herculean effort to maintain an upright pose if his strained expression was any indication.

"Better h-hold off for now, Doc. I'm f-feeling kind of... a smidgen peaked . Cool a-air and moist pores don't m-mix too well. Might end up w-with full-blown pneumonia. D-don't need a-any help feeling like c-crap about n-now."

"Peaked? Son, I'm half-tempted to give the med boys a ring."

Hawkins, the bare flesh of his shoulders, chest and arms gleaming with scattered patches of moisture, raised a shaky hand and waved it feebly back and forth.

"N-no, that isn't... won't be necessary, r-really. I'm... it's just a... I'm in a bad rut lately is all."

"What kind of rut might that be?"

"Just... not getting enough sleep."

"Is that all? No sweat then. I can have an RX of sleep-aids shipped out to you by tomorrow AM."

Hawkins nodded, his baggy eyes fraught with fatigue.

"Not necessary. I'd... rather not start down that particular road."

"Why suffer, man? Stubborn is one thing, damned foolish still another."

The haggard man's pale-lipped smile was misery personified.

"Honestly, I'd rather be a tad worn out from lack of proper shuteye than shuffling atop the sand a mindless zombie."

"A *tad* worn out, Hawk? You study a mirror lately?"

"I'll ...tough it out without a certain rattle to my walk."

The big man shrugged.

"Fine, you're the doctor. Any specific reason for the insomnia?"

Hawkins paused to run splayed fingers over his stubble-infested dome, his breathing as raspy as the tone in which he eventually replied.

"If I confide in you on this matter, Chief, you have to swear it goes no further than this hut."

His own expression atypically bland and utterly without emotion, Zack raised his right hand and flashed a 'Scout's Honor' gesture.

"Not even with your wife, agreed?"

"*Especially* not my partner. Agreed."

"And, even more vital, no giving me up to Dean Graham. Nice enough guy, I'm sure, but those jog and jab counseling techniques he employs unnerve the hell out of me. I'm not due another visit from his mobile couch for another two and a half weeks, and I'd rather not see that date moved up."

"He means well," Zack replied shrewdly, cloaking a small smile with a well-placed palm.

"I'm sure, and I consider myself a fairly well-conditioned athlete, but having my noggin poked and prodded like fried turkey is uncomfortable enough without the added pressure of a full-blown marathon."

"Marathon?"

"We lapped the island forty-six times, Doc. I kid you not. By the last query, I was on the verge of fainting while Graham was hardly winded."

"Yep," Zack nodded, recalling his and Liza's recent session spent laboring inside the Atlantis' gymnasium. "Sounds about right. Mum's the word, Hawk. Now, what's been ailing you?"

"Dreams, Doc. Sounds cliché, I know. *Nightmare on Hawk Street* perhaps."

"Nightmares leading to a sleep disorder of some magnitude?"

"I'll say. Probably averaging two, maybe hours a night, tops, the last week or so. Last few nights, lucky to nod off at all. I've tried napping during daylight hours. I guess vampirism was never my thing."

Zack stood stiffly, strolling toward the kitchen with a noticeable hitch in his giddy-up. He replied only after pulling a plastic cup from a nearby cabinet and filling it to the brim with cool, filtered water from a clear pitcher snatched from the fridge.

"Those must be some seriously troubling dreams. They are ...just dreams, correct?"

"Hope and pray so, Doc. If not, the alternative is a damn sight scarier."

Pulling his chair clear from the table, Zack propped his boots atop the edge of the tabletop with the ankles crossed.

"What alternative might that be?"

Leaning back and hugging himself across his bare midriff as if enduring a sudden chill, Hawkins gnawed his lower lip before flashing a hideous smile.

"What if it's real, Doc? What if ...even a portion of what I'm hearing and seeing is based in reality? Shit, if *so*, the foreseeable forecast is bleak, to say the least.

"If *not*, if it is just my subconscious flipping random channels in some remote corner of hell ...well, Doctor Graham will soon be emptying the pharmacy for every damn psych med available."

"Hey, sometimes such treatment is necessary. It's not uncommon in the regular world, much less in one so ...irregular."

An infestation of chill bumps coated the smaller man's arms; a slight tick forming at the corner of his left eye.

"Not happening, big fella. If I'm going down, swirling downward in a spinning descent into bat-shit insanity, the least I can do is remain stone-cold sober for the trek."

"Um, you want a sip of my water, Hawk? Maybe put on a shirt? We could go outside...sun's up and thus so is the temperature. Might be just what you need to perk up."

"I'm all right, Doc. Really. Just need a few minutes to decompress."

Zack emptied the cup in two lengthy swallows, placed the empty on the table and leaned back with the fingers of both hands snugly intertwined at the back of his neck.

"So, what is it you're seeing?"

"It started with scratches ...scratching at the door ...at the bedroom window. L-like windblown tree limbs scraping across glass, just enough to wake me but not significant enough to instigate a search for the source. The implausible ...impossibility of it didn't hit me 'til the next morning."

"What's that?"

"No trees near that window, thus no limbs to reach out and tap yon window."

"Oh, got'cha."

"That was the first night. The second it began similarly, only this time I heard the front door open. A loud, drawn-out screech that saw me roll off that cot and crawl into the living room on all fours like a cockroach seeking a suitable crevice."

Hawkins wiped a bare forearm across chapped lips, as if to wipe away a build-up of non-existent spittle.

"Of course, once I'd completely shaken away the cobwebs and confirmed the absence of the blood-sucking, flesh-munching sea-monster my inner fear had cultivated, it was easy enough to blame a stout gust and the fact that I'd never checked the entrance to see if it'd been completely shut."

"In all fairness, Hawk..." Zack shrugged, "...it's not as if hut security were a priority, right? Not exactly Grand Central Station on these dunes."

"Most nights I don't even give it a second thought. Why the hell should I? Cat-burglars are few and far between."

"True. So, what then?"

"Night number three saw a massive escalation of similar nocturnal variety. While the scratching noises were bypassed altogether, the door wasn't merely pushed slowly inward but practically kicked in with such force I heard two distinct bangs: the initial impact followed by the door itself smacking the far wall hard enough to leave a clear indention of door knob into wood."

"You left it unlocked again, even after the previous night's weirdness?"

"That's the thing, Doc. I *did* lock it. Swear I checked it several times before traipsing off to beddy-bye, fruitless as that turned out to be, as I'd been wide-eyed and completely awake when that door imploded. Honestly, Doc..." he continued, leaning forward and suddenly whispering, "...this boy isn't easily shaken, must less downright scared shitless. I practically jumped out of my skin."

Zack reached forward to loosen a build-up of sand from the side of one boot, the moistened chunk spattering the beige tile floor.

"I'm guessing further investigation ensued."

Nodding, Hawkins resumed his previous pose, slumping back into his seat and rewrapping himself in a self-imposed bear hug.

"Once my heart had properly repositioned itself from my throat back to the chest, indeed I did."

"And?"

"It gets ultra-strange here, Doc. I'm talking *break out the straitjacket* bizarre."

"Understood. I'm all ears but completely void of knee-jerk judgments."

His tone raspy and gruff, Hawkins no longer quite whispered but was far from regaining the smooth, full volume that was a trademark of sorts.

"Creeping from the bedroom to the kitchen, I heard …first heard footsteps. Pattering steps; quick and light like that of a …small child. Bare feet slapping hard tile. Clear as a bell they were. Following a tense moment or two, during which time I actually pinched myself in order to convince the coward within that it was not a dream, curiosity prevailed and I practically sprinted through the kitchen in hopes of at least catching a glimpse of my mysterious guest."

In the short pause that followed, the senior corrections officer started to intercede but refrained once his client gave evidence of resuming.

"I saw a shadow dash out the door. Narrow and close to the ground and lightning-fast, like its source had taken flight upon my intrusion. I quickly followed, half-tripping over the coffee table and stumbling through the opened door. Of course, the beach was predictably deserted. No tracks in the sand, kid-sized or otherwise, hence no evidence to disprove my own gradual meltdown."

"What about the last few nights?"

"No additional incidents. Hasn't improved my downtime, sad to say. I've …I'm trying alternative methods to increase my level of exhaustion and force the issue."

Zack gestured toward the back door.

"So that's why the *punch 'til your pooped* workout?"

The smaller man grinned despite himself, unlocking his arms from their double-grasp and allowing them to fall limply to his sides.

"Oh, good one, Doc. I like it. Yeah, at this point I figure passing flat out is preferable to full-blown insomnia."

135

"Just a bad spell, Hawk, that's all. Lack of recent episodes probably means it's done."

Hawkins frowned, "Done?"

"Your subconscious is apparently on to other tasks, no longer obsessing with whatever birthed the other."

"Hope and pray you're right. A few more visits from the sand ghosts and I'm liable to attempt a Count of Monte Cristo and dig my way to China."

Raising a shaking finger, Hawkins regarded the larger man through a single, squinting orb, the other clamped tight.

"Remember your promise, Zackary. I don't want to wake up to a med chopper landing at my doorstep in the next few days and Dean Graham subsequently pecking at the door."

"Your secret's safe with me, Hawk," Zack replied with a stern nod, removing his boots from the table before pushing the chair back and standing with a wide, noisy yawn.

"Besides, ragged shape you're in, it'd be nothing short of cruel to send Doctor Super-Abs your way. He'd probably prescribe a quick jaunt around the island."

Try as he might, Hawkins' attempt at a follow-up smile appeared more a warped, pained grimace.

"No joke. Might even follow that up with a marathon swim all the way back to the Isle of Atlantis."

"All that said, Hawk, the boys manning the vital charts won't hesitate to sound the alarm if your BP goes volcanic, and it's a sure thing these little nocturnal trips to the Land of Oz might just do the trick. You sure I can't order you up some sleep meds?"

"Thanks again, Doc, but no thanks. I think I've got it under control, sincerely."

Zack stepped over and applied a gentle tap to the man's sweat-slickened shoulder.

"All right, all right, but if the midnight willies come-a-knocking and you find yourself freaking out beyond repair, do not hesitate to give that big red medical emergency button a stout poke, understand?"

"Yes, Dad..." Hawkins complied, bowing weakly until his forehead hovered mere inches from the tabletop, "...will do. Cross my heart and hope to croak."

Strolling into the living room, Zack gestured toward a trio of unpacked boxes sitting atop an otherwise barren glass tabletop.

"Order's complete, by the way—each and every item present and accounted for— I saw the way you gave the passing *olè* to the inventory sheet. Oh, we were finally able to confiscate a copy of that Vietnam War documentary you'd been requesting—something like one-hundred twenty hours' worth—that ought to keep you occupied 'til the next drop."

Hawkins remained seated, the ruddiness of his complexion appearing to gain a semblance of color as moments passed.

"Appreciate it, Doc, as usual. Wish you had ...more time to jaw. Sure could use the company, but I understand you're ...you two are bound to the strictest of schedules."

The big man paused at the open entrance, donning his sunglasses in preparation for exiting the hut's shaded interior for the dazzling glare of the awaiting beach.

"Truth is, I've already overstayed our set visitation by nearly ten minutes, but then, we've recently had an opening that affords us a little extra time at each drop site. Sorry I can't...couldn't hang out longer, Hawk," he paused, regarding his client through a tint so dark his eyes were completely cloaked and thus impossible to properly read. "My apologies for the wife's lack of sensitivity. In fairness, she's been going through a bad stretch herself recently."

"Don't give it a second thought, big guy. Those in my ...line of work hardly expect an outpouring of sympathy for our plight. Take care ...both of you."

"Steady as she goes, Hawk..." Zack replied, stepping through the threshold, "...and if you must dream, see to it the plot involves, say, an old girlfriend, a picnic basket and a lush, green pasture, all right?"

Pushing back from the table with a weak but steady shove , the initial portion of Tate Hawkins' croaked reply might or might not have been heard over the sudden intrusion of a faraway cutter's blaring horn, "Sounds a bit like Heaven, Doc..." while the follow-up refrain, no more than a throaty, hardly audible mumble, had most certainly not been intended for mass consumption, "...such soothing, joy-filled fantasies are strictly off-limits for those whose soul is branded as permanently damned."

Bypassing the recently arrived stock, he staggered out of the kitchen and through the living room, crashing onto his cot with a low groan and spilling a pile of recently folded laundry into the floor in the process. The low hum of an overhead ceiling fan accompanied Tate Hawkins into a deep, dreamless slumber, the occasional twitch of a finger or flutter of an eyelid the lone signs of life.

~ * ~

Lounging atop the cutter's squared stern, Liza utilized each of the available deck seats by slumping deep into one and propping her booted feet onto the other. Though sufficiently shaded by a domed overhang, she had not removed her sunglasses while using a probing forefinger to peruse the assigned on-board iPad, a woefully outdated model that nonetheless served as the cutter's back-up GPS. For want of nothing better to do as her lesser-half schmoozed with the inmate—an annoying habit she'd learned to tolerate but was unwilling to duplicate—she'd accessed personnel files for a quick go-over, specifically those belonging to one Tate Jerrod Hawkins.

Of the seventy-one so-called clients, formerly seventy-two before the demise of a certain German-born assassin, she and Zackary served on a weekly basis, Hawkins consistently got under her skin most of all. Suddenly, inexplicably unaware of exactly why that was, she decided to refresh her memory by revisiting the man's criminal history via his personnel file.

Listed beneath the main folder, simply titled 'HAWK', were several sub-files, each with their own subheading. Yawning beneath a gloved palm, she purposely bypassed the first three, entitled '*ORIGINS,*' '*EARLY SIGNS/AGENDA,*' and '*PATTERNS/KILLS*' respectively, to one labeled '*FINAL SANCTION/CAPTURE,*' opening the PDF with a single, gentle tap.

Whispering to herself in her native dialect of Bisayan, Liza receded even further into the hard-plastic chair, nearly lying flat across between the two until it appeared she was attempting to undertake a midday powernap. A pair of gulls levitated briefly overhead, perhaps hoping to discover an easily attainable food source on the deck below, before dumping a double-load of moist, whitish droppings onto the cutter's starboard side and sailing off toward the mainland.

Liza spied the circular poop-spatters through the dark tint glass of the windshield and groaned before refocusing on the file, which was in the final stages of opening.

"Yeah, that about sums up the general consensus concerning this line of work...in a peanut-shell."

Eyes rolled upward and forehead creased, she pondered her choice of words just as the PDF flashed to life.

"*Walnut* shell? *Chestnut* shell? Awww, whatever. On to more important issues, like why it is every time I get within six feet of that double-talking jackass I want to deck him? Why *him* most of all?"

She speed-read the document's short prologue before clicking an audio link designated '*In his own words: Official confession to Agents Cartwright and Grayson, Federal Bureau of Investigation.*'

Several bursts of static ensued, followed by the prerequisite intros, exact date and time recorded for prosperity, and finally the clearing of throats and a few scattered coughs before questioning officially began.

~ * ~

For the record, this is Agent Brian Cartwright (clears throat). Mister Hawkins, please elaborate why and how you came to be at the residence of record on the date in question.

I'd tracked Winslow to the Oak Lane home a few days before. Not exactly a monumental feat with SOs...um, that's sex offenders to the layman, as we all know. A quick Google search, followed by the local PD's crime reports website brought me right to his door. From there, I cased the place until I had a pretty decent take on his daylight schedule and nocturnal habits. In such a dilapidated, crime-infested neighborhood, no one sees anything or anyone suspicious; not when residents and strangers alike are equally seedy by nature. I could've slept on the man's lawn without it raising a single brow of concern.

Agent Grayson here...we assume this is your usual...the (clears throat) normal pattern you'd followed when tracking previous targets.

With the SOs, yes, hardly a variation from one to another. There are... were times when the staking out aspect wasn't so easily completed. Some of the more...cramped government housing locales made for quite the challenge.

Agent Cartwright speaking. So what you're saying is that the stalking and ultimate eradication of the judges in these cases was much more complicated and complex a mission than the related registered sexual offenders.

Obviously, yes. Those with the means can afford to employ security measures that others of a lesser pay-scale cannot. Still, being able to overcome said roadblocks only served to hone my instincts and keep me grounded somewhat. That is (laughs) until the amateurish debacle that was the Clint Winslow sanction.

Grayson here. In your initial confession to Detective Jamison, you stated Winslow reminded you, at least some aspects of his facial features, of Peter Rothland. Perhaps this explains the recklessness of your behavior that particular night.

How so, Agent Grayson?

Grayson here. Emotion, Mister Hawkins. Such anger and rage, the savagery of the assault on Winslow. This was, had not been your trademark in earlier eradications. Perhaps you channeled some inner frustration tied to Rothland's memory and worked out same on a man you viewed as a distant relative, both in terms of physical appearance and depravity.

(Lengthy pause) Excuse my curtness, but I wasn't under the impression this session was yet another psyche exam.

Grayson here. Humor me, Tate. I'm thinking my future lies in profiling.

(Groans) Fine, but only because you fellas have kept the Starbucks flowing consistently since my transfer.

(Heavy sigh) Before we discuss specifics, the obvious fact is that the majority of predatory scum such as these often do share many of the same disgusting, deplorable traits: the missing teeth, prison tats, illiteracy. Not always a factor, but they were originally referred to as stereotypes for a reason.

Agent Cartwright here. Agree wholeheartedly. Then there are, of course, those who are the complete, utter opposite of the aforementioned stereotype.

Ah yes, the wolf in sheep's clothing. Such was the case of Professor Cline, he of the perfect haircut, tailored vests, three-decade teaching career and solid family background. Gentlemen, I must confess to a soothing sensation warming the very cockles of my ticker whenever I think of that bitter cold day in February when I exorcised that particular demon.

Cartwright here. My apologies for throwing you off-track. Please, back to the previous subject matter.

That stated, it was true that the curvature of Winslow's fat, repulsive mug did mirror Rothland's to a degree, and both cultivated shaggy, woefully neglected facial hair, no doubt filled with fragments of past meals and an assortment of insect life, but come to find out—the main similarity, as bizarre and surreal as it might be—was the shared tattoo. Talk about a mind-blower! (claps hands) What were the odds, yes? Two individuals, birthed on separate coasts and reared two-thousand-plus miles apart...no six degrees of Kevin Bacon here...absolutely zilch in common save their penchant...their love for molestation of the innocent and....and...wait for it...the same exact body-art, at least in terms of design. Size and placement differentiated, of course, but regardless, I found the discovery somewhat...breathtaking and, admittedly, exhilarating.
(Lengthy pause; inaudible mumbling)

Grayson here. Point of order: Winslow possessed many assorted tattoos. I'm... we're not privy to a similar marking on the body of the late Mister Rothland. Please enlighten.

The dragon, gents. The winged, horned Chinese dragon adorning Winslow's right shoulder and Rothland's left bicep. Same... identical design and, stranger still, nearly identical color schemes.

142

Cartwright here. Similar enough tats, to say, fuel your inner rage to as-yet-unfelt levels?

As in ...blind rage, Agent Cartright? An anger so all-consuming one loses their ability to reason, striking without mercy and usually without memory of doing so.

Grayson here. Textbook definition, Tate. Personal experience? (lengthy pause; muffled laughter)

Not ...a ...chance. Rage, as so defined, has never before and never will dictate or control my actions. Since we all know what you're digging at, gents, allow me to cut to the chase; the Winslow eradication was not unlike all that came before it. Meticulously plotted and mapped out in excruciating detail. That the execution of said plan was thrown so horribly off-kilter by unforeseen circumstances had nothing to do with my ...losing control in any way.

Talk to us ....oops ...my bad. Grayson here. Talk to us about that, Tate, and what led up to those ... unforeseen circumstance.

Cartwright here. From the beginning please, Mister Hawkins, if you don't mind.

Nothing too complicated, really. Mental midgets like Clint Winslow rarely bother to secure their kingdoms, allowing me to waltz through the back door without even removing the hook-pick from my backpack. The interior lights had been doused at must past midnight; Winslow's usual sack-time, I'd assumed from its consistency from the two previous nights. I waited a full hour-plus before making entry, removing the ski-mask and tucking it into a side pocket of my cargo pants but remaining gloved. The uncloaking—full identity reveal— is...was all about allowing their kind a full, unblemished view of the one responsible for snuffing out their miserable existence. Might sound melodramatic and, alas, even a bit corny, but there is a heartfelt sincerity to such rituals.

As with many of his ilk, Winslow was not only a moral degenerate but a slob of the highest order. The kitchen sink overflowed with stained, stacked dishes and bloated bags of garbage that smelled of spoiled meat and long-expired dairy products.

The living room was hardly an improvement, with assorted clothing scattered about as if by a rogue funnel. I'd barely avoiding tripping over haphazardly strewn boots and sneakers, the stench of unwashed feet somehow overwhelming even compared to the kitchen's rancid aura. Disgusting...utterly disgusting. A wolf in pig's clothing was our Clint Alan Winslow. I recall freezing in mid-step at one point, thinking a lumpy, unrecognizable pile dominating the living room couch could only mean that the man had never made it to his bedroom before passing out. A more careful study however, through better adjusted night-vision, found the culprit to be a disheveled wad of tangled bedding.

I seem to remember a stout whiff of urine and pondered if the man owned an indoor pet of some kind; perhaps a tiny dog of toy-breed type or a feline whose litter-box had been as neglected as that sink-load of crusty dishes. This was quickly dismissed as I moved toward the rear of the house and the two bedrooms located directly across from one another.

The door stood wide open to the one on the left; empty except for a raggedy cot, a TV tray and several scattered mounds of clothing, obviously unwashed from the putrid stench, so nauseatingly aromatic as to render all previous stenches nonexistent.

Side-stepping over to the opposite door, shut save perhaps an inch-wide opening, I heard Winslow's throaty snores reverberate from within, the consistency of which was broken sporadically by either an *exclusively nasal snort or squeaking, slightly moist release of gas. Following a short pause, surely no longer than two minutes in duration, during which time I readied the Hand of Justice and meditated briefly—common rituals that had become the norm following the second of the six sanctions—I used my left elbow to ease the door back and was instantly taken aback by the overwhelming presence of the sharp, sour fumes associated with ingested whiskey of no particular stock. No shock whatsoever, considering Winslow's lengthy arrest record, littered with assorted booze-related violations to include a trio of DUIs and a half-dozen public intoxication-related incidents.*

Agent Cartwright here. Apologies in advance for interrupting, Tate, but just to clarify ...the Hand of Justice you speak of refers to?

Oh yes, I get it. The term Hand of Justice could definitely come across as a tad bizarre, perhaps even comic-book corny. Well, gents, its origins are as simple and uncomplicated as the time-period from which it came, a vintage Fairmont four-pound sledge designed and manufactured in the mid-nineteenth century for the blacksmith trade.

I ...came into its possession just over a decade ago, purchased at a garage sale for a mere five dollars.

Grayson here. Pray tell, Hawkins, what ...caught your eye about such an object? I mean (laughs) surely you weren't thinking of actually using it for its designated purpose.

Not quite. Truthfully, I'd had no intention of making a purchase that day. In fact, I'd never been the garage-sale type...just the opposite, actually. Later that same day I began to realize it had been no mere whim, no ordinary coincidence that I attend that particular yard sale, just as that hammer's true use in the day's and years to come began to gradually gain meaning ...and gain power as a source of inspiration for my true calling, my true purpose; something that had been so sadly amiss for the duration of my entire adult life.

Grayson here. Maybe it was the words burned into the handle that ...initially served to inspire. What were they again? (clears throat) Just for the record...

Caught my eye right from the start, though at the time I thought it nothing more than a clever play on words. It read simply 'A pound of flesh,' It would be a full calendar year later before I was to truly understand the significance, as in 'to extract a pound of flesh from the wicked masses.'
I'd run across that particular line in a pulp mystery novel by Douglas Boren, one of my favorite authors who normally specialized in historic or sea-faring tales.

Cartwright here. We'll get back to that initial...mission before signing off, but for now we'd better stay on track in the matter of Clint Winslow. Okay by you?

Certainly. Where was I?

Cartwright here. You'd just entered the foul-smelling bedroom...

Ah yes...nostrils flaring wildly no doubt from the effect of fumes so stout it was as if the man had literally bathed in whiskey. I'd remained instinctively stealth-like, though in all honesty, I'd have been fairly confident the rumble of a full-blown twister would not have held a candle to that worthless bastard's thunder-like snoring. He'd lain on his back, head tilted slightly back and mouth pulled wide, those slug-like lips trembling like worms perched on the edge of a fishhook with every exhale. Other than a pair of cherry-red Fruit-of-the-Looms and a

146

single sock hanging from his left foot, he'd been as nude as the day Satan's bride celebrated his hatching. His left elbow was stuck to and had apparently emptied a small glass ashtray onto the mattress.

By the time I'd reached the edge of the bed and leaned over his sprawled frame, I'd filled both hands with the required tools of the trade.

Cartwright here. Point of order, Tate: the Hand of Justice has certainly been well established as the main…tool. Please specify the other.

A filled syringe containing an ample serving of Thiopentol, mixed with just a dash of veruronium.

Which is …um, sorry …Grayson here. Which is?

A paralysis cocktail of my own creation …well, perhaps not, but I'd venture to say no practicing MD had ever utilized the same exotic mix in fear of felony malpractice.

Grayson here. The effects of said cocktail?

Nearly instantaneous muscle paralysis when administered in the full adult dose. Needless to say, I never shirked on quantity. Once jabbed, ready the slab, you might say.

Grayson here. Once …jabbed …ready th—?

(Laughs) Turn out the lights, agent…the party's over for pervert, get it?

Grayson here. Um …oh yeah, got'cha …crystal clarity, Tate. Please proceed…

Well, from there it was fairly hum-drum ...by-the-numbers, at least as far as the eradication phase. Same old, same old. Sadly, by this time the act of the kill itself had lost the majority of its previous kick.

Cartwright here. Humor us, please.

Fine, for the infamous record then and, hopefully, for the final time. A trio of injections came first: the initial in the upper left thigh, the second in the opposite leg, the last in the right side of the neck just below the ear lobe.

Grayson here. And ...he ...Winslow never stirred while being pin-cushioned?

The soulless bastard was extremely inebriated, Agent Grayson. Regardless, pardon my blowing my own horn, but I have...had by this time became something of a specialist in the fine art of the relatively painless injection. By the time his eyes fluttered and struggled to open and obtain focus, his extremities were already well on their way to almost complete paralysis. Though there is no hard scientific evidence to prove it, at least none I'm privy to, I wouldn't be surprised if the effect isn't at least somewhat enhanced by heavy alcohol intake.
From there, well... (pauses) is it really necessary to rehash the details yet again? I'm starting to feel a sideshow-type vibe.

Cartwright here. Yes, I'm afraid it is necessary yet again, Tate, for our....that is, for the bureau's official audio and video register.

Videoed to boot? (pauses) Well, damn, gents. You could at least warn a guy so he might properly spruce up. I've got nose-hairs poking out like tentacles and this bird's nest hair hasn't seen a comb in days.

Grayson (laughs softly) h-here. Actually, by regulation it isn't mandatory we inform you of either method of surveillance.

Cartwright here. My...our apologies, Tate. Now that the cat's out of the bag, so to speak, just want you to understand there was no attempt at secrecy. It just...truthfully...slipped our minds to mention it.

But...if we're on Candid Camera, what's with the continuing need to identify yourselves as speakers?

Grayson here. Strictly COA, in case the video version is ever compromised. Audio version is recorded on a separate app. Um, just to reiterate, sorry for the info omission, Tate.

No sweat, gents, truly. Appreciate the honesty (pauses, signs heavily). Well, back to it, then...for the record.

Removing the backpack, I exchanged cloth gloves for a pair of latex ones and carefully removed the tools of the trade...the 'usual suspects,' you gents might say, and, in exact order of occurrence, I proceeded to:

A - Duct-tape Winslow's mouth from ear to ear.

B - Light a pair of scented candles and place them on opposite ends of the bed atop matching lamp-tables. Side-note here: the candle-lighting ritual was a staple by then but so ironically apt this particular time considering the many horrid odors their tart, vanilla scent served to mask.

C – Retrieve and unfold an article of newspaper, dated nearly two years earlier and containing a single, faded black and white photo of a smiling, raven-haired, buck-toothed six-year-old girl—the same girl, Constance by name, that he'd confessed to abducting, beating and raping nearly two years earlier...

....and released to probation by Judge Raymond Garto...(clears throat)sorry, uh, Grayson here, whom you'd...tracked to his lakeside home a few months earlier, where he was later found bludgeoned in a style uniquely your own.

...indeed, Agent. You have a point for recycling old news or was this again a case...for the record?

Cartwright here. I must apologize for my cohort—young, brash and overly enthusiastic as he might be—for the rash of interruptions. We profess to be professionals, after all.

(Lengthy pause)

D – I wad the news article into a loose ball and carefully dip it into a mason jar filled with hydrofluoric acid. While waiting for the print paper to reach maximum moistness, I carefully insert sewing needles into each of his eyelids, essentially pinning them open. An extra pillow is placed behind his neck in order to better elevate. This to allow him the best view possible as we near closure.

E – With great care and much disgust, I remove the molester's recently soiled underpants.

F - The print paper, reduced to a blackish glob, is then rung out thoroughly over Winslow's exposed groin.

G - The acid does what comes naturally as I prep the hammer, leaning down amid the choking stench of melting flesh to deliver the bastard's eulogy. Before you inquire, gents, I have never and will never divulge that parting message. It is strictly between me and the demon in human form I've exorcised.

The hammer falls...sometimes more than once, depending on my level of rage at the time. Normally, I'd say it descends three, perhaps four times max. Regardless, if my aim is where it needs to be, only a single ascent and subsequent descent are necessary. In Winslow's case, I was...needless to say, unduly pissed.

Cartwright here. From the crime photos, I'd say that's obvious.

Grayson here. I'll say. A sausage grinder would've done less damage. In addition, that tissue-melting cocktail of yours left nothing behind but a black crater between the man's legs.

As was the intent, gentlemen. I take it (sighs) we now come to the portion of the story you've have been waiting for with bated breath. In my yet-unwritten memoirs, I plan on entitling it the 'Gina Jordan Tragedy.'

(Pauses amid muffled coughs)

I'd only begun to douse the perimeter of the living room when I heard them—faint but relatively consistent and administered in eight to ten second interval—as to mimic Morse Code.

Grayson here. Rewind if you don't mind, Tate. Douse the perimeter?

Lighter fluid, Agent Grayson, a pencil-thin stream, to be ignited from the same back door exit from which I'd entered.

(Lengthy pause)

Sorry, um, Grayson here. Sorry, clarification required. Please resume. I believe you had first become aware of the girl's presence in the pa—

Please, Agent Grayson, allow me to tell the story or tell it yourself, but do not jump ahead at your own convenience.

Grayson here (clears throat). The stage is all yours.

The knocking was, as I'd stated, so light, almost timid in its initial delivery, as if of no urgency whatsoever. Briefly I even considered it might be originating from another residence, perhaps the next-door neighbor or even down the street. That was, until I entered the kitchen and both the frequency and decibel level increased quite noticeably.

In sliding to the side a mostly emptied dishware cabinet, I soon discovered the hidden doorway. The door was thick oak, unpainted and badly scarred, like the entranceway to some ancient, haunted castle. By comparison, the shining, silver padlock providing extra security appeared as if it had been purchased and attached within the hour.

Around the time I'd shoved the cabinet aside, the knocking had ceased. Still, by this time I could practically feel the presence beyond that massive blockade. Smell their desperation...their fractured hopes and prayers for impending salvation.

Two quick, efficient strikes from the hammer, a well-placed boot-heel and presto! No more barricade. The darkness inside was all-enveloping, a pitch-black veil. I took a single, cautious step forward, hammer cocked and at the ready, when a small figure shot past my lunging frame like a phantom bullet, whizzing underneath the three-foot-plus clearance beneath my outstretched right arm with room to spare.

I found her in Winslow's bedroom, kneeled at his side with her head bowed and her thin, frail arms outstretched over his nude, blood-soaked chest. Her reddish-brown hair glowed like live embers, this I recall so clearly, cutting the relative darkness like a beacon powered solely by misery and fear. Decked out in a bright yellow dress riddled with an assortment of multi-colored stains and faded blue sneakers, she'd buried her head into her captor's arm pit, her choking sobs slightly muffled and sporadically mingled with the occasional snort or gagging cough.

I cannot be sure exactly how long I stood at the entrance—perhaps as short a duration as a full minute or as lengthy as five. Could be I was simply awaiting the change in her. It was inevitable, I knew, even in a child of six or seven, as I'd deduced she was. The stages of sudden, unexpected emancipation: elation to sadness, sadness to rage, rage to relief. Although I'd apparently missed elation, or that particular stage had been side-stepped completely, there was little doubt stage two was currently underway in all its tear-duct draining glory.

(Pauses, sighs)

Cartwright here. Tate? You need a fresh glass of water? Coffee?

Jigger of brandy, perhaps? (laughs) No, it's...I'm fine, gents...really. It's just...not one of my fonder memories. Just...give me a minute, please.

(muffled coughs)

Grayson here. Listen, Tate...I...seriously, we can postpone if you need a lengthier sabbatical.

(clears throat once, twice, a third time)

I'm fine, Agent Grayson, and I'm thinking we'd best wrap this up today. Not sure I want to revisit...tread a similar path ever again once we've...concluded, as in a take-it-to-the-grave type scenario—you get the gist—speak now or forever hold my peace.

Cartwright here. Understood. Please resume whenever you're ready. No rush...(chuckles)...we're paid by the hour.

One should never ever assume, gents. I'd...foolishly...naturally assumed she'd been moaning and sobbing in unbridled ecstasy over being freed from purgatory. Sixteen months missing, abducted from an elementary-school playground in broad daylight. Forced solitude, forced to...into all manner of ungodly acts. Surely overcome by a tidal wave of heavenly joy, yes?

(Pauses) Not...even...close. One never quite knows as much as they think they do. Apparently, Winslow had a weapon stashed underneath his bed for just such an occasion. The girl had, upon my casual approach to provide comfort, brandished said weapon and...(pauses, sighs)...c-came at me like a...a feral cat. In that small child's face, all contorted and weirdly disjointed by rage, I saw only madness at its most primal. I had, as you gents well know, faced down many an evil entity by that time, a few of which were roughly twice my size and physical strength. I say that to say this, gentlemen: I had never felt such fear as when little Gina Jordan came at me with that blade in hand, growling and spitting like Winslow's demonic offspring. Not ashamed to confess, in fact, to the later discovery that I'd urinated myself at some point, most likely at that initial moment of sheer terror.

Cartwright here. The weapon you speak of was later identified within the torched rubble, by the way. That is, in case you weren't able to properly ID during the...melee.

The hell you say. I was…always assumed…there's that damn word again…a machete of some type.

Grayson here. A lawnmower blade with electrical-tape handle.

(Laughs) No shit. Obviously sharpened to a fine, razor-edge. Honestly gents, if I'd been leaning even two inches closer, you'd likely be referring to me as Nubs. As it was, I didn't exactly stroll away unscathed. (Pause) Take a gander…took thirty-six stitches in all…of the homemade variety at that. Hey, Boy Scout training finally came in handy after all, I guess (laughs).

Grayson here. Nasty scar for sure.

Cartwright here. Yep. Fortunate it didn't cut through to an artery or sever every tendon below the knee cap. Little ankle-biter wasn't messing around, yeah?

Little ank—(pauses)…Agent, Gina Jordan's…psychotic behavior was, I believe, fully justified at the time. You have heard of Stockholm Syndrome, I take it?

Grayson here. Of course. Logical enough diagnosis. Almost two years a prisoner, and at such in impressionable age.

Cartwright here. Agreed. She was, by that time, probably no more than a robotic extension of her captor.

Exactly. I didn't…have never blamed her for such…blatant aggressiveness. After all, her master was dead—bludgeoned so his features were nearly unrecognizable to her—to pursue the man responsible with extreme prejudice was…only natural.

Grayson here. The...her ending was...I'm hoping, as quick and painless as humanly possible?

I'd lurched back as she'd prepared a follow-up blow, welding that blade like a master swordsman, managing in my overt clumsiness to slip and trip on a pile of kiddy-porn magazines, almost as if that pig Winslow had strategically placed them there to better hasten my demise.

In retrospect, that involuntary breakdance had probably saved my life, as the gir—Gina's back-swipe had barely grazed my scalp as I'd pin-wheeled back, whereas if I'd been standing upright, it most likely would have resulted in at least partial decapitation.

Upon impact with that hardwood flooring, I commenced to scramble frantically to the left. I can recall Gina's animalistic growls as she readied a fresh assault. As God is my witness, gentlemen (pauses) I had no idea the hammer was still in my possession. Apparently (clears throat) it was...had been. Instinct, nothing more, dictated I swing wildly, blindly, in a slashing motion, whether armed or bare-handed. Eventually I felt a slight jarring of my left hand and wrist, as if I'd made contact with nothing more substantial than perhaps a brittle tree limb. As trivial as the force had seemed, the....sharp crunching noise that had accompanied it spoke volumes to its overall effect. The growls, grunts and hissing of my attacker had ceased so abruptly, replaced by a deafening silence that was as mortifying as any force, tangible or otherwise, I'd ever encountered. Sounds...bizarre I know, but it was...almost as if I'd have preferred a sudden resurrection, despite the obvious risk.

Grayson here. So...the kill blow, pardon the bluntness, was delivered by the hammer?

Indeed...yes. I recall...immediately staring it down, blood-soaked and trembling in my grip and (pauses) for the first time...thinking it looked...appeared totally alien to me. I...thought, very briefly, of tossing it aside...permanently discarding it.

Cartwright here. The girl had...passed upon your finding her?

Still as stone, lying on her back with her head turned sharply to the right. Funny (pauses) but in looking straight down at her tiny, prone form, one might have mistakenly her for a peacefully napping child. Her dress, though adorned with newly added blood spatters, appeared relatively neat and trauma-free; her pencil-thin arms folded neatly across an equally narrow midsection. It wasn't until...I gently turned her that the...that the extensive damage (pauses)...her skull had...fully caved.

Grayson here. Did you immediately torch the place or, well, delay the deed due to the circumstances?

Can't say how long the duration between the two incidents, gents. It is, to tread heavily on cliché, a fogbank of mystery. I do recall eventually becoming aware of the possibility of bleeding to death from the severe gash beneath my kneecap. Practically had to tie off that particular vertical smile tourniquet-style, forced to shred a tee-shirt I'd pulled from the lone clothes-dresser Winslow owned. I was in shock, without a doubt. Not so much from the aftermath of the planned eradication but the wholly unplanned one.

Grayson here. Don't want to go all head-shrinker with you again, Tate, but how did the sight of the girl's lifeless body lying there amid the filth affect your usually painstakingly evidence-free cleaning job?

I was shattered, Agent Grayson. A soulless husk. Thus, carelessness saw its head. I made mistakes. Truth be told, I really... (pauses)...believe that a big part of me didn't give a shit about being caught. DNA evidence be damned, I wasn't about to leave her...Gina...inside that degenerate's room to burn alongside him. Placing her inside that second bedroom, atop what appeared to be fairly clean, unslept upon sheets, just seemed the...least I could do. You... (pauses)...there's no way to explain the anguish. I'd taken the life of a child. Circumstances and situation be damned, I'd fatally harmed an innocent...one of the precious souls I'd sworn to protect. There is really no way to come back from that. Future retributions aside, there is simply no way to make full amends.

Grayson here. Not to delve too deeply into your past, Tate—the details of which have been covered ad nauseam by so many—but in ending the girl's life, however justified, is it possible...unconsciously of course, that the traceable evidence left behind was no accident?

Did I secretly want to get caught due to the overwhelming guilt? I'd have to say no, though in truth that's merely an opinion. It could have just have easily been due to extreme carelessness born from the state of walking fugue I'd experienced immediately following Gina's...passing. Certainly the exit torch-job had been, to use the crude vernacular, a half-ass effort at best, not nearly up to previous standards as evidenced by the...fairly well-maintained condition of the girl's remains from which my DNA surfaced. (Laughs) I present the following long-winded reply in lieu of merely spouting the obligatory 'can't really say for sure.'

Cartwright here. To conclude then, please provide your thoughts and opinion on the sentence handed down in your case. The agency requires feedback to use in future congressional deliberations.

Grayson here. Obviously no reason to hold back, Tate. Not to sound overly cold, but unless someone unlocks the key to immortality in the next, say five or six decades, your calendar is pretty much booked.

(Sighs) No salesmanship required, Agent Grayson. I've never been the beat-around-the-bush type, regardless of potential repercussions. My take on the government's...make that the world's newly acquired take on capital punishment is, to say the very least, quite disappointing. You see, gents, I'd long since decided that if apprehended at any point of my mission, a willful confession on my part would surely result in the death penalty—though far from guaranteed by the systematic elimination of child-raping scum like Winslow, which some might actually applaud—but three, count 'em, three state-appointed judges?

I'm not the type who can survive, must less thrive, while rotting in an eight-by-ten surrounded by similarly warped entities as those I'd sworn to eradicate. Once the powers permanently voted the death penalty off the table as an option...(pauses)...I do believe this was mere weeks before my own sentencing, I have to admit I was downright terrified, for want of a less...pansy term.

Cartwright here. So the permanent island setting didn't shed even the slightest ray of positivity?

I must confess it certainly beat out the prospect of the aforementioned concrete and steel bars scenario. I mean, no possibility of gang rape, random bludgeonings or cellmates suffering from intestinal disorders, if you get my drift. However, in retrospect, I cannot help but ponder if such archaic penal colony stereotypes can hold a candle to the suffocating loneliness and desolation of...the permanent island setting. Long story short, gents, as I feel my ever-wagging tongue beginning to waiver, is that I truly wish my capture had come soon enough for the old school rules to apply, as in the biblical sense: an eye-for-an-eye and tooth for a tooth. As it is, I have no choice but to persevere and leave my fate to a higher power.

Grayson here. Now that is the ultimate penal-colony stereotype, if you don't mind my saying, Tate. Finding religion while incarcerated, now that's old school without a doubt.

(Laughs) Correction, Agent Grayson…if you'll check my dossier, you'll find I'd made my peace with the Lord long ago. After all, who do you think pointed me to my life's calling?

(Following a lengthy, static-filled pause, the tape clicks off)

~ * ~

"Ahoy, Mate, mind if I stow away on this here tub?" she heard Zack bellow, resting the pad on her lap while craning her neck forward to squint through the cutter's tinted windshield.

"Advance and be recognized, ya big scurvy lug!" she countered in comically butchered pirate-speak, her natural accent sounding ever-stronger despite efforts to cloak same. Powering down the iPad, she tucked it inside a side pocket while pushing from the chair with a pained moan. Zack hopped aboard in a single bound and soon joined her at the bridge, his forehead riddled with bb-sized sweat-polyps.

"Well, hello there, Miss Congeniality. Hope I didn't keep you too long," he huffed while turning to the console to requalify himself with both touch and voice ID requirements.

"I choose my friends wisely," she retorted sourly, moving forward to deliver a light hip-bump to her much-taller spouse's upper thigh.

"Wish I could say the same for you. Hawkins is a *pekeng*…a fraud. I may be forced to serve him, but I sure as hell don't have to like it."

"Don't buy his story at all, do you?"

"Not a solitary word. Call it female intuition. Tate Hawkins is as evil as his resume states."

Zack didn't response while calmly prepping the cutter for departure.

"If anything, he's a step *below* the rest in my book. Cold-blooded killers one and all, but *that* one…" she pointed in the general direction of Hawkins' abode,"…is a convicted liar to boot. Craves sympathy. Wants to be labeled something other than what he is truly is. Wants everyone to clap him on the back for his accomplishments. Well, not this girl. I know an imitation when I *smell* one, and Mister Tate Hawkins is as fake as a Hollywood tit."

With the gentle push of a button, the anchor withdrew with a smooth hum from the billowy sand-bed from which it had submerged. His jaw set tight in building frustration, Zack steered the cutter around one-hundred eighty degrees and slowly accelerated toward open seas.

"The man's history speaks for itself, Z. Confirmed and set in stone. His agenda was as logic as any serial killer could ever claim."

"Millions upon millions have suffered similar tragedies, Zackary. How many have turned vigilante in response? How many decided to play dark god in the name of revenge?"

"I'm not excusing the man. I'm just saying if such behavior was ever to be justified…"

"Justified? *Seriously?*" she railed, her petite frame coiled as if to spring, her normally flawless complexion practically pulsating in dark splotches of maroon across the forehead and both cheekbones. Eyes front and focused solely on the relatively peaceful waters ahead, Zack meantime remained calm in both tone and deportment, a character trait that never ceased to further infuriate his oft-volatile soul-mate.

"Tate snuffed out vermin to prevent further anguish to future victims. Sorry, but I cannot for the life of me find a reason to label him the true bad guy."

"Horseshit. I can't believe you've fallen for his act. Good thing Graham doesn't feel the same way or that maniac would surely be roaming the streets as we speak, cutting down every man, woman or child that gets in his way, all in the name of repressed anguish."

The big man's shoulders visibly slumped.

"Again, I'm not agreeing with the concept. Outside of the battlefield or protecting one's own life or the life of their loved ones, there is no excuse for taking another life."

Her gestures no longer animated, but sluggish—bone weary—she joined him at the console and hooked an arm around his waist.

"I'm no pacificist, big 'un, you know that. I just can't force myself to place him on a pedestal over any of the others."

"*Pacifist,* Liza, and I get that, but please understand this…" he turned to her, peering downward to meet her gaze with an unblinking glare that was as intense as she'd ever witnessed in their many years together "…if some ungodly monster masquerading as a human being had raped, strangled and then set fire to a five-year-old daughter of mine, I'd more than likely be hanging out a permanent shingle at one these penal isles myself."

Forced to break his intrusive stare, as unnerving as it was intimidating, Liza briefly glanced out at the strikingly clear blue waters parting so effortlessly at their insistence. Upon relocking eyes with her husband, mentor and superior –in-rank, she barely refrained from shuddering openly.

"Hawkins has walked the outer perimeters of hell, maybe even took a quick dip into its churning, boiling, soul-consuming seas, and what emerged was what you and I see now. I truly believe…*he* believes…that he survived his child's murder for…to become what he became. I can only hope and pray that you and I never experience anything nearly as…excruciating."

The next several shifts were as bland as such work could possibly allow and saw no further discussion between the two that didn't involve the most mundane aspects of their daily assigned tasks, that is, until such time a grim, unrelenting bleakness as deep as the ocean they traveled emerged like an all-consuming, ultra-violent squall bent on total destruction.

Nine

Hyde's Slide

Both arms submerged elbow deep in a cardboard box filled with assorted canned goods, Dylan Barnes took mental note of the sudden silence, the familiar clicking of cue against ball having ceased a few minutes earlier. He stacked the aluminum cans, labeled black-eyed peas and green beans, respectively, side by side with a dozen similar containers atop the otherwise bare dining table, shooting his assigned partner the occasional glance. Officer Suzy Hobbs, rail thin and having donned a mask of perpetual giddiness—the corners of her lips seemingly glued into a slight upturn—held the Taser at hip level and swayed it loosely from side to side, its general aim directed into the combination pool room/arcade.

"So what's the story in there, Hobbs? He must be linin' up one helluva trick shot."

As if on cue, a resounding flush reverberated from the playroom john.

"Well, there ya go. With any luck the act itself will trigger a change in personality."

"Geez Louise, mean to tell me you're still unpacking in there? Loafin' fuckers must surely be paid by the hour."

"Ahhh, wishful thinkin'," Barnes groaned with a weary roll of the eyes.

"We'll have this wrapped up in a few, Mister Barton," Hobbs blurted politely, permanent Joker's grin intact while containing to whip the Taser about like a stunt prop. "Again, we're sorry for the inconven—"

"Eat shit, Missy," their client growled sourly, his usually thick, shoulder-length red coif oil-slick and coiled into a pig-tail that lay just over his left shoulder, "don't need your patronizing bullshit...just inventory the goods and make tracks already."

Barnes openly bristled. As irritating, annoying and downright cloying as the Jed personality could be, it was much preferred over his Yankee twin's threatening tone, nonstop profanity and constant berating.

"Best cool those jets, Jessie. Officer Hobbs there might come off as a pushover, but given the word she'll fry those 'Joisey' balls without a second thought."

"Yeah yeah...says you, Colonel Sanders. She's probably moistening up just standing guard, and I'm not speaking of her peepers. Tell you what, sweets, holster that watt-popper, toss away the utility belt and I'll show you a *real* shock-stick. Don't normally cater to skinny chicks, 'specially the type in uniform, but hey, beggars can't be choosers, am I right?"

Pausing the restock to rest a hand on the grooved, well-padded handle of the very weapon Barton had just so rudely referenced, Barnes instinctively stiffened in the remote chance that the blowhard's bluff might actually escalate into something more.

"Oh, Mister Barton, you are a card," Hobbs replied casually enough, though her eyes had narrowed considerably. "How about another game of solitaire eight-ball?"

"I got your solitaire balls right here, Twiggy. I'd bet a stack of Hamiltons you prefer it in the caboose, am I ri—"

"Hey! *Enough* already! How 'bout clamming the hell up and lettin' us finish this and we'll both be outta each other's short hairs, so to speak?"

The Jessie Barton entity paused to stifle a yawn before giggling maniacally while reaching over to snag the cue ball from the center of the pool table. Hobbs took a step back into the dining room as he began flipping it playfully from hand to hand.

"And what if I decide otherwise, Barnes?"

"Then I'm…we're liable to pack this shit back up and leave you sippin' saltwater, lickin' clam-shells and wipin' your ass-cheeks with palm fronds for the next thirty some-odd days. Your call, big shot."

"While you're deciding, Mister Barton, please return that billiard ball to its original position," Hobbs stated respectfully enough but with a definitive undertone of menace, her grip on the Taser no longer flimsy but firm, its trigger mechanism at the very cusp of release.

"Whatever you say, sweets," the Jessie entity replied, instantly backing away in a clumsily executed moon-dance before adhering to said command by placing the ivory ball dead center at the slick tabletop's midway point. "I never argue with a lady packing such…impressive heat, even one masquerading as a rather attractive strand of dental floss."

Even as Barnes dropped his guard and resumed inventory, Suzy Hobbs remained steadfast with a newborn cautiousness, at one point even elevating the Taser's aim until it rested directly between the Jessie entity's far-set eyes.

"Mister Barton sir, may I speak freely?"

The man's smile was textbook sexual deviant; his upper lip curled just slightly to reveal a lower level of bright-yellow stained teeth.

"Please do, sweets. I just adore watchin' those rosy-red lips part. As carnal fantasies go, I do believe I have ample ammo for the next lonely moon or two."

166

Shockingly, considering the ultra-considerate, slickly professional behavior that had preceded it, the young CO used her free hand to blow him a kiss before utilizing the middle finger of the same hand to flash the most common of profane gestures.

"Not if yours was the last working dick on the planet."

Yawning, the Jessie entity raised his arms in mock surrender, his eyes pulled wide and gleaming with renewed mischief.

"Uwwww, I do love it when they start talkin' nasty. You hearin' this, Barnes? Seems my natural manly charms are finally getting your trainee here nice and moist."

"That *trainee* you speak of..." Barnes retorted, having checked off and removed the final item from the list with the weary swipe of a forefinger atop his iPad, "... just graduated from a three year tour at Black Beach in Guinea, this after an initial assignment at San Quentin, no less. Hell, I'd wager your act doesn't even rate in her all-time top fifty. I call that right, Miss Hobbs?"

Fully retrenched in character, everlasting grin firmly in place, her reply was breezy and utterly malice-free.

"Actually, it doesn't even touch the scale. We almost done here, boss?"

"We'll be shoving off as soon as Mister Warmth there graces this here e-form with a signature. Besides, we do seem to be keeping him from his midday nap."

The Jessie entity waited until Hobbs regarded him with a quizzical, raised brow to clutch his midsection with both hands.

"Gonna have to wait, sweets...gotta go mail another package. Must be all that tofu garbage Doc limp-wrist has been stuffin' in on the Q-tee. That, and I can't *rent* a good night's shuteye for all the looney-tune nightmares—wacky mind-bendin' shit I couldn't drudge up with a vein-load of liquid crack. I swear that little weasel is tryin' his light-loafer best to do me in."

Hobbs watched him waddle off with knees practically knocking like a small toddler on the cusp of wetting himself and vanish into the lavatory at the back of the playroom before easing her grip on the Taser and dropping it to waist-level.

"This was...the enforcer of the two? Jesus, evil little troll seems harmless enough save a natural penchant for crudeness. I only had time to speed-read through about a third of his...of their file. Soooo, he...this Jessie version was deemed the catalyst—"

Opening the double-door fridge for a quick peak, Barnes' nostrils flared in reaction to a sudden bombardment of chilled sourness.

"Jed is...was considered the mastermind and Jessie the muscle, yeah. That from a team of Fed evaluators who specialized in multiple personalities. My take, you might or might not ask? Psychobabble of the highest order. I think he...both 'em know exactly what the other is doin' at all times 'cause..." he raised a forefinger airborne before backing away and closing the fridge door, "...there ain't no blessed difference."

"You think it's a ruse?" Hobbs asked in a tone that bordered on hysterical. "Really?"

Barnes frowned while scrolling the inventory e-form, his stubby forefinger a fidgety blur between frozen pauses.

"Hey, you asked, I answered. Hey, playin' the psycho twins bit got 'em off twice before a jury finally got it right."

She shot him a final, disbelieving glance before departing the kitchen for the playroom with cat-like grace, the Taser cupped in a two-handed grip with its short barrel-end pointed upward.

"So he...they pulled the wool over the eyes of not just one but several teams of experienced psychologists?"

"Shit, it's just one man's opinion, Hobbs," he snarled and shrugged out of view, pocketing the sleek, pencil-thin device in a side pocket of his comically baggy cargo pants. "Just check on Mister Loose-Bowels, will ya? We need to be shovin' off pronto."

Strolling between and past a full-sized pool table and trio of vintage pinball machines, the checkerboard bright walls adorned with various dartboards, some equally antique and others fully electronic, Hobbs heard the toilet flush just as she'd reached the sealed door.

"Hey, you all right in there, Mister Barton?"

A muffled cough ensued, then another, but nothing in the way of a verbal reply.

"We're going to have to be leaving, Mister Barton. Schedules to keep and people to see, you understand."

Dislodging her cupped right hand from beneath the left, Hobbs prepared to tap gently, her wiry frame instinctively tensing, her knuckles pausing just before impact at a fresh outbreak of strangely cloaked coughing.

"Hey now, you gonna live, Mister B?" she giggled with just a twinge of inexplicable apprehension. "If it's privacy you need, I guess we could just slide the iPad underneath the door for your John Hanco—"

The door swung inward in a sucking vacuum, effectively pulling her inward just enough as toxic vapors packed her flaring nostrils. Hobbs openly gagged, her eyes instantly tearing as the Taser was pulled from her grip and her right temple was dented by a blunt object of unknown origin.

The door slammed shut behind her just as she collapsed onto hard tile like a marionette with severed strings, its inner lock engaged as thin streams of dark maroon commenced to flow freely from each eye....each ear....each nostril.

At the first clue that something was possibly amiss, Barnes whirled about and sprinted from the kitchen, the bathroom door resealing with a resounding thump at just his third stride.

"Hobbs! Hobbs!" he bellowed, having retrieved both his Taser and Shock Baton and tucking his shoulders for an impending charge.

"Barton, you open this door pronto and I'll consider *not* jamming this electro-club so far up your poop-shoot you'll be pickin' splinters outta your eyelids!"

His upper lip trembled spastically; the attached mustache gyrating like an electrified caterpillar, Barnes cautiously placed an ear to the outer door and detected barely audible shuffling noises, like that of dead weight being dragged across smooth tile.

"I mean it, you loony som'bitch! You got exactly three seconds..."

Hopping back several steps, Barnes plucked the tiny shoulder mic from its strapped holster simultaneously striking a coiled pose with both knees slightly bent and his stout torso bowed inward.

"Atlantis, this is *Glaucus*. Location is Hyde Island. Possible... officer down. I repeat, this is Officer Dylan Barnes of the cutter *Glaucus*. Possible officer down. Request expedited security team response, over."

The scent brushed his nostrils just as he'd prepared to charge; a tart, abrasive aroma that, upon sucking in an initial mouthful felt like a ragged burn torch his throat with an effect similar to the mountain-brewed moonshine he'd once favored during his wild, carefree youth.

"Wha...the fu..." he croaked, stumbling back to elude the intrusive vapors while burying his nose into the crook of his left elbow. His mind raced in a feeble attempt to recall minute details of the man's personnel file—of which he'd previously skimmed only the highlights—in order to possibly mount a successful plan of action and/or counterattack.

A sudden barrage of gut-wrenching sobs, intermingled with the occasional wet, hacking cough, severed his already frazzled train of thought. Barnes backed toward the kitchen with each weapon clutched to his hitching, heaving chest; his eyes brimming with hot tears; his nasal cavities effectively lit aflame. Utterly discombobulated while twisting his head violently from side to side, he was temporarily unable to locate the source of the moaning cries as they seemed to bombard him from all sides simultaneously. One thing he knew for certain: hazy, confused state be damned, was that the source of said anguish was definitely *not* Officer Susan Hobbs. This, he deduced crazily while crashing into and subsequently bouncing off the south wall of the playroom, was your classic 'good news and bad news' scenario. *Good* in the fact that his assigned partner was not the one apparently suffering such anguish—*bad* in the fact that such conspicuous silence might underscore an even more tragic fate.

Half-blind as the eye-pain intensified from mild to severe burn, thick streams of mucus bubbling from each nostril, he discarded both the Taser and baton from badly shaking hands as he stumbled into the kitchen.

Amid sporadic wailing that seemed to grow increasingly distant, Barnes dipped his head over the sink and used cupped hands to splash cool faucet water into both eyes. Throughout this frantic, copious drenching, the result of which was an almost instantaneous improvement of both visual and motor skills, he heard the occasional spoken word shatter an otherwise continuous blast of static reverberating from his shoulder mic.

"...*Glacus,   this*...Atlantis...-*curity   team's   ETA   to*...*isle   is aprox*...*eight   minutes*...*you   read,   Glacus*....-*cer   Barnes,   do*...*read? Over...*"

Upon retrieving only the Shock-Baton, he departed the kitchen in a wavering lurch, overturning the dining table and essentially dropkicking its accompanying chairs into a far corner while reaching around to grope for the com mic.

It wasn't until he stood between the living room couch and two matching bean bags, the mic parked mere inches from his trembling lower lip, that Barnes was able to solve the twin mysteries of both the criers' source and immediate location.

The figure stood poised at the center of a wide, blue-juniper infested dune approximately twenty-five paces in the distance, having halted at the center of the well-worn track leading from the hut to the lagoon where the recently re-commissioned cutter *Glaucus* floated atop clear, still waters.

"….sh-she c-came at m-me…I…s-swear…s-she l-le-left me n-no c-choice…I…it w-was cl-clearly sef…self-d-defense," the man stuttered in a deep, drunken drawl, standing with his legs splayed into the shifting sands as if on the cusp of executing a full split, both hands gripping the sides of his head as to cloak each ear from some mysterious, mind-piercing clamor he alone was privy to.

Barnes momentarily paused, debating whether or not to backtrack to the kitchen to regain the Taser, an argument quickly resolved once he recalled the contamination trapped inside. Eventually he resolved to tighten his grip on the baton, struggling to first read through bleary eyes its tiny digital menu and then reset with quivering fingers its jolt charge to the highest possible reading, Meanwhile the barely coherent rambling from the dune continued unabated, like some sparsely rehearsed Southern Baptist sermon from the mount.

"…the…th-that dense, slow-witted, l-loudmouth c-coward saw…s-sensed the thr—her threat b-but as…us-usual w-was unwell…unwilling to d-deal wit…with it. As a-always I…had no c-choice but…but ta-take the reins a-and e-end s-said th-threat…"

Sprinting off the hut's stone walk onto the beachhead in a wobbly gait, Barnes sucked in the salty air greedily, feeling his vitality and vigor return with each passing stride. Though he had nary a clue what had transpired inside the hut's lone lavatory or the fate of his fellow CO, there was no doubting the one obvious transition that *had* occurred behind its sealed door during that brief, two to three minute span: Jessie Barton, wholly fictitious Jersey knee-breaker with the pit-ball mentality, had given way to his physically *inferior* but intellectually *superior* alter-ego, Jed, he of the borderline-feminine deportment and meek, apologetic tone.

"...b-but I see n-now...I-I realize h-how fruitless th-the effort to s-survive. It...it's a no-win...as my bru-brutish cohort w-would sp-spew. Perha—maybe it's just n-not meant t-to be. I...I only kn-know that I...can't...we can't...take any more. The sleepless n-nights spent sh-shaking in fear...fearing s-sleep most of a-all. I...that we are...s-sufficiently d-drained of wi-will power. At t-this point...the tank is...drained, the well is...b-bone dry, and there is...obviously...n-nowhere else to r-run or...god he-help us...h-hide. I just...*we* just w-want to sleep n-now. Just...lie down a-and...nap...dri-drift blissfully a-away."

In gaining a clearer picture of his quarry's present condition, Dylan Barnes had skidded to an abrupt halt, boots buried ankle-deep in the pliable sands, his forward momentum nearly causing a full-tilt, face-first tumble. As it was, he held steady with perhaps twenty yards' separation between them.

"Shit, B-Barton, what the hell have you...done?" he mumbled, a throaty whisper audible only to himself. He peered over the top edge of the baton, which he'd instinctively placed in front of his face in a blocking, defensive pose.

"Wh-wha-zat?" Jed Barton responded, wide-eyed and staring overhead as if literally responding to a voice from above while slowly, painstakingly removing his cupped hands from each partially cloaked ear and thus revealing an additional snapshot of the extensive carnage beneath. "Wh-who is t-that? Mis...Mister Withrow, I...is th-that you?"

Barnes found the name vaguely familiar, repeating it several times as to perhaps jar free a fragment of suppressed memory, though in light of Jed Barton's present appearance, his powers of concentration were dim at best.

The hands that had previously held Barton's skull in a double-clutch grasp of apparent agony were held out passively—a pleading gesture—clumps of gray-streaked brown hair coating each palm as if he were undergoing a supernatural manifestation of sorts. The world's first schizophrenic lycanthrope, Barnes thought crazily, actually giggling aloud. The bare patches left behind—Barton's mangled coif resembling a comical cross between the stereotypical mad-scientist and a warrior's Mohawk—blistered and bubbled profusely, like broiling cheese atop fully-baked pizza crust. Narrow, dark-maroon streams, no thicker than a number five pencil, flowed freely from each eye and down each cheekbone. His speech grew less comprehensible—a drunken soliloquy—as pus-filled blisters broke out onto grotesquely bloated lips.

"C-come to finish th-the job Miss Da-Dandridge st-started?" Barton blurted, leaning forward while balancing one of the hair-coated palms at his forehead and peeking beneath it, having finally spotted Barnes' wavering frame standing less than sixty feet away.

"Dandridge?" Barnes replied, unaware he was even speaking aloud, "Withrow and Dandridge? Damned if *both* monikers ain't ringin' a bell…faint as that ringin' might be."

Leaning hard to the left as if shackled to that particular section of beachhead, Jed Barton reached back and removed something from his belt, the mystery object effectively cloaked by a curled fist.

"Li-liddle…little l-late in the gammba…g-game for he-heroics…bu-but neber…never for a hearty d-dish of r-revenge serb…served bloody raw, ri-right, b-boys and girb…girls?"

Barnes held his ground, the fully charged and slightly pulsating Baton cocked back over one shoulder, his quarry's next few words lost amid a fresh surge of static echoing from his shoulder receiver.

"Glacus…Security Team Bravo. ETA to your location is approximately one minute. We are approaching from the east toward Hyde Isle. Over."

Gingerly pulling the mic free, its thin cord curling around his wrist like a coiled reptile, Barnes' eyes remained firmly affixed on Barton's filled left hand, which was being waved wildly about as the man's barely comprehensible lecture continued.

174

"Roger that. Current location is opposite side to your approach, approximately fifty yards west of the cutter. Barnes out."

"...if it's a-an apolobe...apology...or r-repentance you s-seek, W-Warton...Warden...I'm afaid...afraid youba...comb to the wronb plate. I...we libed as sinners...we shall die the samb."

"Warden Withrow?" Barnes silently queried as the faint hum of an approaching chopper materialized from the east.

"Call me selb-selfish, Warten...but if I...I'm 'bout to hop abroad...a freight car hee-headed bound for hell...I'd preferb a liddle...companionship for the ribe....r-ride..."

It appeared, at least initially, that Barton was falling forward in a premeditated combat roll, as he'd leaned dramatically forward as if taking a bow. Barnes had taken a cautious step back in reaction to the other man's sudden descent—an enraged, bull-ape charge that gained speed upon descent.

"...this timebaa, Warten..." he warbled, lips like bloated slugs, lumbering forth with the left arm reared back in a pre-toss pose "...I'm personally tearing your boat...boarding pass, m-modder-foooker..."

Figuring the man's blood-smeared vision had to be horribly impaired—Barton rumbled forward with the wild, directionless look of complete blindness—Barnes decided to take the offensive and thus not await possibly enduring a lucky shot of whatever the man was about to fling his way.

Sprinting forward at full tilt, frantic thrusts kicking up mounds of sand, Barnes never intended to reach Barton or, perhaps more vital, allow the mystery weapon to depart the other man's clenched fist. Eight to ten steps into his mad dash forward, eyes peeled as to any clue that Barton was readying to let fly, he skid to a sliding brake while simultaneously triggering the Shock-Baton's wattage control and chucking it forward with all the force he could muster—an end-over-end fastball—just as the separation between the man had closed to approximately five to six yards.

Jed Barton, mouth ajar, devil-eyes darting and tongue lolling, had continued to screech his indecipherable ramble, his throwing arm still tightly cocked, just as the baton creased his skull at full impact.

His stocky frame whiplashed, tensing briefly in mid-flip before going completely limp a split-second later and digging a deep slug-trail upon impact with the supple terrain. Wisely, Barnes had dived to the left immediately following the baton-toss, executing several full-body rolls that would effectively separate him ever further from his fallen target.

Poised on all fours, Barnes approximated a ten yard distance between the two even as, pushed forward by a sudden, stout breeze, a familiar scent assaulted the whole of his senses. His eyes felt an instant irritability, a slight burning as they began to tear, his nostrils and the back of his throat soon equally enflamed. He crawled away like fleeing prey, having first sucked in a single mouthful of air and holding it captive until fresher climes could be found. As it was, he had refused to halt—half-crawling, half-sprinting—until wet sand coated his clawing fingers and he'd reached the edge of the beach with the cutter *Glaucus* floating, literally, into view.

Down on all fours and sucking air like mad with thick streams of mucus spewing forth from each nostril, Dylan Barnes appeared completely unaware of the whirlwind of sand swallowing him whole as the chopper landed just a few dozen yards to his south. His thoughts, predictably scattered and frazzled, could hone-in solely on two specific fact, two facts he'd taken note of before scrambling from the scene like a cockroach from a fine mist of insecticide.

The first? A severely malformed Jed Barton's passing salute; a final, shuddering death spasm that had for all the world resembled an all-approving 'thumbs-up' gesture.

The second and easily most disturbing? The glass jar that had taken flight and apparently ruptured less than an arm's reach from the spot Barnes had initiated what he would forever think of as his 'survivor-roll.'

He snapped to only as a trio of slightly blurry, shadowy figures hopped from the chopper's cockpit and jogged his way, their bellowed dialogue lost in the incessant hum of the craft's swirling blades.

Pushing himself upright with what meager strength remained, Barnes held both arms out with the palms exposed, waiving frantically while screaming in a banshee-like wail and hoping they understood the gist despite the surrounding commotion.

"Back away! Keep... your... asses... *back*! Possible... possi...probable contaminant! Keep the fuck...*back*!"

Obviously comprehending that most vital of said verbiage, the trio did eventually adhere, retreating back to the chopper with hands raised as in surrender.

Dylan Barnes, in response, flashed a meek thumbs-up and, in retrospect, instantly regretted the act.

~ * ~

Mouth hanging partially agape and amid the overwhelming aroma of freshly administered antiseptic, Barnes studied his IV drip with great intensity, as if entranced by the occasional burp and subsequent bubbling within its crystal-clear glass casing. To his immediate left sat Dean Graham, bifocals hanging from the edge of his beak-like snout as he squinted downward at the iPad he'd balanced atop the bed's gleaming metal rails.

"Inventory of all drops to Hyde Isle show no pesticide deliveries. They...Barton was banned from handling such chemicals, for obvious reasons. Certainly an investigation on how he was able to obtain said item is in the works.

"Regardless, the boys in the lab have yet to determine how he managed to successfully concoct such a lethal mix with what meager chemicals he had on-hand."

Leaning back with the iPad clutched to his lab coat's comically oversized lapels, the doctor yawned without benefit of a cloaking hand.

In knee-jerk response, Barnes inwardly cringed at the memory of Jessie Barton's serial yawning episode just before that final, faithful change.

"I knew he'd been requesting bug spray—crackpot kept cryin' about an infestation of mutant spiders or some such horseshit—but had been told no dice on each occasion. So they're thinkin' that Ultra-*Raid* crap was the catalyst? Kinda like a tequila shot to a margarita?"

Graham removed his glasses and tucked them inside the lab coat.

"Indeed, though how in God's name the final result was a combination tear, nerve *and* blister agent is beyond my limited scope of knowledge. A sample has been shipped off to the coast for conclusive results."

"Shit was damn near lethal even from a fair distance. Peeled Barton's noggin like a rotted grape in a matter of minutes once he'd cracked the seal on that Mason jar. And, Hobbs...shit. I can only imagine..." Barnes paused to rub his chin vigorously with an open palm, "...on second thought, I'd...rather not. Moody as your average chick, but a good Joe nonetheless. In the limited time we spent, she...talked about her kids...no more than tykes, I understand."

Forefinger dancing atop iPad at warp speed, the facility sawbones soon locked on and subsequently perused the personnel file of the recently deceased and presently referred to CO.

"A boy and girl, ages...three and five, I believe. She'd been divorced for just over a year, taking on this particular assignment solely in order to build them a better future."

"Figured as much," Barnes croaked wearily. "Damn shame of the cryin' sort, for certain. Blindsided by an invisible enemy that chokes you into submission with that very first inhale. She never had a blessed chance."

"It...wasn't at all pretty, Dylan. He'd...Barton had...apparently stripped her of her all clothing to allow for...full effect and...hung her from the shower rod like an exhibit. She was...from the photos the Hazmat team provided, barely recognizable as hu—"

Barnes openly gagged, his eyes instantly pooling hot tears.

"Please, Doc…s-spare me the gory de-details, will ya? I'm havin' a hard time chowin' down on anything outside of soggy noodles as it is."

"Good lord, my apologies, Dylan. I sometimes lose perspective at the most inopportune times," Graham replied, gently placing a hand atop his patient's shoulder.

Fighting both the overly cushioned bed and comically baggy hospital gown, Barnes struggled to lean up.

"S'okay, Doc. Not exactly known for an overabundance of couth myself, ya know," he replied wearily, having cleared his eyes with the folded edge of bed-sheet.

"Appreciate it," Graham said, smiling weakly. "You'll be happy to know your wounds appear to be scabbing over at a normal rate. I'll keep you here another twenty-four hours just for observation. Nasty thigh bruise appears to be the worst bodily trauma. You might possess a bit of a hitch in your get-a-long for a few days, but it'll pass, as will the associated soreness.

"How's your breathing? Tightness easing up?"

"Yeah, coughin' jags have slacked off 'cept for the occasional hackin' spell."

Barnes cleared his throat, his tone growing raspier with each verbal volley.

"On another subject, ya say it came as no surprise that it was Jekyll, um, that it was the *Jed* persona that went all chemical warfare on our asses and not the *Jessie* version? The MO I read clearly stated that the Jersey side *always* played the Hyde part. I mean, wasn't that the whole purpose for his being, well, the imaginary part of the team?"

Graham paused to reach over and check the IV drip as, somewhere down the hallway echoed the faint sound of a phone ringing.

"During my sessions with Jed Barton, I found just the opposite. Jessie is the secondary personality, obviously, but Professor Timid is…was definitely the aggressor of the two. Jessie was…all bluster and no action. The prof wasn't just the instigator and initiator, but the igniter."

"So why bother with the *Two-Face* crap at all?" Barnes inquired with a pained wince, reaching up to tap the bandage cloaking his left cheek.

"I mean, pardon my backwoods psychology, Doc, but that wacky shit makes no sense at all."

"Dylan," Graham replied with a sly grin while leaning over to inspect the bandage his patient had inadvertently loosened, "the man is...was insane, remember? Clinically so. To answer your first question, he...needed the Jessie persona solely as his personal scapegoat."

Slinking downward with a resounding sigh, Barnes' lone response was a dramatically cocked brow.

"The Jersey brawler's sole purpose was to shoulder the blame...and happily so. Get it?"

Barnes' pasty mug appeared to melt with increased befuddlement at his caregiver's latest pronouncement.

"Soooo, Jessie was his...was Jed's bitch?"

This time, it was Dean Graham who appeared utterly lost.

"His patsy."

The doctor nodded knowingly.

"Bingo. Jed was the mad genius...Jessie the muscle, until such time the plan was hatched and the plan executed. After the fact, Jed, unable to shoulder the guilt, would fade into the background to allow his personal stooge to puff out his chest and take sole credit for the kill."

Barnes ran splayed fingers through an already mangled coif.

"Jeepers, Doc, that boy, *boys*, were a pair of seriously cracked Egg McMuffins...even more so than we were briefed to believe."

"Understated in your own unique way, but yes, I totally agree. You, of course, have read of the incident that gained him a semblance of fame?"

"Um, yeah sure…the details are foggy, but I recall it involved some sorta correctional school near Atlanta and a slew of dead bodies. Hyde flew the coop and they finally caught up with him in…" Barnes hesitated, his eyes rolling upward and forehead creased in deep thought, "…ugh, South America, wasn't it? Bogota maybe?"

"Canada actually," Graham corrected while retrieving the iPad. "The Dandridge Academy for troubled teenaged boys, sadly defunct since the incident. Lawsuits galore." His left index finger slid and skittered across the pad's glossy surface with the sleek expertise and digital dexterity of a life-long surfer.

"No shit, Doc. I'd imagine grieving parents of murdered kids have one helluva appetite for retribution. Since they couldn't get away with a public hangin', shuttin' down the school stone-stupid enough to hire Hyde in the first place was the next best thing."

Barnes coughed into his hand, his voice even hoarser in the aftermath.

"At least now the Dandridge reference makes sense, at least somewhat."

Cocking a brow his patient's way, Graham temporarily broke eye contact with the device parked at his lap, though his finger continued its rapid, side-to-side scan.

"The founder and facility administrator, was one Jacob Xavier Dandridge, a former prison warden who, at the time of the murders, was a mere six months from retirement. Fate can be a fickle entity, Dylan…fickle and at times downright cruel."

"Who's Withrow, Doc? Dandridge's co-warden? Couldn't quite place that one either…"

"The facility's head counselor. According to the Toronto PD detective assigned the case, she'd tried repeatedly to warn Dandridge of Barton's erratic behavior, to no avail. The man was a fine teacher with quite the impressive resume. He…hid the cracks well, at least to most.

Withrow apparently not only spotted them but, in a written memo to Dandridge just days before the killings, warned of a possible breakdown."

"Oh yeah…" Barton said excitedly, eyes sudden aglow and snapping his fingers enthusiastically, "…now I got it! Didn't she even refer to Barton as a 'Jekyll and Hyde' personality, right?"

Scanning the iPad, Graham couldn't help but smile at his patient's sudden surge of vitality.

"Indeed. Authorities and the media soon adopted the nickname and…well, the rest, sadly, is history."

"How many he poison that day?"

"Eighteen. James Kerns being the oldest, at sixteen years and eight months; Wilbur Gentry the youngest, at fourteen and six. Technically, it wasn't a poisoning but death by biochemical."

"Oh yeah…some kinda…nerve agent? I mean, a real lung-scorcher, right?"

Graham peered up from the pad with a faraway look, staring at a nearby wall as if observing home movies projected directly from his mind's eye.

"Death by asphyxiation…proceeded of course by violent convulsions, the release of bodily fluids and uncontrollable spasms. Barton had sealed the classroom from the outside and utilized the ventilation system. Pumped in the cyclosarin through a homemade contraption that included an air needle, hand-pump and pencil-thin PC pipes."

"I sure as hell don't envy the first-responders to that particular scene." Barnes nodded, his cheeks gaining a shade of rosiness that appeared positively radiant when compared to the snow-white pastiness surrounding them.

"Indeed. The school patrol officer and three EMT personnel died almost instantly upon first infiltrating and then entering the classroom.

The hazmat pics are...to say the least...quite graphic. The...students had apparently piled together like blind mice, melding together like some grotesque, abstract sculpture from hell's darkest pit."

Raising a shaky hand, Barnes cheeks suddenly expanded as if on the verge of upheaval before gradually deflating.

"Geez Doc....enough already. I saw the same pics. Remember 'em well, unfortunately. Keep up the color play-by-play and I'll be wedgin' my head into the nearest bedpan."

"Again, my sincerest regrets, Dylan. Such blatant overzealousness is a lifelong affliction, I'm afraid, as my ex-wife often reminded me without reservation."

At least partially baffled, Barnes' timid, mumbling response was delivered in kind.

"Um, yeah, got'cha, Doc. I...guess. My exes adopted a few pet names for yours truly I'd rather not share."

Graham nodded knowingly and smiled in lieu of a verbal reply.

"Say, Doc..." Barnes inquired wearily, his haggard appearance easily matching an equally battered tone, "...you wouldn't have a smoke on ya?"

The good doctor's harsh expression—left eyebrow sufficiently cocked, disbelieving smirk firmly intact—provided the obvious answer.

"Figures. Guess I'll have to tough it out, huh?"

"Indeed. I would advise *toughing it out* for the duration of your life, but then again I assume I'd be wasting both my time and breath in doing so."

A lengthy silence ensued, wherein patient leaned back and dozed while physician casually surfed the 'net between stifled yawns, the latter quietly departing to first track down and then address the sporadically ringing phone down the nearby hall.

Amid Dean Graham's muffled whispers once said mission was accomplished, Dylan Barnes slept uneasily while treading a fear-fueled dreamscape that included standing completely nude in front of a full-length mirror and watching the inhumanly pasty flesh of his chest, abdomen and genitals blister and bubble before peeling away like detached potato skins. Unable to emit anything other than a choking, angst-filled gasp, he was able to identify the looming shadow standing just over his left shoulder even as his vision was gradually cloaked and eventually blinded by a dark maroon haze. The man previously known as Hyde, his forehead, jowls and neck infested in golf- ball sized polyps—some of which spewed thick, yellow ooze while others birthed an army of scuttling cockroaches—danced forward with both hands gripping overturned, lidless Mason jars that he quickly balanced over Barnes' mutilated, nearly skinless dome as to apply a final, fatal application of whatever abominable agent they'd previously held.

"Just as I thought...you are one major-league pussy, Barnes," Jessie cackled gleefully, his left eye popping free and dangling as a scaly slug the color of freshly lain tar pushed its way from the hollow orb. "Shit, even the skinny chick showed more balls..." a short pause as both the tone of voice and accent mutated dramatically to an equally familiar, easily identifiable source, "...in the face of certain death."

He watched the Jed persona lean in, could practically feel the hot breath tickle the lobe of his left ear, the man's blue-tinted lip bloated to inner-tube proportions. "Before going our separate ways, I'll leave you with a clue as to my own sad, tragic demise, Officer Barnes, as well as that of your fallen compatriot. Simply put, its origin might have appeared to be triggered solely by a mental breakdown of epic proportions, but alas, sometimes the blatantly obvious is *anything* but."

"Yeah-buddy, best watch your own government-pimped ass, Colonel Sanders...." the Jessie-voice chimed in a final time, gradually fading as if its originator were slowly descending a bottomless chasm, "...the real culprit ain't apt to take any prisoners, be it friend, foe or co-worker, you dig?"

Dylan Barnes jolted awake with a muted gasp, his exposed flesh saturated with fresh, cold sweat, the blaring echo of Jed Barton's parting words and accompanying, hopelessly maniacal giggling fit still ringing in his ears.

"…trust no one, least of all the one you'd never, *ever* suspect…"

~ * ~

Vance Carmichael, infamous for his serial pacing while addressing subordinates in whatever setting provided adequate space to do so, stood statue-still while ingesting the occasional toke from the vapor-smoke parked between the forefinger and thumb of his upturned left hand. As out-of-character and borderline frightening as this behavior was, the grim seriousness of the situation at hand was made ever-clearer by the overly calm demeanor and tone that had accompanied it.

"Officer Barnes is, at last report, in satisfactory condition, treated for chemical inhalation and a handful of third-degree burns. Officer Hobbs' next of kin have been contacted and her…she'll be shipped to the mainland within the next twenty-four hours for burial in her home state."

The briefing room at five-thirty AM held the usual suspects, that being the three sector teams scheduled for daily drop-ships, their itineraries normally doled out via an automated, computer-generated PDF slideshow. In light of the previous day's incident atop Hyde Isle, revisions to the oft-mundane morning pre-departure session came as little shock, though Carmichael's very presence dictated the highest level of concern. After all, he had junior officers perfectly capable of delivering similar speeches filled with cautionary reminders of not taking for granted the dangers involved with an assignment to Atlantis. To grow comfortable in one's duties, supervision constantly reminded, was to invite death, to essentially expose one's neck to a rapidly descending blade. Never, *ever* forget, it was preached *ad nauseam*, with whom you were dealing and what brought them to this place.

Anchoring the center of a trio of well-padded, high-back chairs at the first of several lengthy conference tables facing a single podium, Zack Gorman peered over his commander's square, buzz-cut inflicted scalp to a brightly-lit image being beamed onto and engulfing the whole of the far wall. As Carmichael waxed on rather blandly on the details of the Hyde tragedy, most of which he and Liza had ingested via facility scuttlebutt the night before, Zack studied the dual chart/mapping image—projected via VR slideshow from a tiny PC tucked within the podium's center shelf—and found himself instantly entranced at the message being conveyed. Liza sat to his left, wide-eyed as much from early morning caffeine intake as their commander's rambling monotone. To their rear sat Officers Jenkins, Peters, Jong and Garcia, all of whom save Garcia—a relative newcomer to Atlantis— he'd once shared warehouse duties.

"...what we have, lady and gents, as of Jed Barton's self-inflicted demise less than eighteen hours ago, is a definitive pattern that the suits on the mainland will no longer just shrug off as being par course. Take a gander," the captain said, pausing to gesture toward the projected image—with its bold, black lettering, blood-red drawn map and light green background, virtually impossible to either miss or dismiss— while maintaining a face-front pose as to better scrutinize the individual attention spans of his troops, "Three, count 'em, three suicides within the same sector in such a relatively short time. What this equates to, people, is that it's only a matter of time before a site visit from the mainland fills my calendar. Zack, you and Liza have the honors, I believe, of wading those potentially treacherous waters on this date, correct?"

Still under semi-hypnosis as he continued to scan the interactive map, with its sporadic blips and gradually mutating multi-screens, Zack merely nodded without verbal reply, leaving that chore to his jittery better half.

"Fuck the luck, Cap, but that be us in an eggshell."

While a spattering of nervous giggles and at least one full blown guffaw emerged from the peanut gallery, Zack merely groaned with a roll of the eyes while Captain Carmichael resumed the briefing presumably unfazed.

"Needless to say, you two, increased security measures are now officially in play. Before you arrive at that first drop-off point this AM, revisit and re-familiarize yourself with the reg. Lock, load and keep the required distance while sharing space with the inmate. Do not make yourselves a single target to whatever carnage he or she might have in mind. It goes without saying, lady and gents, carelessness can be fatal. Apparently, something plenty rank has gotten into the water, so by all means…"

"Don't dreeeenk the waaaater!" Officer Juan Garcia blurted, shamelessly mimicking an exaggerated hybrid of Speedy Gonzalez and The Cisco Kid's Pancho. Despite being born and raised in the American Northwest, he had, somewhat predictably, been the target of any and all south-of-the-border-aimed humor since his arrival a few months previous and didn't at all mind playing to the stereotype.

Once the scattered laughter, mostly half-hearted and somewhat forced, faded to a stiff, uncomfortable silence, Carmichael regarded his young charge—Garcia had not yet reached his twenty-fifth birthday—with a tight-lipped grin that all save its intended target instantly recognized as anything but mirthful.

"Perhaps, Officer Garcia, you're not grasping the direness of this particular scenario."

Garcia shrugged good-naturedly, his naturally dark complexion taking on a darker shade of maroon.

"Sorry, sir. I just was, you know, thought injecting a bit of hu—"

"Three corpses. Corpses we were tasked to maintain as live entities. Such vile statistics will most certainly mandate a full-blown investigation of not only our procedures for dealing with the inmate population but also seriously question those individuals presently assigned to follow said procedures. There is, of course, the major issue of just how inmate Barton came to be in the possession of insecticide.

"It is not at *all* out of the realm of possibility that, at the conclusion of said investigation, all presently assigned personnel of Atlantis will not only be removed from their present duty status, but suspended without pay for what might well be deemed as a severe case of dereliction of duty. This still strike you as a particularly jovial sequence of events, Officer Garcia?"

"No, sir," the young officer replied after a labored swallow and ragged series of coughs into a curled palm, "not at all, Cap."

Either satisfied with the young officer's apology or simply too time-pressed to berate further, Carmichael turned to the VR image with his hands crossed parade-rest style at his lower back.

"Good to hear. Take a moment to eyeball this layout. I'd say the pattern is fairly obvious. As we all know, inmate self-eradications are not uncommon out here. Then again, we're talking a viral rapidity in Sector Two. Therein lies the problem.

"Now, I'll keep everyone updated as to the fallout. In the meantime, no matter the sector to which you're assigned, initiate security level Bravo until further notice. Drop by the armory before shipping out for additional weapon and uniform issue. Zack, you and Liza hang out a sec. The rest of you move out and watch each other's rears."

Moments later, Zack and Liza stood elbow to shoulder directly in front of the periodically mutating image, each silently mapping out that day's drops in their individual minds-eye as their CO hopped up onto and sat upon the same table they'd previously occupied.

"Graham completed site visits to each of your drop-off sites last night," he announced wearily, stifling a yawn with the back of one hand while gripping an as-of-yet unlit vapor smoke in the other. "Regulations call for immediate counseling sessions following self-erads....suicides for all remaining sector inmates, usually within twelve hours if it involves a staff fatality."

"For what purpose, Cap?" Liza asked, sipping steaming black coffee from a Styrofoam cup and wincing in the aftermath.

"Doc's attempting to find a common denominator in order to nip future episodes in the bud," Zack interjected, turning from the image back toward Carmichael, pasty-faced and toking heavily from an ultra-slim, back-filtered, aqua-blue cartridge.

"Bingo, big man. Graham left me both voice and electronic messages…emphasizing in both tone and type a stern warning for whatever team was assigned to what the boys are already referring to as 'The Suicide Sector'."

"Any clues on the pesticide thing, Chief? I mean, I just want to make sure we're…Liza and I are cleared of any, well, suspicion."

Carmichael raised a hand, almost defensively, his stony mug temporarily softening.

"If that were an issue, Zack, we wouldn't be having this conversation. Your…both of your job histories speak volumes in terms of both the trust and respect of this agency."

"Appreciate that, Chief."

Joining her spouse in facing their CO, whose noticeably shaking hand belied his otherwise uncharacteristic calmness, Liza laid her half-filled coffee cup aside with a suitable grimace directed at its obviously aged, overly stout taste.

"Of the six isles on today's agenda, he sensed a strong vibe of potential behavior issues in but one."

"Let me guess, Cap," Liza interrupted only as Carmichael had paused for a fresh inhale of lung vapors. "Jugular Jane."

Carmichael nodded, spewing thick, snow-white vapors from each flaring nostril.

"Two for two, Gormans. Not exactly an O.Henry revelation I know, but up your guard several levels regardless."

"Check," Zack replied while peering down at his partner with his enormous jaw in full jut mode. "She hasn't given us any guff in the last few drops, but we normally assume a Bravo stance in her presence as a steady rule."

"According to Graham, she's antsier than usual with the news that certain government higher-ups in both Seattle and Portland are pushing for another vote to extradite. Just watch her psychotic, teeny-bopper ass for contraband." The captain paused for an additional toke, his hand so racked with tremors it took cupping it with the other to fully quell the effect. The Gormans would, upon their departure later that morning, openly broach the subject and discuss that neither had ever witnessed such open unease in the man.

"Amazing, isn't it?" Carmichael resumed amid a cloud of exhumed smoke.

"What's that, sir?" Zack replied, secretly holding his breath as said cloud drifted by his freshly shaven mug in the shape of a levitating noose.

"How is it such a heartless, cold-blooded reaper can be so damn frightened of her own mortality? God's honest truth, people…thirty years of housing the worst of the worst, and it never ceases to amaze that, deep down, the majority of their ilk might as well have a bright yellow streak tattooed down their collective spines in regards to that eye-for-an-eye thing the good book speaks of."

"I get it."

Both men regarded the only surviving female CO assigned to Atlantis with a dramatically creased brow.

"I mean, why they fear the consequences of their actions to such a degree."

Again, neither her hulking spouse or perpetually frowning commander felt obligated to speak, no doubt understanding a further explanation was forthcoming.

"Think about it. If one undertakes such unspeakable deeds, I can only think they'd fight tooth and nail to avoid meeting their maker. Though most claim atheist status, we all know how many true believers are found in foxholes…or death row for that matter."

Meeting each other's gaze, Zack Gorman and Vance Carmichael shared a slight nod, the latter even bowing toward the former's spouse as to better highlight the gesture.

"Big man, may I state you have most definitely outkicked your coverage with *that one*."

"Yes sir, Cap…" Gorman beamed, flashing teeth as blindingly pale as the vapor-trail snaking from the smaller man's flaring nostrils "…without a doubt."

Liza Gorman's own grin appeared slightly warped, said malady birthed solely from the uncertainty of whether she'd just been complimented or insulted.

Ten

The Isle of Lost Youth

Liza emerged from the hut wearing a sour smirk, popping the fat end of the shock baton into a gloved palm while staring into churning, dark gray skies. Despite the severely overcast conditions, she had insisted on donning her Ray Bans, the top edge of which she peeked over and past her husband to the sunbathing figure a dozen or so feet north of his position.

"*Dili-katuhoan.* Incredible…isn't that just precious now? Sweet sixteen is certainly growing up and, if not quite ready to leave the nest, she appears more than ready to fill it with newborns."

"Enough already. Unpack this last duffel and let's shag tail."

"All she requires is the seed of a strong, virile, willing young buck. Hey, perhaps even a *tikaedad*…an aging buck will do in a pinch, huh big 'un?"

"Mocking tone aside, Z, your feral side is showing," Zack fired back stiffly, standing at the center of a circular trench he'd so effectively dug in the moistened sand using only the edges of his boots

192

while maintaining a full visual on the client. The butt of a slick, black-handled stun rifle tucked against his right shoulder, his forehead, cheeks and neck infested with pea-sized sweat beads, he'd chosen a spot approximately halfway between the hut and the subject of what was their second of six scheduled drop-ship targets.

"It never fails. You only mix Tagalog and English when the jealousy bug sinks its fangs into that pretty little head of yours."

Poised directly between senior officer and inmate, Liza alternated glances between the two, the smirk slowly transformed into a full-blown sneer.

"That's it...make light—double-talk, change the subject, shift the focus—I've got eyes, big 'un. I *saw*."

"I'm sure you did, Z. Saw whatever that endlessly scanning, overworked imagination wanted you to see."

Zack paused, forced to shift the stun-rifle's aim as Liza had briefly crossed into his line of fire with the last of four off-loaded duffels slung over her right shoulder. Her left hip jutting out seductively, Liza studied the subject of this present jousting session, equal parts humorous and deadly serious, while chewing her lower lip and lightly patting her left thigh with the shock baton.

"Uh-huh, that being the case, my...imagination simply *insisted* that you stare twin laser burns into that little girl's exposed ass-cheeks. Care to object and/or deny said accusation?"

Much to his chagrin, Zack briefly broke character by flashing a toothy smile that he quickly retracted without the better half having ever witnessed its birth.

"Well, um, Missus Prosecutor, being that said butt-pads weren't merely exposed but practically levitating in mid-air for all to see upon our arrival, I'd have to plead guilty. Then again, other than poking out the aforementioned laser-orbs with the nearest pointy object, I'm must argue that refraining from receiving an eye-full wasn't just improbable but damn near impossible."

Liza giggled aloud without meeting his gaze, using the crook of an elbow to muffle further revelry.

"So then, do we have a verdict?" he chastised without a tint of humor, squinting through the building haze at what he perceived to be movement from the prone form sprawled face-down on a multi-colored lawn chair less than a dozen strides away.

"Fine, fine…not guilty by circumstance. Doesn't change the fact she's hot for your bulging bod. Girl appears to be coming of age at a rapid rate due solely to your manly, macho presence."

Raising the shock baton shoulder-level, she sustained a firm grip despite extending a forefinger.

"Best take into account, in case you do find yourself falling for those innocent, youthful charms, the fates of her previous beaus. You heard it here first, big fella."

With that, Liza whirled about and trudged purposely back toward the hut, having never met her lover's and superior's, stoic gaze.

From the corner of his right eye, Zack watched her step through the hut entrance while taking note of more obvious movement straight ahead.

Yawning beneath a cloaking palm, the girl performed a leisurely rollover, her tiny, two-piece string bikini obviously struggling to remain in place.

"You two an item?" she inquired lazily, looking toward Zack through rose-shaped sunglasses. Her voice, normally fluttery and waif-like—not unlike that of an animated heroine of some Pixar children's film—showcased a tint of seductive maturity that her assigned sentinel found simultaneously creepy and oddly arousing.

"We'll have the list ready for you in a few, Miss Jane. Sorry to interrupt your …tanning session."

Zack immediately cleared his throat, a tinge of guilt tightening his gut at the thought of Liza's good-natured ribbing actually coming to light.

"But she's so…petite. How can you two possibly, I mean, like…do it? You'd squash her like a toad or split her in half like kindling."

Readjusting the straps of the bikini top with a probing pinky, she smile mischievously and, while awaiting a response, licked each heavily-glossed lip slowly from corner to corner.

"Miss Jane, you'd, um," he paused to clear his throat, suddenly as parched as if he'd coated his tongue with a layer of nearby sand, "you'd best consider relocating soon or risk a pretty nasty burn. Far as I recall, you requested only the tanning lotion but zilch in the way of sunblock."

"Why, I appreciate your concern, Officer Gordon, but I'll be just fine and dandy. Like, seriously…you must really…hurt her when you two…bump and grind, right? I mean, looking at you, I figure you've got to be as hung as a Kentucky Clydesdale," she giggled, spreading her legs and running splayed fingers from each upper thigh to the knee and back again, her olive-shaded flesh glimmering despite a woeful lack of sunlight.

"*Gorman*, Miss Jane. Officer Gorman. Li—…my partner is probably wrapping up as we speak. As usual, once you sign off the inventory sheet, feel free to add any and all requests for next drop."

The girl leaned up and brushed back her straight, tar-black locks before lying back and removing the sunglasses, placing them in the moistened space between her breasts.

"I have an immediate request, Officer Gorman, if it's not…against regulation."

Zack swallowed nervously but did not reply, inwardly both shocked and embarrassed by the high level of unease he felt from merely conversing with the girl, who obviously fed off said vibe and thus reveled in the continual verbal bantering.

"I mean, like, I understand you and…your partner have a schedule to keep and all, but…well, would it be out of order to suggest…a little threesome action?"

Reaching up, she lifted the colossal sunglasses just enough to allow him to bear witness to a playful wink before dropping them back into place.

"As you might already know, I kinda, well, have a thing for older guys. As for your lov—...partner, it'd be a kick to say I got it on with an Asian chick, not to mention politically correct, right? I mean, like, the younger generation is always being taught the virtues of race relations."

"Miss Jane," he croaked, unable to completely shake the 'older guys' remark, "I'm afraid that would be, extremely inappropriate."

"Oh, how so, cocks-man of my dreams?" she practically purred, reaching between her legs and stroking ever-so-gently.

Briefly and for the first time since their arrival, Zack broke contact with their client by turning toward the sound of Liza's voice as she emerged from the hut entrance, shutting the door with a resounding thud.

"Well, for one, Chicky-pie, it is, most *definitely* against regulations. Number two and much more relevant, neither this Asian chick or the senior *cocks-man* there are into the whole child molestation thing."

She approached the girl with the required caution, iPad held palms-up in her free hand with the shock baton cocked overhead in the other.

Jane Savoy Clayton, age sixteen and a quarter and convicted killer of six in almost as many states, retrieved the iPad with her free hand while sighing wearily, an obviously forced exhale that reeked of stereotypical teen angst. Following a final, spastic session of genital massage, she moaned softly before commencing to administer her electronic signature without benefit of reading the attached form.

"Oh, forgive the interruption..." Liza chastised, hopping back as if goosed, "...but before you even ask, sweet pea, the government will not fund sex toys of any shape, size or form, to include any and all vaginal stimulants."

"Bummer," the girl pouted while offering the pad from an open palm and inserting the forefinger of her signing hand between pursed lips with a faint, slurping sound. "Mind if I ask a personal question, Officer?"

Gripping the iPad loosely and away from her body as if it were coated in flesh-eating toxins, Liza backed away in virtual slo-motion with the baton still cocked to strike.

"Like you won't inquire regardless. Fire away, Lolita. Just make it nice and loud so my superior can take in every saucy syllable."

Leaning up until she sat splayed-legged at the lower edge of the lawn chair, the girl reached back and detached the bikini top, which she then flung casually over her left thigh, all the while peeking past Liza toward her male counterpart.

"Well, like, just between us girls...what's it like humping the Hulk over there?"

Having tucked the iPad into a side pocket of her parachute-pants, Liza gripped the baton at each end, balancing it at eye level.

"Well, truth be told, sweet cheeks..." she beamed, slowly sliding one hand toward the other to reveal the final twelve to fifteen inches of the baton's fatter end, "...it hurts...so...damn...gooooood."

Vigorously massaging her tiny, tan-line accented breasts, the girl practically swooned in jaw-dropping, eye-rolling ecstasy, be it sincere or wholly manufactured.

"Time to go, Li...Officer Gorman," Zack groaned, spinning around on a boot-heel with the stun-gun slung over a shoulder and marching forward at double-time pace. "We've got a schedule to keep."

Liza tossed Jane Clayton a brisk salute and followed suit, sheathing the baton and kicking up a virtual sandstorm in her wake.

"If, like, you two change your minds, you know where to find me!" the girl shrieked gleefully at their backs.

The Gormans converged at the beached cutter amid rapidly stiffening winds and a steady mid-morning shower.

"My heartfelt apologies," Liza cracked as Zack boarded with a resounding grunt. "Little nympho craved *both* our bods."

"Creepy as hell, that one," he replied curtly, helping her board with a stout tug. "Honestly, Z, I felt more at ease with Bertha Wolf."

"Probably because Brenda Wolf wasn't at all interested in your, um, *baton,*" she giggled, patting the club hanging from her belt.

"Yeah, well, more so because I have nieces the same age and they're not even allowed to date."

"That and your average tweener isn't into stalking, slashing and stashing the diced up bods of their former teachers, all in the name of puppy-love rejection."

Zack cleared the final security measure and punched the ignition amid a steady downpour and the occasional flash of lighting overhead.

"I'll say. If they hadn't nabbed her for decapitating that biology teacher's wife. What was their names? Gilford? Garfield?"

"*Gilmore.* They'd practically been newlyweds, married less than year, I think. With hubby out of town on a teachers' conference, sweet pea had holed up in the backseat of their unlocked SUV and waited for the wife to run an errand."

Grimacing as if from a sudden onslaught of severe intestinal gas, Zack steered them toward the west and directly into what appeared to be a minor squall.

"Peeled her off at the neck with a homemade, razor-wire garrotte and stuffed the head in their mailbox. Charming little minx."

"Couldn't been worse, big 'un. If she hadn't gotten so careless at the ripe age of thirteen, Jugular Jane would likely be prepping for college as we speak. Talk about a potential body count."

Zack nodded, squinting through a torrential downpour as the cutter rocked and swayed atop increasingly troubled waters.

"Well, she was a straight-A student, after all. Honor-roll intelligent and just as conniving."

He peered over at his perpetually frowning better half, seated at the bridge and checking various dials, and decided perhaps an unexpected injection of humor was sorely needed to dilute the present aura of doom and gloom that had trailed them since their pre-dawn departure from Atlantis.

"Bollocks, my dear, that devilish, pigeon-toed sprite might even have wiped out a faculty's worth of tenured profs at dear old *Haaaa-vaad...*" he spouted in his best UK accent, a broad bit of Brit mimicry that she'd often found knee-slapping, snot-dribbling, eye-watering hysterical, "...or worse yet, those uppity bugger-pickers from the campus of Yale *unnivaaaaasity...*"

"If you don't mind, I'll take a shot at writing the site report for this one," came Liza's stoic reply, as if totally oblivious to his admittedly feeble attempt at jocularity. "Chick is coming unraveled. I want to make damn sure the instability is noted in case she decides to commit SE by masturbation."

Clearing his throat, Zack gently eased the throttle forward before twisting around for a final glance, wherein a single, jagged lightning strike appeared to pierce the center of the island like a giant, fiery spear.

"By all means, it's all yours," he replied morosely, a palpable sense of relief growing ever stronger as, not uncoincidentally, the distance between the cutter *Proteus* and *The Isle of Lost Youth* gradually increased.

~ * ~

Carmichael leaned back on a well-padded Nautilus machine boasting the label 'Chest-Buster,' the entirety of his frowning visage cloaked by a cloud of e-cigarette vapors, as, less than a dozen feet away, the facility physician paused between poundings of a well-scarred heavy bag to lean against its rounded bulk for support.

"So what's the verdict, Doc? Barton manage to procure all those skin-peeling, lung-blistering poisons from Mother Ocean or what?"

"Believe it or not, such a wild, off-beat assumption is, in truth…" Dean Graham huffed, his light gray sweatpants so saturated in fresh sweat as to appear a dark shade of brown, his naked torso equally drenched, "…not *that* far off. In addition to an extremely *unhealthy* dose of one of the stronger pesticides known to modern man in the form of Rodenticide, long banned from commercial use I might add, a *hydroxycoumarin* on steroids, one might say—the chemical breakdown also included several unique toxins found only in certain organisms found only in salt-infested bodies of water such as the great lakes or…well, the great oceans."

"Jesus crow, for *real*, Doc?"

"Very much real, Captain. Jed Barton held several degrees outside his chosen field, as you well know, to include years of study in the fields of oceanography and marine biology. Little did we…did *they* know that in exiling him here, it was akin to handing him the keys to his own vast, well-stocked science lab. The hydro-…um, pesticide was just the catalyst he needed—the trigger if you will—to complete his own personal weapon of mass self-destruction."

The facility gym was otherwise deserted at just past noon, par for the course considering the majority of assigned personnel were currently on the clock and, unlike Dean Graham, preferred to spend their lunch hour eating.

"Speaking of said catalyst, any luck tracking the source?"

"*Nada.* Frustrating as hell, Doc. No history of ever stocking anything nearly that stout on this burg. Mostly just assorted mosquito repellant other than a case of Black Flag and a few scattered cans of Spectrum, all of 'em coated in dust so thick you could barely read the labels."

Graham had resumed pummeling the bag with various jabs and hooks, halting abruptly once Carmichael had paused for a fresh toke.

"Smuggled in? I mean…possibly?"

The captain exhaled a trio of only partially circular smoke rings.

"Safe wager, as much as I hate to admit it. I mean, unless Barton had a third personality tucked away—*Aquaman* by name—back-stroked ninety-some-odd miles to the mainland and made a random purchase, there's just…few other options."

Graham pulled a glistening bottle of vitamin water from his gym bag and chugged greedily before responding.

"Investigative team on the way, I surmise?"

"Should arrive no later than noon tomorrow, weather-permitting, though I'm thinking they're gonna be held up an additional twenty-four to forty-eight. We've got a nasty tub-churner headed this way that's either gonna slide just to our south or hit us directly between the peepers. Storm-jockeys have it rated less than tropical storm strength at the moment, but it bears watching. Anyhow, we won't know for sure for a new moon or two."

The doctor nodded knowingly, removing battered, thinly-padded punching gloves that had seen better days.

"Those guys are legendary for getting to the bottom of things, Captain. The team usually includes a veteran psychologist. Perhaps they can even shed some light on the sudden surge of self-eradications. Personally, I welcome their intrusion…" he paused upon observing Carmichael's soured expression, "…at least from a mental health standpoint. I mean, anything to help prevent continued incidents."

"Um, yeah, sure, Doc…certainly that is a…the goal," the facility chief sighed despairingly. "I just hope we all don't end up staring down at a freshly typed pink slip as a consequence of not being able to figure it out on our own, because other than…getting to the bottom of things as you said, ICIT teams are also legendary for one other thing; rolling the heads of those they deem responsible."

Strolling over to a nearby mat, Graham knelt and began a series of leg and back stretches, pausing to resume dialogue before collapsing onto his back for a frenzied set of bicycle crunches.

"Should I expect alterations to my schedule, Cap? As of now, the docket shows five island visits per day for the next two-plus weeks. That is, weather-permitting."

The e-cigarette put away, at least temporarily, Carmichael paced a far wall lined with free weights and their accompanying racks, peering up occasionally to catch his own haggard reflection in the mirrored wall to his left.

"Status quo. Nary a single variation that I've been made aware of. HQ isn't normally big on going against regulation, and those clearly state individual psych evaluations are mandatory for each sector inmate in the face of such a sudden…barrage of suicides. Just keep on keeping on, and for god's sake…" he paused, halting in his tracks to eye Graham through a floss-thin squint, "…those emailed reports you're required to turn in within twenty-four hours of each session?"

Graham halted in mid-crunch, regarding his CO with a creased, sweat-coated brow.

"Yes sir?"

"Don't leave out a single nugget of info, no matter how inconsequential it seems at the time, or our collective butts might end up boiled, broiled and served on a dereliction of duty platter."

Perspiration flying from his drenched noggin in a wild spray, Graham nodded vehemently before resuming his set with increased fervor.

"Will do, Captain. Dot all 'I's' and cross all 'T's'. Leave no stone unturned and subsequently unreported."

Wearing a smile so unsubstantial as to barely rate as such, Vance Carmichael departed the gym with hands tucked loosely at his lower back.

"Or in this case, Doc, no potentially *loose marbles*."

~ * ~

Dylan Barnes, bandaged and buzzing quite nicely thanks to a recently ingested Percocet of ten milligram stoutness, leaned awkwardly against the entrance to Zackary and Liza Gorman's two-bedroom barracks abode, occasionally applying a weak, half-hearted knock which echoed eerily down a lengthy, otherwise deserted hallway. The 'couples' housing unit contained four separate condo-styled apartments, two of which were currently vacated and the one other *not* occupied by the Gormans currently home to a lesbian couple who plied their trade in the communications center.

"Hey Zack, Lin—…Liza, ya two got a sec? I mean, if you're nappin' or bumpin' uglies I suppose I can come back in a half-hour," he giggled, a droplet of foamy spittle hanging freely from his lower lip. "That is, if I can remember how to find the place, or, come to think of it," he hesitated, reaching up to scratch the side of his head with one hand while using the other to soothe a similar itch at his groin, "why the hell I came to see ya in the first place."

Meaning to use the solid oak door as leverage to push off and exit, ungracefully as such an attempt might be, Barnes instead found himself lurching forward to chest bump the deep shag carpet of the Gorman abode's living room threshold.

"C-crap-o-la on toasted rye, what a clumsy bastard your poor ol' mama raised, DB," he mumbled, rising slowly onto all fours before pushing himself upward with supreme effort.

Brushing nonexistent debris from a badly fading, light blue Houston Texans tee, he started to turn and depart but instead maintained a slightly shaky stance with his tattered sneakers set wide apart.

"Geez, nice digs," he blurted so loudly he actually winced in the aftermath, his nostrils flaring wildly below his bushy, slightly disheveled 'stash.' "Smells like…cinnamon…no…banana bread…freshly baked and ready to ravage! Hot damn but don't that takes me ho—"

He spotted the incense on a nearby coffee table, thick, diamond-shaped glass atop a steel frame positioned between a wall-sized plasma and tar-black leather sectional. The walls were adorned with various prints—some abstract and others as everyman common as a pastoral or bowl of assorted fruit—all framed in gold-tinted metal frames of various styles. Dominating still another wall was an enormous, multi-shelved entertainment center that served as a combination movie/music disc library, along with a top-of-the-line, four-speaker stereo system.

"Holy rockin' Moley," Barnes practically gasped, reaching over to snag the upper-edge of the nearby recliner, also genuine leather and black as the ace of spades, for much-needed support, "Now how in the *hell* did you two avoid a full-blown internal investigation? Place is right outta the lifestyles of the filthy rich and infamous."

Stepping past the recliner, he peeked over to the left, craning his neck as if hanging off the side of a protruding cliff-wall. Nothing nearly as spectacular stood out save a pearl-shaded Samsung refrigerator complete with French door and stainless-steel finish—easily a major step above the facility-provided icebox currently adorning his own modest one-bedroom bachelor pad.

A few tentatively-executed steps down a surprisingly wide hall led to the first of two bedrooms to Barnes' right, the door fully ajar and the squared, rear edge of a California-King swimming into view, along with a PC workstation that included various accenting hardware, all balanced on top and around a burnt-finish oak desk that appeared every bit the refurbished antique.

"All right now, this shit just ain't right," he whispered, taking a cautious step inside in order to obtain a full, panoramic view of a bedroom he instantly noted was twice the size of his own, if not three-fold. The PC, actually a colossal—perhaps twenty to twenty-two inch screen's worth—laptop with connecting keyboard, possessed an engraved label which read *Acer Ferrari 1100*, a sleek, stylish model even a relative novice such as Barnes figured wasn't exactly chump-change at the register. To its left sat a combination printer/scanner along with a trio of modems, all of which sporadically blinked as if perpetually forced to recharge in the absence of their masters.

"Well, I'll be a butt-pickin' chimp. Street cops have been grilled, peeled and tossed into general population for ownin' and showin' off much less in the way of material possessions. Hell's bells, how much does a Senior CO make anyhow? If this haul is any indication, Iron-Jaw Carmichael must be savin' up for his own gold-plated palace."

Finding the neatly-made bed—cloaked in a chocolate fleece blanket and assorted pillows—far too enticing to pass up, he lumbered over and slumped cautiously onto the outer edge, facing the computer workstation while wearing a warped, buffoonish smile, much like that of a mischievous child having pulled off the ultimate prank.

"Must be one of them tempurpedic jobs," he giggled sheepishly. "Feels like my flabby ol' ass-cheeks have been dipped in pudding."

He stood gingerly and turned to inspect the blanket to ensure no dramatic alteration of the blanket's shape and, satisfied his actions would forever remain a secret, practically tip-toed toward the bedroom entrance.

There was a sudden whirring sound, freezing him in mid-strike, followed by a ringing beep that, in comparison to the deafening silence that had proceeded it, was akin to a pyrotechnic explosion ignited within narrow cave walls.

Wind-milling back, Barnes collapsed back onto the bed with arms swirling and mouth agape in silent horror, convinced he'd somehow set off some type of motion-detector alarm. Sitting back up and reaching for a trio of throw pillows he'd accidentally knocked onto the carpet, he winced at the continuous beeping coming from parts unknown, figuring it was only a matter of moments before he'd be surrounded by armed security.

He'd just managed to push himself upright and was planning on yet another resetting/straightening of the bed when the incessant beeping halted and the computer monitor awakened in a bright flash of light.

"Livescape call incoming. Call directed to a Zackary Gorman," an automated voice droned, obviously female and wholly manufactured, *"Livescape call directed to Zackary Gorman from..."* the drone paused as to property obtain the video caller's confirmed ID, *"...Suckersneednotapply.com. I repeat...video call originates from website Suckersneednotapply.com, aforementioned site originating from the United States West Coast...Southern California region. A Mister Marlon Green incoming in...five...four...three..."*

Lurching clumsily away, Barnes first eyed and then practically dove from the monitor's line of sight, having spotted a tiny, mounted camera at the monitor's top left.

"Mister Gorman, my name is Marlon Green, newly assigned collections specialist here at SNNA Inc. Mister Gorman, are you present? If so, please respond."

Barnes fought off a building cough by continued swallowing, breathing through his nose and praying a sudden sneeze was not forthcoming.

"Mister Gorman, I understand wanting to keep this rather substantial debt solely between us and yourself and not divulging its existence to the...your wife. Big G...*Gaylord* mentioned her rather fiery disposition. Know I would not have forced this call upon your device without much deliberation. You have, according to records, been a fine customer for several years, never failing to pay your debts on time and with complete resolution.

"As for myself, I am officially calling on behalf of Big G...um, Gaylord Woods, whose employment within the firm is presently being reevaluated. I understand you'd given Gaylord specific instructions never to call unless you'd first initiated a 'coast is clear' warning signal, but I'm afraid things...the urgency of this situation has escalated in light of the last extension he granted you having expired four days ago. Mister Gorman, I understand Gaylord extended these extensions out of personal friendship, the last two without authorization from his superiors within the company, thus, I have been assigned your case."

Backed flat against the same wall hosting the rear of the work station, Barnes leaned forward and peeked around until he was able to view the monitor from a side angle with the understanding that his surprise guest was unable to view anyone not staring almost directly into the mounted camera's dime-sized eye. From what he could ascertain from such a skewed angle, Marlon Green was a pale, bespectacled white male sporting a blond coif spiked high with some sort of hardening gel, the man's dark blue eyes appearing freakishly buggy from beyond thick black frames propped high atop the bridge of a sizeable, freckle-infested snout.

"Now, down to the undeniably *grim* bottom line then, Mister Gorman: as in the case of simple mathematics, the present totals literally drenched in bold red lettering. As I mentioned a moment ago, that last extension, written up and agreed upon as interest free, expired over ninety-six hours ago. As of said expiration, the daily interest rate for accounts over one-hundred twenty days in duration automatically kicked in at twenty-four and one-half percent.

"Mister Gorman, you can imagine how just how increasingly dire your situation is becoming, literally by the hour. In a week's time, you're adding just over one-hundred six dollars of added debt. As of this minute, said debt sits at…"

The man paused, temporarily lurching off screen before reappearing as if magically teleported.

"…three-thousand, one-hundred and eighteen dollars and sixty-seven cents. In two weeks, you're looking at thirty-three-hundred plus. In a month, over thirty-six hundred."

Marlon Green sighed in mock misery, *the bug-eyed web-cam enforcer with a heart of gold*, Barnes deduced groggily, almost laughing aloud at the mere thought. Once the spiel resumed, it was in a softer tone, almost regretful.

"Hey, it may come off as insincere considering the business as a whole, but I...we do sympathize, Mister Gorman. Losing streaks in sports betting are as common as rainstorms in the Amazon, and they happen to even the most astute, most experienced men of wager."

Slapping a bare palm over trembling lips, Barnes barely avoided cackling aloud at the *men of wager* remark, delivered with all the emotion of a house plant.

"Alas, Mister Gorman, the time for understanding has long since passed. This is a business, after all. Now, the last thing we want to do is involve your employer. The garnishment of wages is, seriously, a last resort from the company's standpoint. I would assume, being in your line of work, such heavy wagering is frowned upon more than others. Gaylord informed me of your long, illustrious history with IC. I'd...we'd truly hate to see that jeopardized and, believe it or not, would not enjoy in the least being responsible for such a sad downfall in stature.

"Therefore, I'm here with a final option. An...ultimatum, if you will.

"As of this date, I'm allowing you a five day grace period to pay the debt off in its entirety. This is not business days, but five days *period*.

If this doesn't happen within the timeframe allowed, we'll be left no choice but to contact your superiors at International Corrections. We welcome your kind cooperation, Mister Gorman. You may, if you wish, contact me personally at the number provided on your screen. We are all adults here, Mister Gorman, and I certainly hope we can settle this matter without further difficulty.

"Good day, sir."

Barnes waited until the screen sufficiently blackened to come out of hiding, side-stepping from the bedroom before breaking into full stride through the living room while making a frantic bee-line toward the apartment entrance, which he'd inadvertently left slightly ajar.

"Soooo, the big man is up to his bulging lats in gamblin' debts. Shit, and he always seemed so damn squared away on *all* levels."

Swinging the heavy door inward, he took a single step into the eerie stillness of the hall before stiffening, the silver knob slick in his palm.

"Wait...waitaminnit there, pard. I ask myself once more...just what in the hell did I come here for anyhow? Borrow a cup of sugar or fresh roll of crap paper maybe?" he croaked, his forehead acceptably creased for such a frustrating, internal quandary. "Jeez...maybe that bug-spray skin-peeler of Barton's wiped away the majority of my brain cells after all."

The notion did not come to him gradually, a fragment at a time until full comprehension was achieved, but in a single, blunt-force wave of understanding. Backtracking with a fluidity and grace he'd rarely attained in the whole of his three-decade-plus existence—an impromptu breakdance accompanied by a double snapping of fingers— Dylan Barnes then quietly, ever-so-gently as not to wake some nonexistent, lightly slumbering neighbor, shut the door behind him while donning a wide, satisfying grin, his eyes pulled wide and gleaming and strangely, unblinking as if utterly entranced; the cold, guileless eyes of a ceramic doll.

"Oh yeah...*now* I...I got it. Like a bolt outta the clear blue sky, she was..."

He crept toward the kitchen, his gait as stiff and strangely alien as the weirdly robotic tone of his voice.

"...appears a little scavenger hunt is in order, pard, and I'll be damned if I don't have a pretty clear notion of where to start."

Eleven

Flameout

Liza stood legs wide apart, at least as much as her petite frame would allow, her boots submerged almost to the ankle in the aftermath of the retreating noon-day tide. Though no longer a torrential downpour, the rain remained steady; the accompanying winds as stout as ever and thus pointing the descending wetness straight across like an endless swarm of tiny, flesh-stinging missiles.

"Seriously, *Senior Officer Gorman,* do you have any idea how hard it is for me to play the by-the-book hard-ass? I'm having a hard enough time believing you'd risk this, much less that I'm standing here in the middle of this monsoon scolding *you* for it."

Roughly ten minutes earlier, she'd discovered entirely by happenstance the secret stash he'd intended for Marquez Chandler. The cutter had lurched violently to the left, struck by a colossal rogue wave that served to toss Liza head-first into Zack's hunched frame as he battled to maintain control in the churning, weaving aftermath. Meaning to wrap grasping hands around his tensed, muscle-laden midsection, her left hand had instead groped and finally clung to the side pocket of his camo-parachute pants, the palm instantly filled with a cylinder-shaped object of vague familiarity.

Once the vessel had righted itself—assisted greatly by the steely resolve of its square-jawed pilot—she'd removed the mystery item with only token resistance from its previous possessor.

It had taken an additional twenty-five minutes to reach their destination, the duration spent in total silence save the surprisingly soothing resonances of the storm. It wasn't until they'd beached that she'd broached the subject, forced to tuck the circular object beneath one arm as each hand clutched a separate weapon.

"I mean, damn it, Zackary, with all the extra scra—shrug—ahhh, shit…"

"Scrutiny."

"Exactly…*that*. They're watching our every eye-twitch like a chicken hawk and you're smuggling in illegal contraband? Strange timing, I must say."

Hugging a pair of overstuffed duffels to his chest, Zack trudged past his frowning spouse without ever daring to meet her stern, tightly-squinted gaze.

"He needs them, Z, badly. If he didn't, I surely wouldn't risk it."

"Yeah? Well, what happens if an investigation reveals their presence? All it takes is a simple blood test and you have to figure a full medical exam is just over the horizon for the whole sector."

"I'll take the heat," he replied, mounting a sizeable lead atop despite the beachhead's slight upgrade. "Besides, it's a moot point now, right? Once said contraband landed on-shore, we are officially liable for its presence."

Liza broke into a lumbering jog, the moist, sucking sand serving to slow her progress.

"We, *amigo*? *We* did you spout? From that I assume you've tossed me into the guilty mix without approval?"

"Sorry as I can be you fell upon my dirty little secret, Z, but yes, that much I do indeed assume."

Marching between familiar, bookending shrubs and cresting a final dune, Liza gained ground until he held only a three to four yard lead and the hut assigned to Marquez Chandler swam fully into view.

"Yeah, well, I get the feeling we're both gonna be sorry," she groaned, sprinting ahead and passing him on the left, aided greatly by a consistently stout gust at her back.

"For Sam's sake, Liz, it's a month's worth of antibiotics, not crystal meth," he shouted, slinging the heavier of the two duffels over one shoulder while maintaining a fireman's grip on the other.

"Well big fella, as our superiors view such matters, it might as well be."

They reached the porch with Liza, as planned, on point with the stun rifled aimed directly at the center of the hut's secured entrance. Tossing the duffels onto the rain-drenched stone to the right of the door, Zack kneeled over and clutched both knees in open palms while discharging a trio of increasingly violent sneezes, a fine mist of collected precipitation sailing free from his buzzed coif.

"Extreme *guilt* makes one susceptible to colds, I've often heard," Liza chided, wiping a similar build-up of moistness from both eyes with a less saturated shirtsleeve as Zack straightened with a pained grimace while massaging his lower back.

"Did...do you..." he stuttered, eyes widening, "...you smell something?"

Her nostrils flared even as Zack fronted the door and appeared to size it up for impending assault.

"Smell what? I got nothing..."

"You know my sensitivity to chemicals..."

"Yeah, so? Chandler isn't allowed any such produ—"

Kicking aside the duffel closest to the entrance, Zack quickly filled both palms with shock baton and stun-gun, respectively, his neck and shoulders visibly tensing; his bulging arms like coiled springs.

"This we both know and understand. Regardless, my spider-sense is tingling like a thousand-volt shock."

Having removed a glove and tucked it into a side pants pocket, he reached out and eased the palm of his left hand against the door, pinning it there for several seconds before pulling back.

"No sign of any interior heat build-up."

Liza frowned, the tension in her voice growing thicker by the syllable as her native accent began to dominate.

"What do you mean? Like…a fire? But, we didn't see or smell any smoke to indicate—"

"Chemical backdraft perhaps?" Zack inquired, though clearly not expecting an answer.

"Chemical back…I don't get…"

Liza backed up and off the porch, burying both boots into the wet earth with a moist, muffled thud—like drop-kicking a pair of soggy sandbags—while aiming the stun-rifle's twin sights just over her spouse's broad left shoulder.

"Oh, okay…okay, I'm getting it now. Like some kind of oven cleaner or maybe a floor stripper."

Sheathing the baton, Zack reached into a small pouch hooked to his utility belt. He instructed without turning; a harsh, guttural whisper. Rearing back his left leg, his next move appeared fairly obvious.

"Strap on your MCU, power up your shoulder mic and cover the back exit. We'll meet in the middle."

Liza accomplished the first in less than eight seconds—textbook when facing imminent chemical attack—and did not speak until after properly clearing the gas mask's built-in filter.

"Regulation calls that we stay together. No more than five yards separa—"

"That 'close-knit is a safe fit' reg is bat-shit crazy in this scenario. Manages to transform a pair of targets into one big-ass bulls-eye," he scolded, the goggles of his mask slightly foggy at their circular edges.

In response, he performed another clearing of the filter before retrieving the baton.

"Damn but ain't you the rule-breaking rebel all of a sudden?" she replied, practically forced to shout in order to be heard.

Though he'd already turned back toward the door, it was obvious this feeble attempt to break the tension had fallen woefully flat.

"Just do it, Liz, but watch your ass. Do not, I repeat, *do not* enter the premises until I give the word, clear?"

Once she'd activated the small mic—hanging from just outside her left shirt collar from a pencil-thin black wire—Liza shouldered the rifle and broke into a cautious jog toward the left side of the hut.

"Mic check."

"Loud and clear."

"Ditto, and watch your own rear end as well, big fella."

"Will do."

Three solid blows to the center of the door, delivered with machine-gun quickness ensued, after-which Zack backed completely off the porch with weapons drawn.

"*Marquez! Hey Marquez, you got visitors, man!*" he bellowed, the effect still partially muted due not only to the attached mask but consistently gusting winds.

"*It's the Gormans! We come bearing gifts! You all right in there, man?*"

His mic came alive with static, initiating an involuntary wince.

"I'm in position, Zack. Back entrance secure. Not a peep from inside," Liza conveyed, sounding as if she were standing at ground level of a deep abyss. "Any sign of our client?"

"Negative. I'll sound one more verbal alarm before breeching the entrance."

A trio of fresh, sharp, static zaps preceded her next reply, the tone noticeably clearer, as if she'd at least partially removed the bottom

214

edge of her mask. Unlike her initial transmission, this one wasn't nearly as inundated with the moaning shriek of a continuous, unmerciful gust.

"Maybe…you…we ought to reconsider the present plan of action."

"Reconsi—"

"Call in the ETU, just in case."

"No time to debate. It'd take a tactical unit thirty-forty minutes to arrive on site."

"Instead of skin-melting poisons, what if Chandler has a nasty, *explosive* little surprise awaiting? What good are plastic facemasks when things go bo—"

"Liza, I'm going in. Radio for the TAC team if it eases your mind, but I'm not waiting on 'em to make the scene.

"Now, on my signal, clear?"

Another burst of static, followed by an exasperated sigh.

"Shit, *fine* then. Whatever you say, as usual."

Straining to acquire an adequate supply of oxygen within the mask's limited confines, Zack sucked in several deep breaths before blurting out a final salvo.

"G'day in there, mate? Give us a fair go, yeah? We got some real lollies for ya this time around! Marquez! Talk to me, bloke!"

The rain briefly intensified even as, thankfully, the wind died to no more than a mild breeze. Regardless, Zack was forced to briefly discard his shock-baton, leaning it against his left calf while frantically wiping spatters of freshly applied saltwater from the mask's hard-plastic dome.

"Marquez, if you're in there and are harboring some kind of surprise—be it exploding parrot or land-crab flash-fire—be warned that we are definitely…not…in…the…mood!"

Pausing to loosen the building stiffness at his neck with a quick set of neck twists, Zack reclaimed his grip on the baton with one hand while tightening the same around a slick-handled, triple-pronged stun-gun with the other.

"Going in three," he whispered into the mic. "No matter what you hear, *do not* crack the seal of that rear door until given the word."

The lone reply was a single burst of static just a split-second before he charged toward and onto the porch in four lengthy strides.

As promised, Zack planted a size thirteen-and-a-half boot into the center of the door precisely on the count of three, reeling back in the aftermath and nearly toppling backwards off the cement porch. A second kick, delivered with equal if not more force from the opposite boot, resulted in an almost perfectly horizontal hairline fracture that ran the width of the door. Backing away to prep a third attempt, Zack paused just long enough to peel the bottom of his mask upward and suck in a fresh breath. A burst of static and familiar voice delayed the next charge just as the warm, gusting winds shifted, spattering his mask with a barrage of saltwater pellets which stung the exposed flesh of his neck like red-hot syringes.

"Zack, are you in? I heard the...you engage the door...are you...have you breeched the perimeter?"

"Door's on the verge of splintering but I think it's...he's got it blocked—maybe with the furniture or somehow nailed shut. Stand by...one more time oughta do it."

"Tactical unit is on its way. ETA is fourteen minutes. You sure we can't just sit this out until backup arri—"

"Fourteen minutes might be thirteen too late, Liz. Standby."

Changing up to ease the pressure on his battered knees and ankles, he opted for a reverse kick instead, digging his heel into the already semi-fractured oak and essentially snapping it in half with a resounding crunch.

Utilizing the baton, he batted away each severed half of the jagged door from either severely warped or broken hinges before ducking his head cautiously inside the opening, peeking through the rain-spattered mask into the darkened interior. As hazy conditions at his back did little to provide illumination, he waited for his eyes to adjust before moving forward, already aware of a monkey pile of scattered furniture that had obviously served to barricade the entrance.

"Zack..." his mic blared, "...you oh...you all right in there? Shit, Zack, I heard a shatt—"

"Got through the door," he interrupted upon hearing the panic-level in her voice intensify, "Looks like he blocked the door with every stick of loose furniture in the joint; the bed and headboard, the couch, both clothes dressers, the fridge and...*damn,* even the toilet. It would appear he yanked the bowl, tank and even the seat..."

Liza's stammering interruption was delivered in a high-pitched wail.

"But...why would...Zack, just hold position! TAC team is twelve and a half minutes out. I mean, *why* chance it?"

"Stand by...I'm...heard something...bedroom I think. Stand by ..."

"Zackary for god's sake, there could be...it's got to be a trap. Just back out and wait or by god I'm about to bull-rush through this door..."

Pushing his way past both the overturned couch and fridge—the latter's double-doors hanging ajar and emitting a rancid stench from whatever ruined content remained tucked inside—Zack waited until he stood at the center of the carnage before responding.

"Hang on, Liz. I'm inside. I'm going to check out the bedroom."

"Not without me you don't, you stubborn, m-mule-headed lug. Just give me a minute to join you..."

"*Negative,*" he countered sternly, pausing to ensure each weapon was set to maximum charge, "Hold position until I signal otherwise."

Kicking away the remains of a shattered dresser drawer, Zack took note of scattered clothing, shards of jagged glass and dishware lying about what little free floor space remained. He'd taken his initial step into the kitchen—the dining table and chairs conspicuous in their absence; several cabinets pulled ajar while others had been ripped away altogether—when the sound of an anguished moan first *merged with* and then *emerged from* the gusting winds and torrential rains pounding overhead.

"Marquez, this is Off—…it's Zackary …Zack Gorman," he bellowed, miraculously without a tint of apprehension. "Sound off, mate! I'm…we're here to help!"

Outside, Liza's entire frame trembled from Mother Nature's continual bludgeoning.

Upon hearing at least a part of her husband's plea—testament to his foghorn pronouncement—she first backed up several steps, her boots instantly sinking into the sandy slog, before charging forward with the stun-rifle slung over her right shoulder and the left tucked for impact.

The implosion of surprisingly brittle wood and razor-thin glass mingled with two distinctly different species of shrieks, the first that of a veteran law enforcement officer reacting on pure instinct at the sight of his wife sailing into the kitchen head first amid a shower of debris, the latter a cry of pure agony from an as-of-yet unknown source.

"What the hell, Liz?" he scolded, reaching down and acquiring a solid grip beneath her left arm and pulling her upright with an effortless yank. "Other than telepathically, I surely don't recall requesting your pres—"

"Enough already, *Dad*," she snarled, forced to reset both her mask, pulled partially askew from either impact or landing, and the trajectory of the stun-rifle toward the sealed bedroom entrance. "I'm here…deal with it already. Is he…in there? Did he speak?"

Zack took point with the shock baton cocked, gesturing toward their ultimate destination while inexplicably feeling the need to whisper his reply despite the explosive ruckus that preceded their teaming.

"Not…really sure, but I heard something, and it came from in there. C'mon then," he whirled about and shot her a harsh glare. "But keep two steps behind me, clear?"

"Yes, master," she countered with a slight bow, her mask littered in plywood dust.

They crept ahead in single file, covering the twelve-to-fifteen foot distance between kitchen and bedroom with all the speed of heavily-sedated sloths.

In lieu of a direct stance, Zack stood to the left of the brown-stained, oxford-style door, using the stun-gun as a pointer to call Liza's attention to the numerous smears along both walls and the entrance itself, most of which involved easily identified finger and palm prints. The smears were, for the most part, shaded a light crimson, though a few appeared much darker and were accompanied by flecks of jagged tissue that protruded from the mystery masses like badly peeled paint.

"Marquez! Its Zack and Liza, mate! You just napping in there or is there something we can do to help?"

As if on cue, the battering winds temporarily subsided, leaving the drum-echo of hard rain pounding overhead as the lone competition to a possible reply.

"Hey! Pyro! Best provide some feedback or we're liable to take this prolonged silence as a symbol of aggression!" Liza blurted at full volume, the mask only slightly buffering the effect.

Groaning beneath his own water-stained dome, Zack nodded angrily, waving her off with the baton until both movements ceased abruptly in reaction to the very sign they'd requested.

"Well, g'day then, mate! I heard ya knockin'," the voice shrieked, slightly familiar but oddly alien, each word enunciated in a deliberate, drunken slur. "Can't say I'm even a little gobsmacked by your arrival, as I've been waitin' ya know…waitin' and preparin' for the midnight hour to chime forth and for you to come a'knockin'. This…daylight visit must…has to mean you're on Aussie time. How very…fitting!

"Hey, hey, hey, well then…come on in…you know the way. No need for shyness 'tween the likes of us. It ain't like we're strangers, you and I! Far from it, yes? Just a couple'a mongrels fated to reunite. Aces! Your Shelia's welcome as well."

The accent shifted, instantly transforming into an equally slurred, urban hood-rat motif.

"All right then, motherfuckers...let's...do this thang!"

Poised at either side of the door, the Gormans exchanged equally perplexed glances.

"I take it I'm Shelia?" Liza inquired in a barely audible whisper.

"Aussie slang word for *woman*, so I'd assume so," Zack replied a bit louder than he'd intended and instantly dropping his voice several decibels upon finishing the thought. "He sounds altered. Chemically I mean, even butchering several accents simultaneously."

The junior guard shrugged before checking the setting of the rifle for at least the third time since making like a human battering-ram just minutes before.

"You all set?" Zack asked, taking a full stride away from the door with his back to it. She replied only after shooting a quick glance at her left wrist.

"Affirmative, but check it out—the team is less than six minutes out. I say we host a meet and greet down by the cutter."

In studying his ultra-calm demeanor and utter lack of obvious apprehension, she figured any such suggestion was fated to fall upon woefully deaf ears.

"Buck up, Z...it's the classic boot and reel on three," he said, confirming said deduction.

The 'boot and reel' was an archaic but amazingly effective precautionary forced entry technique, first implemented by inner-city SWAT teams in the mid-sixties. At countdown's conclusion, Zack would execute a fierce reverse kick and immediately join Liza in reeling back from the breeched opening, thus hopefully avoiding any possible booby-trap of an explosive or poisonous nature. Considering Marquez Chandler's specialty, a front kick and full-body exposure in the aftermath was not the wisest of choices for those who'd grown fond of their appendages.

"Hey, what you waitin' for, yo? I hear ya whisperin', ya wankers! Now get your stinkin', decayin' asses in here already! I ain't gettin' any younger and ya'll sure as fuck ain't gettin' no spryer!"

A low gurgling noise—like sink water chugging down a recently cleared clog—followed, then a raw, choking, chest-originating coughing jag that concluded with a wet, strained wheeze.

"Still think we have five minutes?" Zack asked with a raised brow. "Whatever he's done or is doing to himself, I'm of the opinion another sixty seconds might be too much. On three then…"

"H-hurry up, y-ya bl-bloody fruit-loops," a croaked whisper pleaded from behind the door a mere split-second before it was flung open with a resounding thud.

They crouched in the narrow hall for a full ten seconds before daring to lean up and over for an initial peek, just in the outside chance that a time-delayed explosive device had been set to detonate after the fact.

Squinting into a bleary cloak of dancing shadows, Zack duck-walked over the threshold while displaying the baton in a blocking stance toward Liza, the stun-gun's snub-nosed barrel unwavering as it blazed the hazy path.

"J-Jesus, Marquez? What in the…" he managed, a faint chemical scent filling his nostrils despite the filtering. Less than a foot to his rear and rapidly gaining ground, Liza was forced to stand full erect just to gain a workable visual.

"Wha-what is it? I can't see shit—" the curse word hung in her throat, suddenly so parched it felt as if she'd swallowed a handful of the same sand that currently clung to her boats like semi-dried cement mix.

As their eyes adjusted to the murky interior, made so by what appeared to be multiple layers of blankets nailed over the bedroom's lone window, the Gormans literally gasped as one.

221

Chandler sat yoga-style at the center of the nearly empty room—the twin size bed and bookend dressers having been relocated to the living room for barricade purposes—wild-eyed and completely nude, white froth dribbling freely from the corners of his mouth. The unscarred portion of his face, along with the whole of his left arm, hand and a large section of his upper abdomen and breastbone appeared coated in soot, as if he'd smeared moist ashes onto his bare flesh. Resting directly in front of him sat a clear, two-liter plastic bottle and just to his left, several empty, overturned cans of various shapes and sizes, their exact color or label content impossible to distinguish within such feeble lighting.

"Well, I…it is a-about time. Th-thought I was gonna h-hafta st-start this party without ya," he rambled, spattering his own chin and lap with foamy spittle.

"Chand….Marquez, what's up, man?" Zack asked with remarkable ease, his tone steady and, amazingly, unwavering considering what both he and Liza had initially identified as dirt or soot splotches of some sort riddling the man's face, arm and torso was soon found to be from a different source altogether. "You join a deep-sea cult since we last jawed or what? By all means, let us in on the ritual, mate."

"Y-yeah, Py…Chandler, maybe we can…help," Liza chimed in, not nearly as convincing once she'd successfully identified the dark, glistening splotches as burns so severe the man's flesh had either melted away or been manually peeled, the thought of the latter causing her throat to fill with warm, fresh bile.

The squatting man's reply was at once timid and aggressive, depending on the syllable uttered. His eyes were glazed…gleaming like marbles, as he appeared to stare through them and into an alternate universe only he could visualize.

"S-so I take it by th-this little d-drop-in th-that you t-two never d-did buy the ol' collateral d-damage defense, yeah? Well p-piss off! I kn-know the truth. Don't mean shit to me what y-you think. I mean,

222

crikey! Th-this is ant...ancient h-history, ya wankers. Wha-what in blazes t-took ya so long to get your mad on?"

"Zack, he's...he's not speak—even talking to us. See his eyes? He's nesting at the funny farm," Liza said, reaching up and over with the barrel of the stun-rifle to gently prod her husband's left shoulder, "Tactical team is better qualified and equipped to handle a code-nine."

The big man shrugged the narrow barrel away, maintaining a defensive pose less than a full yard from their client, who had begun to sway back and forth as if hitching a ride on an invisible porch swing.

"He's hallucinating. Something he's ingested," he replied curtly, nodding toward the empty cans. "Probably from those *and* whatever's gestating inside that soda jug."

Chandler abruptly halted swaying and leaned forward, whispering through cupped hands that levitated mere inches from the top of the soda bottle.

"It appears, Stoney you...o-old rat-bag, that y-your Shelia there can't take her eyes off my donga, no doubt mesmerized by b-both its enormous girth and a-amazing length. Tr-try to control h-her, will ya? Personally, I'm just n-not in the mood."

Liza giggled nervously even as Chandler resumed his snaky gyrations, complete with a mumbling, incomprehensible chant.

"Wha...did he just call you...*Stoney*?"

With a knowing nod, Zack inadvertently lowered the aim of the stun-gun from Chandler's ever-rotating form to the bottle the man appeared to be coveting.

"So *that's* it. Will Stone from the Viking sanction. Remember Chandler's case file? Stone and his dau—" he paused, crouching onto his hunches, "...Liz...reverse field, A S A and P."

"Wh-why? What'd you see—"

"That-the bottle...it's...swell—...expanding..."

"Expad—"

"Liza, double-time it, and not just into the kitchen. Get clear of the hut."

"What about you? I'm not about to leave you alone with this...this glazed nut-sack—"

Turning on her like an enraged jungle cat, Zack's eyes were huge, pulled saucer-wide. His appearance alone was enough to motivate her semi-frozen limbs to snap to with renewed fervor.

"Damn it, GO!"

Shouldering the stun-gun, she did just that, legs pumping at full gallop as she practically sailed through the kitchen and out the same shattered opening she'd so violently created minutes before.

By the time her left boot struck the wet sand, instantly submerging to the ankle and causing her to slide off-balance and eventually tumble face-first onto the water-logged terrain, the hard rains had eased a degree, as had the sporadic bursts of typhoon-level winds. The stun-rifle had flown from her grip upon impact, and Liza, having ripped away and discarded the sand-coated gas mask, located it a half-dozen yards to her left, sticking from the mushy grounds barrel-first like a grave marker.

Her mind reeling, she instinctively checked its setting before jogging back toward the hut. She'd not quite reached its flooded porch when the soggy earth beneath her feet served to intervene, essentially tossing her airborne to land within a full dozen feet from lift-off, her lungs emptied with a resounding huff upon impact.

Zack had considered, ever-so-briefly, inquiring about the contents, the mystery ingredients tucked within that gradually bloating soda bottle as to decide on a proper plan of action.

That was, until, exchanging frenzied glances from the overturned cans to the soda bottle and back again, he was able to put two and two together, the severe twist in his gut nearly instantaneous as a reward for solving said enigma.

"Stoney, d-do not f-fear...I mean, how could y-you really, considering y-you w-were blown to f-fucking fragments y-years ago?" Chandler beamed, mustard-colored pus streaming down his cheeks to pool at his chin like bright yellow birth pods. When he actually locked eyes with Zack for the first time, it did very little to sooth the CO's splintering nerves.

"Well then..." the Aussie assassin codenamed 'Blaze' concluded with a playful wink, "...G'day then, m-mate...and I p-pray to m-my demonic s-sire it's the last fuckin' t-time for the both of us."

Initially, Zack lunged forward at the sight of Marquez Chandler leaning down with his mouth pulled wide to suckle the top of the sealed soda bottle, nearly slipping to one knee as he reversed field upon witnessing the bottle bloat to nearly twice its normal size.

He managed to clear the bedroom threshold in two leaping strides, diving chest-first into the middle of the kitchen floor when a massive shockwave threatened to bring the surrounding walls, drenched in fire, collapsing down on top of his sprawled frame.

~ * ~

In-between steely-eyed stares at a nearby framed photograph displaying the whole of the Atlantis facility from high above the island, Carmichael chewed the filter-end of the e-cigarette like a well-gnawed stogie, sporadically shifting its location from one corner of his mouth to another without benefit of hand and/or finger assistance.

"Drano bomb. Simple, old-fashioned, homemade explosive device that pimply-faced teenagers from coast to coast have been posting on YouTube for more than a decade. Nothing fancy by any means, but fatal enough if detonated improperly, as in...well, swallowed."

Slumped on the edge of a sparsely padded exam table, Zack winced with even the slightest shift of his rear. Liza stood at his side, an elbow propped gently atop one naked shoulder. Shirtless, the senior CO's back, chest and abdomen were littered in a sporadically connected roadmap of scrapes, cuts and bruises. His forehead held a perfectly circular splotch, about the size of a half-dollar, where the gas mask's filter had pelted flesh upon his rather awkward landing, face-first onto the hard tile floor and waking with the severely mutilated apparatus coiled around his skull like a turban.

"I…saw the cans but…realized too late," he managed, swallowing with a pained grimace as Liza handed him a Styrofoam cup of water.

"Realized *just in time* I say," she cooed with a gentle pat of his left forearm, the elbow of which appeared to be housing a dark patch that was, in reality, a deep bone bruise in the process of manifesting itself to the outer layer of skin.

"She's spot on," Carmichael added as he commenced to pace the tiny exam room with hands tucked snugly at his back. "A split-second more spent inside that deathtrap and they'd probably be surgically removing Chandler's brain fragments from your backend, at the very least."

Zack cringed internally at the thought while attempting to maintain at least a partial bead on his ever-mobile commanding officer through eyes that remained slightly bleary despite a deluge of administered drops meant to soothe.

Barely ten hours removed from the latest in recently client-vacated sites, there was still a vague ringing in both ears and a dull, unrelenting ache at his lower back that a thousand set of disc-straining, thigh-blasting squats couldn't touch. Though his full-body dive had prevented him from witnessing the actual event, each time he'd closed his eyes since and managed to doze, such blissful slumber was invariably interrupted by the image of Marquez 'Blaze' Chandler's shiny bald head expanding like an overfilled balloon before blowing apart like a melon stuffed with TNT.

The sound of distant thunder accompanied the occasional shaking of nearby walls. Liza openly winced each time the former sounded off like cannon-fire that, with each new booming retort loomed closer to the sandy shores of Atlantis.

"Getting dicey out there, huh Cap?" she asked, failing miserably to mask the deep concern in her high-pitched tone. "What's the latest?"

"Well, what we appear to be facing is the classic good news, bad news scenario. Currently just spitting rain and those typhoon level winds from overnight are starting to level off."

The captain hesitated as if expecting a verbal reaction from the peanut gallery, but soon resumed once this did not come to fruition.

"As for the bad, well, we may or may not get hammered by a second wave within the next ten to twelve hours. A stronger wave, according to the Doppler analyzers on the mainland. Currently, the odds of Atlantis and surrounding isles catching the blunt edge is sixty-forty in the red."

If anything, Liza sounded surprisingly relieved at such potentially grim news, actually giggling girlishly while applying a playful pinch to Zack's bare left triceps.

"Soooo, possible lockdown?"

Carmichael nodded.

"I'd say more like probable. Regardless, you and the human cannonball here are on med leave for the next seventy-two hours. Hopefully by the time he's able to be reinstated, this nasty stretch will be ancient history."

"Hear-hear," Zack injected, weakly raising a clenched fist and shaking it as in mock victory, "Three days of watching Liza's Filipina soap opera blu-rays and I'm liable to *backstroke* to the drop sites."

The couple exchanged a light jab even as their CO circled them like a spying vulture.

"Zack, I know it's damn early to be hitting you with this, but the Tactical Team CO reported you'd mentioned a reference Chandler kept repeating."

"Will Stone, yes sir. Kept...referring to me as 'Stoney' and...well, looking through us both like we were a couple of wandering spirits."

"I concur. Pyro wasn't even seeing us. No acknowledgement whatsoever," Liza said, switching locations on her continuous massage to the back of Zack's neck.

Carmichael halted in mid-stride, reviewing the Atlantis pic again as the e-smoke wriggled and squirmed from the left corner of his mouth like a probing mandible.

"So, in his warped state, he was conferring with his final victim back in the world?"

Zack nodded timidly just as Dean Graham reentered the room palming a syringe in one hand and what appeared to be a donut-shaped heating pad in the other.

"That, and well, there was a Shelia reference or two, if I remember correctly."

Carmichael's brow severely creased.

"Shelia? Who in blue bla—"

"An Australian slang term meaning female," the doctor contributed matter-of-factly while raising the loaded syringe to an overhead light to check its content.

"Jeanna Hill, Will Stone's teenage daughter," Zack said, shrugging weakly and wincing in the aftermath. "She was…listed as collateral damage in the father's sanction."

The captain snapped his fingers in sudden comprehension.

"Oh yeah, now I remember that file entry. He'd booby-trapped Stone's office not knowing, at least on his word, that it was 'bring your kid to work day.' Wasn't enough left of either of them to spread on a biscuit."

"That's the one, Cap. Um, back to Mar—Chandler. It didn't take a Harvard grad to see he was delusional to the max—eyes rolling like marbles—had managed to burn himself to a crisp long before we got there, no doubt from some reckless experimentation."

Graham stepped forward and, gripping Zack's bulging left biceps, gently submerged the syringe into a waiting vein just above the crook of the elbow.

"Muscle relaxer," he said, applying gauze and affixing it with a short strand of clear tape. "It's on time release—very gradual effects and it won't put you in an incoherent stupor—I'll allow you six more in pill form. Take two a day as needed. Also a seven-day supply of antibiotics for the lacerations. Liz..." he paused, turning toward her with his arms crossed over a body-hugging white tee that read 'Doctor's Orders' in dark red lettering, "...make sure he cleans said wounds at least three times daily."

"Affirmative," she replied with a sigh, resting a hand atop her slumping spouse's tree-trunk thick left thigh. "Hardest part will be keeping him from sneaking in a workout."

"Oh, not to worry," Zack groaned, reaching up with a shaky hand to scratch the grayish stubble build-up atop his squared chin. "Only lifting I'm planning on doing the next few days involves prescription tablets and however much cold brew it takes to wash 'em down."

With that, Graham retrieved two small, dark-tinted bottles from the left-front pocket of his parachute-styled pants and placed them into the big man's open right palm.

"Considering the full-body thumping you've taken, I have little fear of you overdoing much of anything, at least for the next forty-eight hours or so. Oh, with that freshly in mind," he retreated briefly to a rear closet, emerging with a set of wooden, half-cuff crutches that had obviously seen better days.

Frowning, Zack took possession with obvious disdain.

"Just learn to love them, big guy," Graham scolded with a creased brow. "Old and well-used as those babies are, they'll haul your big rear around just fine."

The two men nodded in unison and the doctor turned to depart only to be halted in his tracks with one sneakered foot still inside the exam room and the other atop the infirmary's thinly carpeted hall.

"Um, Doc? Don't you think that *now* might be a convenient time to get the prerequisite trauma brief in the books?" Carmichael inquired in a tone that, at least initially, reeked of desperation. In the short span that Dean Graham had been conversing with the two Gormans, their CO had managed not only to activate his e-smoke—on which he puffed madly away—but also retrieve a palm-sized communicator commonly referred to by staff personal as *static ticks* due to its tiny, circular, bug-like appearance and less-than-stellar performance, consistency wise.

"Well, yes, I don't see why not," Graham shrugged, turning about, tilting his head slightly and studying Zack Gorman's fatigue-ridden deportment with a worrisome scowl. "Although I'm not certain Zack is quite up to it just now."

Stepping over amid a haze of vapor fumes, the captain put an arm around Liza's shoulders and gently nudged her toward the door.

"You game, Liza? Sure would save some time, mandatory-report-wise. You can imagine the level of manure the higher ups are giving me on this one."

She forced a smile while glancing back at Zack, who nodded his apparent approval.

"Sure, why not? You sure I don't need to piggy-back your massive ass back to the hacienda, big 'un?"

"Positive...and my ass isn't that massive."

She soon found herself trailing Dean Graham down the narrow, twisting hall.

"Doc, is it just me or do we have to stop meeting this way?" she quipped, her heart not all in it despite the valiant effort. Still, she couldn't quite help but cop a stare at the good doctor's meticulously chiseled buttocks as they flexed and gyrated directly into an admittedly limited line of sight.

"It's *not* just you, and *yes*, we most certainly do."

They'd drawn to within a half-dozen yards of his office when they were forced to turn sideways to allow passage to a slender, painfully young CO whose face Liza couldn't quite place. They'd nodded amiably upon passing, and Liza felt a sudden knot clench at the center of her gut.

"New blood, I take it," Graham commented blandly as he keyed the door.

Liza had swung around for an additional look but the unknown officer had already cleared a sharp curve in the hall.

"*Young* blood's more like it, Doc. Kid's barely shaving."

Graham's laugh sounded as *faux* as her earlier attempt at jocularity.

"Yes, ma'am. I swear they recruit them right out of high school these days."

As the two entered the doctor's office, so neat, spotless and meticulously arranged—reference books perfectly lined and stacked by size and thickness, glass cabinets utterly smear-free, desk and accompanying furniture appearing freshly dusted—Dean Graham gestured for Liza to take a seat in a well-padded recliner before sneaking a quick peek at his watch, his normally staid, unreadable expression anything but.

Twelve

Lies and Segregation

Propping the crutches in a nearby corner, Zack collapsed onto the padded couch with an exasperated groan, having struggled mightily to remove his rain gear due to the stiff, sore condition of his entire frame, most notably the neck, shoulders, arms and upper back. The captain had excused himself and exited the office, where the painfully youthful-in-appearance CO awaited. Zack could hear his commander mumbling through the thickness of the sealed barricade, but was unable to distinguish any of the actual dialogue. The relatively short stroll from the infirmary to the Admin building had taken roughly twice the normal duration due mostly to his own shambling gait but also the straight-line winds they'd encountered between structures. Though the rain had indeed subsided to a light drizzle, sporadic gusts had threatened to topple him from the concrete pathway, a viable occurrence at several intervals if not for the assistance of both Carmichael and the junior officer.

Clearing his throat and coughing into a curled fist, the captain reentered the office and shut the door behind him, but not before Zack caught a passing glance of the young CO standing across the hall, having struck a parade-rest pose.

Perhaps it was the muscle relaxer somehow easing his inhibitions, but he felt an uncharacteristic urge to cut immediately to the chase, proper protocol be damned.

"With all due respect, Cap, what's the *real* story behind the...my escort?" he croaked, "Damn greenhorn appeared to be one 'boo-scare' away from soiling his undies."

Carmichael eased behind his desk and into his chair before reaching forward and scooting the computer monitor to one side as to allow an unobstructed view between them. Reaching into a desk drawer, he retrieved a vapor smoke and immediately popped it into one corner of his mouth and commenced to gnaw.

"Well, since we're being so forward, big fella, allow me to fire one off that might provide an answer you seek, at least in a roundabout sort of way."

"Please do, sir. I'm feeling a bit perplexed and hoping it's just a symptom of having my noggin jostled severely about."

"A veteran law enforcement officer should never doubt his intuition, Zackary, slight concussions aside."

Leaning forward with a pained wince, Zack was utterly oblivious to a thin stream of blood seeping from one of a dozen lacerations dotting his face and neck, no doubt reopened during the recent trek.

"*Shit*, I knew it. The way you nudged Liz away with the doc. What's the question, Cap? I'm guessing *scapegoat* is my new middle name."

Unhinged by fatigue, he collapsed back into the couch while running bandaged fingers over his buzz-cut coif.

"No argument to make that stands up, no matter how I try to justify in my own mind. Tact team was on its way...just minutes away. I

233

just…felt…*knew* that Chandler was alive but didn't know for how long and figured there wasn't a second to wa—"

"Not the issue," Carmichael interrupted with a vehement nod, reaching down into a separate desk drawer. "This isn't about the tragic demise of one Marquez Chandler. Then again, maybe it is at that. To be determined. As for that initial query, Zack, and pardon me for drudging up old news."

A weak shrug served as the big man's lone response.

"Those pesky financial issues from last year getting squared away or still…lingering?"

The dramatic raising of a brow spoke volumes in terms of Zack's apparent befuddlement.

"It's a process, Cap, slow but sure. Um, I have to wonder what that has to—"

"That pesky gambling Jones still holding tight?"

The veteran CO's eyes widened, a wild giggle escaping from between chapped lips.

"Say wha…? Cap, are we *really* having this conversation? I mean, isn't this strange timing for some kind of half-assed rehab attempt?"

In lieu of a verbal response, the captain scooted his chair back just enough to gain access to a bottom desk drawer, which squeaked sharply upon being pulled ajar.

Pushing forward, he then placed two items atop the desktop—the larger of the two easily identifiable by its labeling, the smaller one enigmatically alien—even as Zack pushed himself back upward and squinted mightily while studying each.

"Same-sized can Marquez had in his possession," he said softly, as if to himself, pointing toward the white-labeled tin container.

"Drano, or the equivalent. Clog-buster of consideration strength. Plenty enough, when mixed with a roll of tin foil, to say, blow a man's head into bone and gristle puree. As for the vial, more than likely a manmade hallucinogen of sorts—think *twilight sleep* clone—it's currently being evaluated on a mainland lab. Should have results within twenty-four hours."

"Fascinating, Cap, but...what exactly does this have to do with me or my...current money situation?"

Removing the vapor smoke from between clenched teeth, Carmichael rested both elbows atop the desk and replied while peering over entwined fingers that appeared almost prayer-like in pose.

"We both know there is that element out there willing to pay a steep price to see what they deem the scum of the earth...*eliminated* as a tax-payer burden."

"I attend mandatory training classes on such matters, sir, as you well know," Zack retorted, his tone openly defensive for the first time—his pasty complexion gaining several shades of maroon. "So, am I to assume that I...that the suspicion is I'm somehow involved in Marquez Chandler's decision to swallow a homemade bomb because I have a few unpaid debts?"

Carmichael reinserted the well-chewed filter-end of his e-smoke before leaning back with his arms crossed and trademark steely glare set firmly in place.

"Not exclusively, no, but there are additional factors, Zackary."

Briefly breaking eye contact with his commanding officer, Zack's jaws visibly tightened with a sudden surge of thinly veiled frustration.

"Those being, sir?"

The captain's gaze instantly shifted to the objects which beaconed so powerfully from the far edge of his desktop—the same two articles which held Atlantis' Senior Corrections Officer utterly mesmerized.

"You're looking at 'em. They were retrieved from your assigned housing unit."

~ * ~

Seemingly oblivious to the booming thunder that sporadically shook the walls around him, Dylan Barnes regarded his coffee mug with a single, twitching eye, the other temporarily stuck shut due to a build-up of crusty gunk. Having rolled from his bunk a half-hour earlier, he'd since roamed about in a slow-motion haze, his thoughts frazzled, his head heavy and his appendages equally so, as if adorned with a lead-laden suit of armor instead of a gravy-stained tee, jockey briefs and athletic socks.

Cripes, but what a bender. Haven't felt this level of mule-kicked since...shit, ever. Queer thing is, I can't for the devil recall suckin' down a single shot of firewater, unless I snuck into the kitchen and slept-guzzled down that en-tire pint of Evan Williams.

Sipping noisily from the steaming mug, he winced at the slight burn to his tongue before retrieving an additional spoonful of cream. Upon checking his facility-assigned iPad for any overnight duty-related messages—a daily, procedurally mandated task—he'd read of the possibility of a facility-wide lockdown, dependent greatly upon the ever-changing weather conditions. Being that this was to be his first day back on drop-ship duty since the Hyde Island incident, he felt an inexplicable need, a stout 'chomping-at-the-bit' motivation, to hop back onto the saddle...inexplicable hangover be damned. Never being one prone to such self-dedicated behavior, he could only logically conclude that the combination of cabin fever and light inventory duty served as viable culprits.

Regardless, he couldn't shake the overwhelming sense that there was someplace he had to be, as if his absence, no matter the reason, could result in a tragedy of unparalleled circumstance.

Must be all those nutty nightmares. Thank the big guy above the details fade with sunlight and a strong cup of Joe—otherwise I'd be dwellin' on 'em 'til or worse, tryin' to make sense of 'em. From there, Dylan ol' sap, you're one maniac's giggle fit away from bein' tied to a gurney with Doc Graham leanin' overhead with a loaded syringe.

Another sip produced a similarly pained expression before he was able to push himself upright and prepare a bowl of cereal. Gazing out from between barely parted blinds from his twelve-by-fifteen barracks room's lone window, he noted the rain's intensity was moderate at best, the facility's assigned flags blowing only casually.

Can only hope that damn typhoon makes a sharp turn and blows in another direction. A day or two holed up in this cave or spent counting off tubes of suntan lotion and Graham might as well start prospectin' for just the right vein to prick.

Dylan Barnes proceeded to forced down a small bowlful of cornflakes and sliced bananas, all the while secretly pondering the true source of his physical and mental ills, as a tentative check of his private bar had revealed a fifth of the aforementioned Evan Williams rot-gut with its seal firmly intact.

~ * ~

Hands atremble and sporting a pronounced limp, Zack winced with each thumping step down the iron-mesh ramp leading toward *Proteus,* his tunnel-vision-like attention span relegating Juan Garcia's passing inquiry utterly non-existent.

"Hey, Chico! Where's the fire, man?" Garcia had inquired casually with a hand raised in greeting, standing at one of a dozen computer-operated, individually maintained cutter lock-docks with his free hand resting on the exposed keypad.

"Gorman! Zack Gorman! Old age done confiscated your hearing, big man?" he'd continued, though several decibels higher in both pitch and volume.

Hitting the brakes approximately ten yards from his destination, Zack felt compelled to reply for no other reason than not raise unnecessary suspicion, something his frazzled appearance—uniform shirt badly wrinkled, drenched in fresh sweat and only semi-buttoned, pants equally infested with a plethora of creases that gave the entire ensemble the dreaded 'slept-in' look— all but begged.

"Oh, ye-yeah, hey Juan. Just coming off?" he managed, only half-turning while keeping his badly shaking hands strategically hidden.

"Affirmative. Half-schedule only."

237

A double-retort of metallic clicks ensued, echoing loudly inside the domed marina, and Garcia powered down the tiny PC before climbing onto the walkway. Short, stocky, and nauseatingly upbeat, the Oregon-born but Hispanic of descent, Garcia paused to eyeball his daily ride a final time before turning back Zack's way. They were alone in the massive marina, all assigned cutters locked into place save two, at least one of which Zack deemed highly questionable in its absence.

"Blow's sweeping our way so they didn't want to take any chances, y'know? Just between us peons, I tread water like a sack full of bricks, so I'll gladly spend a half-shift restocking supplies."

Though a complete turn to face his addressor was briefly considered, Zack inside strolled purposely forward, flashing a raised backhand as he neared the lock-dock which held *Proteus* securely in place.

"Got'cha. Getting nasty out there, is it?"

"Waves are steeping a bit, but it's easily navigable for now. Still, best place pedal to the metal, *amigo*. I figure the lockdown order will be coming down within the hour. Besides, you ain't looking too spry, truth be told."

Standing with his back to Garcia, Zack powered up the computer and poised trembling fingers over the keys as to enter the password as quickly as possible.

"Just a routine maintenance check. Been out a few days and I wanna make sure ol' Bessie here is firing on all cylinders for when we get the all clear."

Garcia started to stroll away in the opposite direction but hesitated, studying the larger man's ramshackle look while reaching up to scratch the wax-shined bald head beneath his cap.

"Hey, so where's the fireplug? Strange to see one without the other."

"What's...who's that?" Zack stuttered, finally able to type in the required code and standing back as twin-clicks ensued and the *Proteus* was subsequently released from its steel-piston auto lock.

"The ol' ball and chain, *amigo*. You know, your wife?"

Zack forced a laugh that was more a strained croak.

"Oh yeah. Back at the hacienda doing her nails, I guess. Liza couldn't care less *how* this exquisite baby provides us quality transportation, only that it *does*."

"Understood. Typical *senorita*, right? All it takes is to feed 'em right and lay the pipe."

A cool chill trailing his spine like a slowly descending sliver of ice, Zack waited for the computer screen to go black before departing the console, thus giving Garcia time to hopefully saunter away without additional inquiries.

"You got it, Juan. Suck down a beer or two for me, okay?"

"Will do for sure, big man. Hey, I'll be in the Lagoon if you and Liza wanna join me later on." The lagoon was a small rec room that, other than a pool table and several vintage pinball machines, also contained assorted vending machines stocked with soft drinks, cold beer and assorted snacks, both microwave-ready and packaged.

Avoiding obligation, Zack shrugged before reaching for the side-ladder and hauling himself aboard.

"Can't promise anything. I'm pretty well bushed. Only thing keeping me upright is an bi-hourly visit from Doctor Feel-good and his many miracle cures in capsule form."

"I'll bet," Garcia replied amid the clanking echoes of his own boot-steps, his words growing fainter by the stride. "Brother, after the beating you took, I'm surprised to see you moving around without crutches. You're one tough *hombre*. Well, if you do change your mind, you know where to find me. *Adios*, and if you have to go out there, watch your ass, man. Like most of her gender, Mother Nature is one unpredictable bitch."

Positioning himself behind the wheel, Zack suffered a sudden wave of dizziness and fell to one knee as a precaution, his face dotted in fresh beads of sweat.

"Don't I know it," he whispered, peering through splayed fingers resting atop the wheel to ensure he was finally alone inside the marina. Rushing through starting procedures as quickly as his frazzled mind and physical limitations would allow, he powered up the vessel and backed slowly from its assigned space.

"Sad thing is, in terms of what's to come, the unpredictable bitch in question just might be *Mother Teresa* by comparison."

As signing out any suitable weaponry from the armory had been completely out of the question due to time and procedural restraints, he checked the vessel's tiny, cramped hold for the lone defense tool allowed in case of emergency and unsnapped it from its binds with a single, forceful tug. The shock-baton felt much heavier in his grip than it should have, no doubt due to his woeful lack of stamina, the majority of which had drained away during the verbal volley with Juan Garcia.

Moments later, the cutter *Proteus* exited the calm waters of the environmentally-controlled marina for the increasingly choppy Pacific at an usually high rate of speed, its slightly slumping skipper having donned a frozen mask frighteningly void of expression.

~ * ~

Liza stood statue-still with her boots set shoulder-length apart, both only partially tied due to being so haphazardly donned, her jaw drooping and mouth hanging ajar.

"He's...he's really...he really left without....without me. *Diyos*...H-how c-could he...I don't...under—..."

Eyes glazed and teary, she stared at the empty space reserved for the *Proteus,* the blackish sea as calm and still as stagnant bathwater.

Edging closer while still allowing an arm's reach between them, Dylan Barnes' tone was stern, but void any semblance of building apprehension, a true struggle to maintain for one so characteristically accustomed to going off the deep end at the slightest annoyance.

"Liza, Garcia said he and Zack jawed less than a half-hour ago, remember?"

The back edge of her white tee hung loosely from her camouflage pants, her hands curled into tight fists that jabbed either side of her lower waist.

"How cou....is he...is he really *gumagana*... running? I mean... r-running from...what we..."

"Liz, his head-start ain't much but its gainin' with each passin' tick. Let's motivate," he prodded, taking a genuine risk by placing a hand gently atop her left shoulder, which he nearly drew back as if from a nasty burn upon her sudden, visceral reaction.

"Oh *abnoy*...and j-just how the fuck are we supposed to catch up, genius? B-backstroke?" she spewed, turning like a hissing cat while swiping his hand away with red-painted nails that left a trio of similarly-shaded scratch marks in their wake.

Clasping his wounded mitt, Barnes laughed wildly while gesturing with a fervent nod to their immediate left, where the cutter baring the moniker *Pegasus* stenciled to its bow gently rocked.

"Liz, *Liza*...I get it, okay? I know...*understand* you're stressed to the max about now, but get a grip woman and *think* for a sec...concentrate...it'll come to ya."

Regarding him with a raised brow, creased forehead and slightly tilted head, it was obvious she had not yet comprehended. Perhaps, he mused, her occasional use of Tagalog was having the opposite effect as well, as in struggling to comprehend plain English.

"*Pegasus* there is my baby...newly assigned."

She stole a quick glance to the cutter and then back to Barnes, her befuddled expression still firmly intact.

"No better time for that initial test-drive, right? Half a blasted hour away from an oncomin' shit-storm," he continued, holding up a hand and wriggling the fingers as to jingle a set of non-existent keys.

"Aw, what the hey? If Davey Jones' locker beckons, who am I to deny? Jump aboard and extract the panic from your voice at least long enough for ID purposes."

Four choppy strides and a coiled leap later, she dashed across the narrow deck to do just that. Dylan Barnes meanwhile, still moving quite gingerly despite a supreme effort, was first tasked to release the vessel from its steel-piston-inserted servitude before dashing over to board as best he could.

"Might you please remove the lead from your ass, Barnes?" Liza snarled, sizing up the console like a rival prizefighter. "Once they order lockdown, these gates do just that."

"Hey, mind your attitude, Gorman," he replied curtly between strained huffs and stepping past her toward the voice-ID mechanism, "You're damn lucky I'm going along with this lunatic mission to begin with. If not for this...this recent *curse* of male intuition I've been saddled with, I'd have told you to go to hell without hesitation."

"Whatever. C'mon...let's go, let's go...chop chop!"

Barnes groaned, typing in the required passcode before scooping a small mic from its stand and bringing it to his lips.

"Man, oh man, it suddenly comes to me just why all three of my marriages fell so pitifully short of the 'death do us part' stage."

Decked out in full duty garb sans any of the required drop-ship weaponry, he staggered over to the console and completed the ID process with his regulation cap turned backward on his slickly shaved dome. Liza meanwhile, had collapsed into the co-pilot seat with an exasperated sigh just as the cutter backed from its squared slot.

"So, we...um...headed where I think we're headed?" he inquired approximately four minutes later as the cutter sliced effortlessly through an increasingly raucous procession of waves, the dimness of the domed marina lit like a flashing Broadway sign when compared to the dreary bleakness of the open sea.

Liza nodded stiffly in lieu of a verbal reply, her naturally dark complexion having lightened several degrees, her fiery gaze unblinking despite the occasional intrusion of mist that splashed and coated the whole of her face. Her normally tucked hair had been tied into a tight bun at the back of her skull that was slowly dissolving, leaving several lengthy black strands trailing between muscular shoulder blades like strands of moist, silky seaweed.

With that, Barnes gradually increased the speed until the cutter *Pegasus* reached its maximum, his thoughts as scattered and frazzled as his nerves. A loud clap of distant thunder echoed, followed by a trio of jagged lightning strikes that appeared to point the way directly toward their ultimate destination like some unworldly navigational device.

~ * ~

Roughly ten hours earlier, Liza had arrived at the Gorman abode following her debrief in Graham's office feeling slightly off-kilter. Upon keying the door and stepping inside, she'd detected two faint but distinct sounds… the former being the unmistakable crooning of John Fogerty belting out "Who'll Stop the Rain" from their living room stereo system, the latter the nasal snores of her lesser half emanating from the sleeping quarters.

Having ingested what Dean Graham had described as a mild sedative, she hadn't felt the initial surge of dizziness until exiting the outer drizzle for the housing unit's dimly lit, eerily silent interior. Peeking inside the bedroom, she cracked a tiny smile despite it all at the sight of her buffed hulk, pasty-complexion and all, passed out with his lips wide ajar and his massive form spread-eagled in nary a stitch of clothing save a pair of slightly yellowed briefs, a dark maroon iPad balanced atop his gut like a fleshy prosthesis. He'd laid the crutches on the floor beside the bed, one crossed neatly over the other.

Tiptoeing into the kitchen, she pulled a pitcher of cool water from the fridge and poured herself a full glass, drinking greedily while reentering the living room. The back of her skull pulsating like a gaping wound, she placed the empty glass on a nearby tabletop and struggled mightily to remove her boots before collapsing into a leather recliner that appeared to swallow her petite frame whole. Despite an relenting barrage of worrisome thoughts, she soon enough drifted into a troubled slumber only to awake nearly eight and a half hours later to XM radio and the less-than-soothing vocalizations of Axel Rose belting out 'Welcome to the Jungle,' the dull headache having given way to a severe case of cotton mouth and vision so badly blurred it took a full minute of alternating eye-rubbing and rapid blinking to clear away an infestation of floaters.

Lumbering into the kitchen like the recently unearthed undead, she retrieved a fresh glass of H2O and gulped it down in four lengthy swallows before replaying the same. Placing the glass in the sink, she felt a hitch at her throat and soon retched at least half what she'd ingested back into the same glistening crystal container.

"Z-Zack?" she croaked weakly, wiping moist remnants from her chin before pushing away from the sink and staggering toward the bedroom.

"Hey…you in permanent hibernation or wh—"

The bed, sans a few creases and a dramatic sag at its center, was empty.

Subsequent checks of the bathroom and outside patio revealed similar absenteeism, wherein Liza, figuring he'd either hoofed it over to the infirmary or chow hall, perhaps even both, attempted to hot shower away the web of fuzziness cloaking her senses.

Roughly forty-five minutes later, she stooped over a plate of scrambled eggs and microwaved sausages—picking through the jumbled pile more than actually ingesting—when the first of two successive weather alerts blared through the hallway speakers of the housing unit like a baying Klaxon, warning of impending high winds and torrential rain.

Abandoning the barely half-eaten meal, she moved back into the living room and pulled a fresh uniform from her side of their shared closet, struggling to pull on her pants without tilting forward just as a repeat of the same warning blared. Reaching for her alternate set of combat boots—the first propped just inside the apartment door—she halted in mid-reach. A true creature of habit in every sense of the word, Zack had always hung a fresh ensemble at his end of the closet for the next day's duties. She had, in fact, noted this the day before and even joked with him about the lack of starch in his camo shirt, quipping something to the effect of '*not being sure it could stand on its own*' if it had accidentally become dislodged from the hanger. The outer knob of the closet that he'd always utilized was conspicuously bare.

Her scalp tingling, she retrieved a fresh tee from a dresser drawer just as a loud clap of thunder boomed overhead, triggering an involuntary flinch and accompanying curse as she frantically begun to lace the boots.

It made little if any sense that he'd bothered to dress out, considering an impending lockdown seemed likely, much less knowing he'd been under direct order for a seventy-two hour medical leave. She could only figure one of two things: his meds were wigging him out to the point where logical decision-making had gone the way of the rotary phone, or, and this is most likely where the tingling noggin and building knot at her gut came in: Zack was bound and determined to clean up some unfinished business before lockdown became official. Either way, dashing from their abode in a full sprint and leaving the front door unlocked and slightly ajar in the process, Liza was just equally resolute to track him down for an answer.

She had slowed just slightly while negotiating a sharp curve in the hall, her early haziness long forgotten as every muscle, tendon and connecting nerve-ending blazed to life, when a form appeared from seemingly out of nowhere and she was forced to swerve awkwardly to the right to avoid collusion. The combination chest-and-belly bump that followed sent her and the mystery barricade sprawling onto opposite ends of the thinly-carpeted hall.

"Jesus Crow, woman, you blind as a mole or just *into* clothes-linin' partially crippled middle-aged men?" Barnes spouted with no trace of actual malice while helping Liza to her feet as the potentially dire forecast was rebroadcast again. His dark green rain gear, already comically large and hanging like an oversized curtain from his slouched frame, had been warped until it literally appeared to be binding his shoulders and neck like a full-body noose.

Squirming from his grip on her left forearm, Liza blew a loose strand of hair away from her eyes and pointed down the hall toward the structures exit, the glass doors of which were being pelted by blowing rain.

"B-Barnes, have you seen Zack? I mean, in the last hour?"

"Nope, can't say that I have," he replied wearily, eyes sagging from recent sleep. "Then again, just fell outta the sack about ten minutes ago." Between a lazy attempt to rub the drowsiness from each, he stole a quick glance at the exit and shrugged with equal languor.

"Should I have? I mean, unless he's got a serious storm-chasin' fetish, I don't see where he'd be go—"

"Something's wrong. I… know something's… happened."

"Ya mind clarifyin' the vagueness of that little ESP nugget? After all, something pretty damned *wrong* is stirrin' right outside these walls."

Her eyes were as round as her natural slant would possibly allow, her movements uncharacteristically animated.

"With Zack, dumbass. He's…he was asleep in our hooch, doped to the grills and snoring like a runaway freight. Now…now he's just…gone. Crutches and all, just vanished from sight…and decked out in full-duty garb. I have to check the admin building. Maybe he's just wandering about…disoriented. Damn that Graham and his muscle relaxers."

Covering his grin with a curled palm, Barnes regretted the reply almost immediate upon its release.

"The gills."

"Wh—...excuse me?"

"Um, nothin' really but I think ya meant *doped to the gills.*"

Liza huffed and puffed her chest aggressively, her lips pulled over her teeth in a reptilian-like grimace that struck Barnes as equal parts frightening and knee-slappingly hysterical.

"My bad, Liz. Timin' nor tact has never been my strong suit," he interjected with hands raised in surrender, "By all means, let's go find the big lug."

Resetting his gear, including the loose-fitting hood, he took a step toward the exit and paused, regarding her with a cocked brow.

"Um, wanna grab your raincoat first? It's a tad moist out there, ya know."

Her answer came without verbal reply as she dashed by him in full stride.

"Guess that's a no. Women."

Barnes soon followed, albeit at roughly half her speed.

~ * ~

Staring into the hand-print-smeared full-length mirror that adorned the inside of his bathroom door, Tate Hawkins inwardly gasped at the sight of his own physique. Once, actually mere weeks ago, he'd showcased a moderately slim but tightly-muscled temple of extreme fitness; complete with washboard abs, chiseled pecs, biceps, forearms and a set of well-rounded calves any seasoned Bi-athlete would've been proud to claim. Having found that staying in tip-top form was not only a boon to his overall well-being but also aided greatly in the performance of his self-proclaimed *mission of perversion-eradication*, he rarely skipped daily workouts, no matter the obstacle, distraction, or even periods of temporarily illness. Once, he'd even managed a jogging session and subsequent weight-lifting regimen despite fighting off chills from a one-hundred-plus degree temperature.

In taking in the full-body horrors of the sickly, scrawny, peg-legged impersonator staring back at him through droopy eyes underlined by bloated, black-tined bags, Hawkins was reminded of a carnival he'd once attended as a young teen. In perusing the infamous *Chamber of Terrors* attraction with his childhood buddies, how they'd cackled and guffawed while standing before a wall of mirrors designed to comically warp and distort the physique to outlandish extremes. The thin suddenly appeared grotesquely obese; the even-slightly chunky transformed into a human beanpole with bug eyes and knobby knees. Sliding an open palm over his sunken midsection and concave chest, warm tears pooling at the corner of each wilting eye, he felt a sudden, unmistakable wave of resignation—unbridled relief of a purely spiritual nature—toward his impending fate: a set-in-stone resolution that reduced the rapid, shocking deterioration of his physical shell to a mere footnote of little or no consequence.

Nearing a full seventy-two hours spent hunkered down in the six by ten lavatory with only a gallon jug of filtered water (long since drained), assorted fruit-and-nut laden power bars (long since consumed), a half-roll of duct tape (only the cardboard tube remained), a foot-long portion of shattered table-leg (carved from stout, fine oak) and a pair of freakishly oversized, oblong sea shells as company, he'd recently experienced the ultimate in epiphanies.

Simply put, there was no justification for further cowering. He'd always been of the belief that his old friend the Reaper was the relentless sort, no matter the level of avoidance skills its prospective target might possess. Death kept the book, he'd long ago deduced, the journal of finality. Everyone who is born does so on a particular date, said date scribbled in the book of life. On the flipside, perhaps *dark*-side was more apt, the journal of expiration also contained a date jotted on the opposite side of each individual moniker. Penned not in bright, cheery shades but in dark red jagged markings that appeared to actually melt and drip like seepage from an open wound. There was, Hawkins had often spat, no avoiding that fateful day when the bell tolled and the razor-sharp scythe drew its deadly bead to effectively separate one's soul from its physical shell. Reaching for the door knob after a final, forlorn peek at his own, borderline-emaciated shell, Tate Hawkins filled the opposite palm with a recently completed creation of his own ingenuity and sucked in a deep lungful that was strangely void of all apprehension.

Minutes earlier, he'd heard a window implode from either the kitchen or living room, possibly a result of the approaching storm nearing full strength or, and this he favored as the genuine culprit, his frequent guests had arrived for a final chat—face to face to face—and he wasn't about to play the rude, snobbish host.

Pulling the door ajar with a single, vicious jerk—a task noticeably harder than it should have been due to both his weakened state and a high level of suction created by storm-related air pressure—Tate Hawkins didn't have to wait longer than a single blink for his answer.

~ * ~

After finding both the infirmary and dining hall deserted save the latter's trio of assigned kitchen workers, Liza had, in obvious desperation, suggested they pay a visit to the CO's office. Barnes had started to argue, his half-hearted objection getting only as far as a raised hand and mumbling stutter that was never able to articulate any actual words before Liza turned away and darted through ankle-deep water toward the double doors to the admin building.

He caught up with her just as she'd accessed the dispatch center, her hair matted, and her petite frame drenched to the bone, thus leaving an easily followed trail. Pausing at the sealed doorway, he removed his raingear's hood and gave it a courtesy shake before extending a moistened forefinger and entering the required entry code into a tiny keypad mounted just to the left of the reinforced steel barricade.

"...we've gone from one extreme to the other on vitals, sir..." he heard a female dispatcher with a slight Spanish twang announce—a rail-thin but breathtakingly attractive young Hispanic he only knew as Flores from their occasional radio banter—the 'sir' in question being the OIC in charge.

"Specifics please, Flores," Lieutenant Dirk Boland retorted politely enough. A towering presence at just over six-feet-six, wide-shouldered and slightly bowlegged, the man possessed a perpetually calm, expressionless demeanor of icy coolness that bordered on downright creepy, "What extreme to what extreme *precisely?*"

"BP has been a bit anemic for the past...."she paused to check an alternate monitor other than the main, "...seventy-two hours-plus. This morning it hit its lowest point at ninety-five over forty-eight before leveling out." Having thus far gone completely unnoticed, Barnes moved slowly past through a small foyer that served as a mini-kitchen for the on-duty dispatchers—a microwave, coffee maker and sink made up the gist—and took up position a foot or so behind a dripping, panting Liza, who herself knelt just to the left of a deserted dispatch console with both arms crossed atop a bent knee.

"Approximately eight minutes ago, there was a definitive upswing...rather dramatic," Flores concluded, peering up at the main monitor while adjusting her headset.

"That being?" the lieutenant inquired, shooting the two new arrivals a passing glance before returning his gaze to the same bright-green monitor flashing separate, jagged chart-lines bolded in yellow like continuous lightning-strikes. A center monitor, the largest of all mounted onto the circular-designed wall, displayed a live weather pattern that, at the moment, resembled some hellish psychedelic painting come to pulsating life. Mutating swirls of red, blue and bright orange approached Atlantis from the east, of shoehorn shape and churning like a funnel-cloud with an infinitely wide base that appeared to be rapidly massing.

"Awww, shit...that particular *tropical tumor* appears to mean business," Barnes babbled wide-eyed, though effectively drowned out by the dispatcher's response to her CO's uncharacteristically impatient query.

"Current reading is one-eighty-five over one-hundred twenty-five, sir…and climbing."

Boland openly scoffed, obviously more intune with the weather situation as his unblinking gaze remained glued to its continued progression.

"Well, the man is…*was* a beast in terms of his daily workout regimen. Perhaps a strenuous set of push-ups or shadow-boxing, perhaps even masturbation."

"One-ninety over one-thirty-five, sir," Flores chimed in, apparently unfazed by her superior's apathetic stance.

"Gena, I'm not unsympathetic, but from a safety standpoint, we have little choice but just continue to monitor the man. Regardless if his ticker implodes or he keels over from a massive brain hemorrhage, an official lockdown order is impending. No medical team can or *will be* taking flight with that…" he nodded toward the center monitor, "…prepping to pucker up and give the entire region a big wet kiss.

"Could be that Hawkins might book a one-way ticket on Tsunami Airlines and pay *us* a visit a hell of a lot faster than our boys could ever get to him."

"Sir, um…" Liza stuttered, wiping a pool of moisture from her lower lip with the inside of a bare elbow before resuming, "…how many cutters we have out? I mean, shouldn't they be…all be on their way back in at full throttle?"

Boland's eyes never departed the center console while replying, his long, slender arms crossed and right leg propped, its attached, spit-shined boot resting in the lush padding of an empty dispatcher's chair.

"Two incoming as we speak, Gorman. Jenkins and Garcia still outside the perimeter, Flores?"

Gena Flores briefly studied the monitor to her left.

"ETA for Jenkins is around six minutes, inbound from the northeast sector. Garcia lagging perhaps two, two and a half minutes behind from the southeast."

"T-thanks...thank you, sir," Liza babbled, already backing out in an awkward gait and nearly delivering a solid elbow-shot to Barnes' exposed midsection in the process. "Great. Surely don't want anyone caught paddling around in th-that shit-storm."

Boland turned, perhaps intrigued by the flighty tilt of her voice, a bushy brow creased with a sudden curiosity.

"Not a problem, Gorman. Nice to see such deep concern for your fellow officers. You too, Barnes."

Barnes nodded, Liza having already shot past in a blur, straining mightily to manufacture even the tiniest of smiles.

"Yeah, well, we're all on the same team, LT, right? Besides, I just ain't up to pullin' double-duty if one of those reckless jack-offs manages to drown, ya dig?"

"Uh-huh, yes," Boland replied behind a playful wink, "Now *that's* more like it. Carry on, Officer Barnes, and please pass on to Gorman that it might be best if you restrict yourselves to the housing building until further notice. We...we're getting an as-of-yet unconfirmed report of some seismic activity some forty miles to our north. That...Officers, is unofficial, got it?"

"Aye-aye, sir. Duck and cower 'til someone spouts all clear....got it."

Figuring Liza had not, in fact, utilized even a shred of common sense and retreated back to the barracks building, but instead continued on her quest to seek out and converse with no less than the facility CO, Barnes made a sharp left and negotiated the long, winding hall with all the quickness his weakened, over-medicated state would allow. Light-headed and heavy of foot, he huffed and groaned as if he were in the midst of scaling some great jagged wall of loose gravel with few solid footholds. In order to maintain a tiny semblance of normalcy, he focused not on his many physical ills but instead on a recent influx of telepathic phenomenon that had become, of late, as par course as dope-related powernaps and frequent urination. Of note was his erstwhile partner's sudden exit upon Boland's lack of mentioning a third cutter being tracked outside Atlantis' marked perimeter, meaning that if indeed the senior Gorman had flown the coup, he had done so without initiating radar; a clear, premeditated case of subterfuge. Question was, why all the cloak and dagger antics from a man legendary for following regulations to the tee, no matter the circumstances?

Clearly, Liza had at least an inkling, though it was just as apparent she was totally clueless on some aspects.

Regardless, he was knee-deep into the mix and hapless not to quench his own natural curiosity.

Clearing a final curve just past an empty break-room on the right and community bathroom on the left, Barnes paused to refill his lungs with the palms of both hands resting gently atop slightly bent kneecaps. He saw the door to Carmichael's office standing ajar perhaps five yards ahead to the left, a petite shadow filling the outside hall from the dimly lit interior.

The scream that soon pierced the otherwise still air began innocent enough...similar to the faint whistle of a tea kettle in its initial boiling stage. As for its ear-splitting crescendo, a high-pitched screech that forced Dylan Barnes to reach up and clasp tightly at each side of his skull, the lone comparison that provided equal credence involved a dozen or more wavering Klaxons cranked in unison to glass-shattering extremes.

Thirteen

The Age of Treason

His bare left foot gashed at the heel and sole from marching across shards of shattered glass, Tate Hawkins left behind a reddish/black trail of smeared prints across the shrapnel-coated tile as he passed freely from kitchen to living room. His most recent creation was cocked over his left shoulder, the attached arm in a state of permanent flex while coiled like a steel spring.

"You know, I see no reason for all the hide-and-go seek shenanigans. It's not like we're lumbering around inside some fifty-plus-room gothic mansion. It's just you and me with the raging sea as our witness," he bellowed, crouching slightly while periodically peeking back over his shoulder as random shadows danced and gyrated through the shattered kitchen window. The living room itself, its lone entrance sealed with the dead-bolt wedged securely in place, was approaching midnight-hour darkness level despite the relative earliness of the hour.

"If the plan was to drive me bat-shit, you're to be congratulated. Then again, if that is the case, I'm more than likely conversing with myself so the only *actual*, present danger is that rumbling typhoon tap, tap, tapping at the door. Of course, that too could be a figment of a deranged mind."

The entire hut trembled from a thunderclap of near-nuclear-blast proportions, followed by a powerful gust that entered through the kitchen like a funnel-torpedo, blowing open cabinets and tossing dishes, pots and pans against the walls and floor, the majority shattering like plastic and ceramic explosives. With a sarcastic roll of the eyes, Hawkins side-stepped over to a small storage closet at the rear of the room that stood slightly ajar, a potentially ominous detail, being as he had no memory of ever opening it since the day he'd booked in.

"Fine, fine...so the state of my lunacy isn't quite *that* creative. Must say that's of very *small* comfort at this point in the game."

Squatting on his hunches, he slipped a moistened palm over the knob, a predatory grin parting his purplish lips as he slung it open while simultaneously hopping back a full body-length. The hand that had been cocked over the accompanying shoulder instantly wilted, dropping loosely to his side as if suffering a sudden fracture.

"Bat-shit it *is* then, in a landslide..." he mumbled, barely audible over the gradually building commotion that sounded as if it were perfectly capable of pushing in the hut's foot-thick stone walls, "...unless the vengeful phantoms of my past prefer to wait me out amid less-than-ideal conditions on the front por—"

The front door exploded outward as if sucked from its hinges—one of which slid across the tile floor to halt mere inches from Hawkins' seeping left heel—the gaping hole instantly filled by a relentless tempest that nearly shoved him backward into the same empty closet he'd so casually left accessible. The floor and walls were soon lathered in a gritty mix of saltwater and sand, the latter riddled with assorted abstract spatters. Pushing forward on all fours, he used the largest portion of the sectional as cover from the bee-like stings pricking his exposed flesh.

"Yep…no doubt about it…" he chuckled hysterically between spitting specs of sand from between gritted teeth, "…a figment *she* is definitely not."

The figures filled the empty doorway as one, twin silhouettes bathed in shadow as if magically teleported and seemingly unfazed by the level four winds at their respective backs. The larger of the two stood to the left, towering the other by a full two feet and at least twice the bulk.

Gripping the top edge of the rain-soaked leather sofa with his free hand, Hawkins stood upright with great effort, his face contorted with a sudden, all-consuming rage.

"You know…th-that storm ou-out there…that fucker's as r-real as the floor 'neath my f-feet…" he screamed while pointing above and past the unmoving heads of the intruders, his bony frame wracked with tremors save the curled fist coiled tightly behind his drenched skull, which held as steady as the stoutest of solid oak branches against Mother Nature's unrelenting fury, "…but a-about you two, y-you see, I have s-some *serious* r-reservations."

Without benefit of taking any actual steps, the pair appeared to levitate several feet ahead until they stood on the opposite side of the sofa with perhaps a foot to spare.

"Well, as they say, the proof's in the puddin', you chicken-shit child-killer…" the larger figure replied calmly, the familiarity of its slightly-slurred, booze-soaked tone sending an icy-shiver down the spine of Tate Hawkins, who instinctively backed up a step. "So what say you come over here and get'cha a heapin' helpin'." A mousy giggle was heard escaping the smaller figure's tightly-pursed lips a split-second before all three lurched forward in synchronized perfection.

~ * ~

Steering the *Proteus* through what seemed an infinite series of raging swells, Zack maintained a square jaw, steely stare and rigid, double-handed grip on the sweat-smeared wheel even as his many scattered thoughts—as fractured and random as any recently diagnosed schizophrenic—pinged and ponged about the inside of his noggin like ricocheting shrapnel.

He figured Atlantis was currently under lockdown, perhaps initiated mere minutes past his hurried exit. Even so, it was only a matter of time before someone took note of the cutter's absence from its assigned slot, more than likely whoever was assigned hourly security checks. Deactivating the vessel's radar was a temporary fix at best, as once reported among the missing, he could easily be tracked via a simple override code from the command post.

However bothersome such details might be, they were in the end, just that... annoyances to be dealt with at a later date and time. No, his main worry, the lone *authentic* concern that threatened to twist his wrought-iron gut to mush and effectively shut down his every working function while flat refusing to be shoved to the rear of the class no matter how concerted the effort, it could be summed up in a single, haunting word. *Liza.* He'd debated long and hard whether to involve her, though in the end it was quite the one-sided argument to leave her stranded a good distance away from the impending mayhem. There had been other options considered amid the chaos that had been his final half-hour atop Atlantis, all instantly cast off once logic dictated the *too little, too late* label had been permanently applied.

Lost in a fog of contradiction in terms of past decisions versus future actions, he was literally caught napping as a wave of considerable girth struck the vessel's starboard side with sledgehammer force. Lurching hard to the left, Zack's hung to the wheel as his boots slid in opposite directions, forcing the painful execution of an awkward leg-split until both knees pummeled the soaked deck with a muffled, double thump.

Cranking the wheel to the right, he felt the *Proteus* lifted airborne from bow to stern, respectively, before splashing down with the port side taking the brunt. Freeing a hand to reach toward the console, he reduced speed while continuing to wrestle the wheel with his considerable bulk practically lying spread-eagle.

By the time he'd righted both the vessel's positioning and course—a bleary span of time that seemed like hours but in reality took mere minutes—Hawk Isle loomed, at least according to the console's seawater-coated radar screen. Between the torrential rainfall, battering waves and near zero-visibility past *Proteus'* bow, Zack deduced he'd run ashore long before actually visualizing the nearest beachhead. Much to his surprise, just as he'd veered a tad off-course in a rare moment of recklessness no doubt tied to extreme fatigue, the island did indeed swim into view in the shape of a bobbing mass that appeared only sporadically, depending on how dramatic the ship's dip first deep into and then out of the churning, watery bowels of Mother Ocean's maniacal carny-ride.

Upon closer inspection once sufficiently beached, the cutter effectively buried to the gunwale, he was able to peer beneath cupped hands through a virtual waterfall toward a familiar shape similarly submerged within the soggy dunes. Retrieving the lone weapon at his disposal, he hopped over the side and instantly sank to the ankles. He approximated the trek to the assigned hut of one Tate Hawkins to be in the seventy-five to one-hundred yard range, a distance that, under more favorable weather conditions, could be covered in less than half a minute at a steady jog and perhaps half that at a full sprint. As it was, he deduced a realistic ETA meant multiplying the latter total by at least three, despite legs and arms that pumped at maximum bore.

He reached the midway point only after slogging up and over the steepest, soggiest dune Hawk Isle had to offer. Huffing and puffing like an overwrought, coal-chugging freight car on the cusp of a skidding derailment, Zack pondered with a heavy dose of inner bemusement just *how* he'd ended up a prime player in such a bizarre, tragedy-riddled stage-play. No matter how he twisted or distorted the facts as he knew them, the answer was obvious.

The fate of potentially innocent victims be damned, there was, after all, no stronger self-motivation than one's *own* survival.

~ * ~

By the time Dylan Barnes had fast-limped his way to the facility CO's open office door, Liza had backed out with one hand secured over her mouth and the other pointing shakily forward as if foreseeing her own impending death. Barnes reached her just as she'd bounced off a far wall, nearly displacing a nearby wall painting—ironically displaying a high cliff wall being bombarded by skyscraper sized waves—from its mount. He could hear her muffled gags beneath a tightly clamped palm, intermingled with the occasional low-pitched squeal. Unable to pull her tear-filled eyes from whatever horror held her entranced, she never appeared to acknowledge Barnes' presence, even as he stumbled past and, mercifully, blocked her line of sight.

"Cap, are you al...ohh, f-fuck...me," he whimpered, standing with a single boot poised just inside the door and each arm spread to the side with the accompanying hand clasping the outer frame.

"C-cap...Jesus cr-crow."

Upon first glance beneath the blinding ivory cloak of overhead fluorescent lighting, it appeared they had walked in just as Captain Vance Carmichael had been attempting some bizarre yoga stretch and had frozen in place—a twisted statue of flesh and bone—and had perhaps suffered a fatal stroke in the process. The leather recliner had been pushed back—possibly even scraping the back wall—as if to provide the maximum space for an afternoon power-slumber.

Propped behind the massive desk and partially concealed by the computer monitor positioned at its center, he appeared to be reaching forward with both arms with his head tilted back to such an extreme that the whole of his face was effectively cloaked from clear view.

That was, until a few rapid blinks teamed with a gradual adjustment to the harsh lighting revealed the grisly truth behind his bizarre pose as something far more sinister.

"What the h-hell is... his eyes... I've... h-hey... ain't those... I mean... they l-look damn familiar s-somehow," he stammered, thinking he'd instinctively backed into the hall only to discover he'd remained firmly in place, as haplessly paralyzed and unable to budge as the obviously deceased man propped an arm's length away.

"On the fl-floor in front of Cap's desk ...it's...it's the... they were...the one's d-doc gave Z-Zack....I...I think...I pr-pray not, b-but..." she stuttered haplessly between hacking coughs, choking gags and the occasional spat of bile onto the hall carpet. Obviously transformed by extreme stress, her accent was gradually reverting back to her native tongue.

"Hang... just hang back a sec. I ne—have to get a closer look," Barnes said, sweeping back an arm with the palm out as to keep her at bay. Sighing nervously, he drudged up the required courage to take an additional step inside—then another and still third—until a full visual of the desktop and beyond was, unfortunately, achieved.

Lying shattered on the dark brown shag carpet were several jagged pieces of what remained of a double-cuff crutch, its fully intact partner propped innocently a few inches away against a metal file cabinet. A single sliver, perhaps no wider than a twenty-penny nail, protruded from the captain's left temple like a recently sprouted devil's horn, the wound around its squared edge weirdly bloodless as if effectively corked to prevent the expected leakage.

A low, wet clicking noise escaped Barnes' throat upon acquiring a closer, unobstructed view of his former commanding officer's brutally mutilated eyes and the strangely familiar accessories that had been so forcefully applied. Twin test tubes, clear glass vials with blue striping at their circular ends and roughly the thickness of a number two carpenter pencil, jutted from each eye while leaving thin slug-trails of reddish gore sliding down the man's clean-shaven cheeks.

Almost instantly upon casting slightly bleared vision upon their glistening shells, Barnes had been struck by a stout wave of *déjà vu* that, despite the ghoulish circumstances of their discovery, ignited a jolt of undeniable exhilaration.

Carmichael's mouth was, predictably, considering the positioning of his head and neck, distended to grotesque proportions, the exposed chasm leaking whitish foam from each corner.

Barnes' top lip began to tremble beneath the heavy dampness of his mustache as a suitable replacement for his earlier eye twitch, which had abruptly halted just seconds before. Shifting his sights downward with great effort, he noted first the partially dented can balanced between Carmichael's outstretched hands; its generic white label with the letters 'PE CLEANER' clearly visible from its rounded frame, tiny bubbles of the same whitish foam visible around its rounded, only partially sealed top. The hands in question, the adjoining fingers of each spread and grasping like the splayed legs of a daddy long-legs spider, had essentially been nailed into place between bloodied knuckles by matching envelope openers, the old-fashioned silver-coated type that were as much cutlery as office tool. This revelation, above all other, spelled out one undisputable fact about the person responsible, Barnes observed.

Took one bull-stout som' bitch to drive those paper-stabbers deep into solid oak. Power-lifter kinda strong.

"Li-Liza…we have to get some…we have to tell somebody," he croaked, the involuntary tick having returned with a vengeance to the corner of his left eye. "Head back to the command cen—"

"Like h-hell I will, Barnes," she retorted angrily, still hugging herself tight even while creeping slowly forward until her slightly slouched form filled the entrance threshold. "You…see what I see, and…know full well what they will take from thi—— what they… belie-…will speculate."

Whirling about clumsily, he avoided tipping forward only by reaching up with both hands and gripping the door frame.

"Well *shit,* Liz, I'm as sorry as I can be as how this looks, but we *have* to report it or be viewed as suspects ourselves!"

Liza lunged forward, fists clenched tightly at her sides. Though not nearly as large as her husband, Barnes still had her by at least five inches in height, forcing her onto tiptoes just to bark into his stubble-covered chin.

"Be my guest then, asshole! Toss me over the bus while you're at it! I'm paddling out of here before they lock the gate…before it's…too late for…to save…there's nothing more we can do here…"

Choking off in mid-rant, Liza stared wide-eyed past his left shoulder as if spotting a levitating phantom at the rear of the cramped office, just past the late Vance Carmichael's desk.

"Listen up, ya stubborn fireplug…I ain't about to heave anybody over *or* under any damn bus!" Barnes retorted, oblivious to her renewed state of shock until she'd backed away and allowed him a full-facial view of her startled expression.

"I told ya to stay back, damn it. Last thing we need is to barf our DNA-*flavored* cookies onto the crime scene," he rambled on, until taking note that she was actually looking past the original horror scene to potentially another tucked away in the shadows between a three-tiered bookcase and four-drawer metal file cabinet.

"Awww, what the holy hell *now*?" he murmured, half-stepping forward while struggling to win the battle with creeping hysteria, a fight his newfound partner wasn't nearly as successful in staving off.

Careful to scoot past the dead man's desk without touching or altering anything along the narrow pathway, he covered the three to four yard distance in a semi-crouch, his calves and thighs burning from the effort.

The rear of the office contained not only the aforementioned bookcase and cabinet, but a full lavatory, a necessary luxury afforded only to facility commanders due to an average workday that routinely spanned twelve to fourteen hours.

Despite the relative dimness provided by a burned out fluorescent, Liza had first spotted the upturned combat boot sticking from its open door.

Leaning into the fray with far less hesitance, likely due to a cloaking numbness that had set in from studying the gruesome slaughter of his former commander, Barnes casually stepped over the upturned boot and its attached leg—the latter cloaked in the familiar camouflage of all assigned correctional officers—while reaching in to trigger the bathroom's interior light.

Though the kid's name escaped him, he'd seen him around the dock and dining halls in the past few weeks.

More than likely a virgin to drop-ships, as all newly assigned COs were tasked with inventory and security duty for their first month on site, it was fairly obvious the kid would never know the experience, what with a neck so severely twisted his face kissed the hard tiled floor while his splayed torso rested squarely on his back.

Barnes stumbled back with his nose and mouth tucked deep with the raingear's thick folds at the crook of his elbow, the stench of recently expelled urine and feces easily as offensive as their mutilated source. Strange, he pondered, how similarly offensive scents weren't nearly as prevalent near the fast-stiffening corpse of Vance Carmichael, though in hindsight perhaps the presence of both the pipe-cleaning chemical and whatever had once filled the mystery vials might've served as a type of shrouding antiseptic.

"What…w-who is it?" Liza inquired, crouched on her haunches atop the hall carpet, periodically twisting her head about as her tear-filled eyes darted wildly up both sides of the hall like a cat-burglar on the lookout for a potential eyewitness.

As Barnes had exited the office, his nostrils flaring with the intake of semi-fresh air, she'd reached out a badly shaking hand. They clamped palms and he pulled her upright with a low groan, his lower back feeling a sharp pinch.

"Young CO. Neck's been snapped," he replied as coolly as possible for one whose mask of sanity was slipping ever-so-precariously away.

She sighed, remembering Zack's assigned escort, so painfully youthful he appeared to not yet have begun daily shaving.

"So, what's the decision then? You coming or…going?" she dually gestured, first toward the hall leading out and eventually to the dock, then to the opposite end toward the command center.

"Shit, woman…" he grumbled, hands on hips, "…I can't let ya just sail away on some suicide mission by your lonesome."

With that, she nodded stiffly before sprinting down the hall with renewed spark, having seemingly shrugged away just enough of the recently viewed horror to re-don her own mask of barely-surviving saneness.

Tough as nails, Barnes concluded, lagging just far enough behind the fiery trailblazer to not worry about her overhearing the words he felt an inexplicable need to vocalize between the passing walls that at times appeared to be closing in, perhaps in order to stop him dead in his tracks and squeeze some common sense from his tattered psyche.

"Yep, tough…as nails and…twice as loyal," he mumbled between limping strides and the accompanying labored huffs, his back and legs screaming their disapproval. "Well then, Liza Gorman…here's hopin' those dogged…loyalties ain't as…sadly misplaced as they…appear."

Less than fifteen minutes later, the cutter *Pegasus* departed the mapped perimeter of Atlantis and directly into the swirling maw of Mother Ocean, approximately four and a half minutes, give or take a click, before the dock's metal-bar gates lowered and were subsequently locked into place and lockdown became official.

~ * ~

Tate Hawkins stirred amid the warm stench of rotted meat smacking his left cheek in two to three second intervals and thus flowing freely into his flaring nostrils. Like half-cooked pork left to simmer and sweat beneath a blazing, midday summer sun, or perhaps raw chicken-skin tossed onto smoldering asphalt until it mutated into an army of bloated, wriggling maggots, he heard himself gag even as his eyes fluttered like the wings of a drunken butterfly.

"Hey, hey, hey…looks who's finally decided to rejoin us, hon. I was beginnin' to think the yellow-streaked bastard was gonna croak on us before this here party ever got o-fi-cially started!" Hawkins heard the familiar voice bellow—putrid breath intact—while seemingly parked mere inches from his left ear.

"Cool!" came a youthful, feminine response that Hawkins instantly recognized, triggering a twist of his inner gut that even the sickening aroma of her partner's breath couldn't touch.

"He looks so pale, C.A, kinda like a vampire who's went too long without a blood fix."

"Sure enough does, honey-bun. You know, Hawkins…" the male voice, equally familiar, chimed in with a bit more distance acquired between speaker and intended audience, a fact for which Hawkins took great solace, as the accompanying smell, as horrid as he could ever recall bearing witness to, had subsided at least a degree "…you ain't nothin' but skin and bones, boy. All bug-eyed and chalky. Lost your appetite of late, I'm guessin'. Damned shame, that. Cuts me and Gina deep you ain't gettin' your beauty sleep. Really does.

"Hell, you weren't much to look at in your prime, but these days I figure to find a photo of your ugly mug in Webster's next to the words 'walking dead.' Hey now…" stinky breath howled, "…now *there's* some irony, huh boy?"

Lying prone on his back, Hawkins reached up and began to message both eyes with a thumb and forefinger, blinking rapidly in the aftermath but still only able to make out a single, bulky shadow to his right.

"W-where a-are...wh-who..." he stammered, becoming aware that he was either lying in a building pool of his own sweat, or the storm was in the process of flooding the hut's leak-proof, solid tile flooring. He dimly recalled a window shattering, a door blasted open by same. The brutish winds responsible were still slapping his bare flesh, meaning he'd probably not been out that long. As the building grit—no doubt sand particles—was gradually being forced from each eye by a build-up of warm tears, so did his hearing regain a level of normalcy and the fact confirmed that the storm was indeed still raging with considerable ire.

"You ain't serious. You hear this, honey-pie? Jackass coward has the gall to play the amnesia card! Priceless. Fuckin' priceless."

"He's what he is, C.A," the girl replied solemnly. "Born a coward, die the same."

"My little princess, you are soooo right. Never heard it said better. The dam holding back the ocean of pride I feel is showin' some major structural damage, girl."

Straining to roll over onto his right side and away from the pair's saccharin-laced dialogue, Hawkins felt a sharp shooting pain at the back of his neck, an electric shock that easily overrode all other ills currently racking his decrepit frame.

"Bi-bingo," he muttered, reaching over to first seek out and then gently massage the trouble-spot in question, "I no...k-knew it."

"Knew what, buttercup? That this was the day you're destined to *bite the big one*? Well then, congratulations are definitely in order to celebrate those extraordinary powers of prognostication, 'cause you are, pardon the funny....dead on."

"T-this may be true," Hawkins replied while first rolling over onto his belly and then pushing himself up onto all fours, his spindly but tightly muscled arms shaking mightily from the effort. "Admittedly, th-the odds for survival aren't looking too...positive at thi-this juncture, but it's to an altogether different revelation that...I refer."

"Is it time, C.A? I'm getting, like, really, *really* bored..." the girl's voice pleaded, though there was a bizarre alteration in her tone that, despite the natural childish whine, came across as faux as any adult-produced voiceover.

"...and the storm's starting to...scare me a little."

"Not to worry, sugar-plum, we're almost done here, aren't we, Tate?" the male answered, roughly every-other word faded and garbled as if from a fading radio station.

Balanced uneasily atop legs that quivered like a toddler taking its first steps, Hawkins slowly turned toward the intruders with his arms held out wide and the palms of each hand upturned.

"Yes, I expect w-we are at that, as is this pe-pathetic c-charade."

Having mentally marked the location of the object he would soon lunge toward in a last-ditch attempt at self-preservation, he watched without a shred of awe or surprise as a final transformation ensued within the dull reflection of his badly bloodshot eyes.

"Credit where credit is due..." the newly formed entity announced in a voice as real and true as the previous two had been artificial, "...you, sir, are definitely a tougher nut to crack, or should I say...*crack up*...than your average serial killer."

Hawkins bowed slightly in lieu of a verbal reply, his mind's eye trained solely on the object at his back.

"Well then..." the lone intruder crooned, puffing out its chest even as its lower appendages visibly tensed, prepping to uncoil, "...let us dance."

Hawkins took a single step backward, his bloodied heel leaving behind a perfectly formed print that was quickly dissipated by the pooling water. His left arm gradually reached behind his back, the fingers splayed in anticipation for an impending pounce.

"By all means...let's."

The intruder sprung, a brownish blur with outstretched arms, just as Hawkins spun around, ducked and lunged, the fingers of his right hand brushing the object of his desire.

He heard a brutish growl just before impact, the object slipping from his grip as he was driven into the closet door head-first and snapped back viciously upon said door slamming shut.

Waking from a pitch-black cloak of unconsciousness, Hawkins lay flat on his back in an inch-deep pool of swirling, debris-filled precipitation shaded maroon with his own leakage.

Temporarily unable to lift a single finger to clear the cobwebs from his sagging, bloodshot eyes, he heard a distant commotion not at all associated with the storm; the sound, however muted, of a life and death struggle and the animalistic grunts and groans associated with same.

By pushing forward with both feet, he was eventually able to raise his head just enough to tilt it against the closet door—the frame displaying a hairline fracture across its dented midsection—and thus visualize a bleary outline of the combatants in question, the identity of the newest arrival still a mystery.

Filling a curled palm with a cool mix of rain and seawater, he commenced to splash his face and eyes with several handfuls even as the battle royal in question intensified, at least from an audio standpoint, a mere six feet from his prone, temporarily paralyzed form.

"W-well, I'll…b-be…double-d-dog d-damned…" he croaked in wide-eyed awe upon finally clearing away the majority of the haze, "…if this *is* just a-another hellin…hallucination, at l-least it's of t-the p-positive variety f-for a c-change."

Flashing a hideous grin—blissfully unaware he'd lost not one but two teeth upon impact with the cracked doorframe—he attempted to haul himself upright with an awkward, ill-advised thrust of his upper body, resulting in a severe wave of dizziness and almost instantaneous unconsciousness.

Left leaning with his head cocked crookedly against fractured pine—his hair matted in both his own blood and a spattering of wood shavings—Tate Hawkins nonetheless did so while wearing the same imbecilic grin.

~ * ~

The cutter *Pegasus* didn't so much as slam the beachhead but meld into it, its V-shaped bow slicing into boggy sand like scalding cutlery through a soft mound of salted butter.

Just seconds earlier, its sea-water blinded skipper had been bludgeoned to the deck, forced to release his grip on the wheel once a wall-sized wave had impacted the port side like a liquid flyswatter. Hoisted airborne from the sudden alteration in gravity, the top of his skull had smacked the metal dome and left a circular dent in its wake with a few extracted scalp hairs glued to its otherwise slick surface like flowing tendrils. Landing hard on his left side, he groped for the nearest hand-hold as both lungs deflated and his tightly squinted eyes were filled with separate lightning strikes.

Even as he crawled atop the slippery deck like a crippled, gasping crustacean toward life-sustaining Mother Ocean, Dylan Barnes could hear select segments of a human voice, female in origin, bellowing from what sounded like a distant mountaintop, or in this particular case, a faraway dune.

"...looks like ...starboard si ....*Proteus* ...to the hilt ...keeps up we'll ....dog-paddle ba ....to Atlantis ....Barnes? Mind joining...? Barn—could use a li ....Earth to Barnes! Co ...in ...Barnes!"

Using the side rails, he'd just managed to pull himself upright when a rogue gust literally scooped him by the ankles and slung him overboard. In the aftermath, it took what seemed like an eternity to first dig himself free from the sandy quagmire that had served as his landing pad, mercifully padded as it had been, crawl free from the sucking pull of outgoing waves that had first so furiously rabbit-punched his neck, back and thighs, and finally slither forward on all fours toward the source of the quasi-incoherent ramblings.

"...out time, Barnes...no time...for a nap. Zack's here...landfall already. Let's get inside before...storm swallows...whole!" she shrieked, a petite shadow bouncing perhaps ten yards ahead, her waist-length hair having broken loose form its binds to whip about like billowing, blackish flames.

He stood three separate times before managing to make the position stick, having twice been forced to his knees by swirling, punishing winds that pummeled and shoved from what felt like all sides simultaneously.

Forced to grip the inner sleeves of his raingear to prevent it being ripped from his torso, he eventually broke into a slow but steady jog while stepping either directly into or near the deep, grooved boot-steps carved into the wet sand by his trailblazing cohort.

Barnes didn't break stride until the hut assigned to Tate Hawkins swam blurrily into view within a narrow, v-shaped space between thigh-high, bookended reed-growths that had been neatly parted by the continuous gusts.

He bent with his hands atop his knees, bowing and tucking his chin to briefly escape the unrelenting barrage. Inhaling and exhaling with his face buried as far within the raingear's hood as possible, he became acutely aware of his state of unarmed vulnerability upon nearing such a potentially dicey scenario. He figured, certainly *hoped*, that Liza had at least possessed the good sense to procure their one-and-only shock-baton upon exiting the cutter ahead of him, as the notion of walking into a serial killer's abode empty-handed was, at *best* reckless, at *worst* a mistake of fatal proportions.

Restarting with his head bent and shoulders tucked like a fullback into a stacked, goal-line stand, Barnes resigned himself to the possibility that the ferocious tropical tempest that currently served to shove him onward might well eventually serve to exterminate his existence long before a human source ever had the chance.

By the time he reached to within fifty yards of the entrance, he could see it was ajar, either blown open or forced by other, more sinister means. A final push to increase his foot speed fell woefully short as the direction of the squall had abruptly shifted until it was like ramming directly into and through a level-four strength wind tunnel.

He was, through squinted eyes stung by sand, slush and tiny, narrow spears of blowing rain, able to make out Liza's rapidly pumping legs as she dashed onto the porch and vanished into the hut's darkened interior. Though it was small consolation, he believed he'd spotted the shock-baton cocked high over her left shoulder as she'd entered.

Just as he'd cut the distance roughly in half, a booming thunderclap was soon followed by a lightning strike that, ever-so-briefly, lit up the landscape in nova-like fashion, allowing Barnes a quick peek, literally a split-second in duration, into the approaching abyss.

Four figures in all—one laid out on the floor against a far wall amid overturned furniture and ankle-deep floodwaters…still another standing directly between the fallen and the remaining pair…that particular pair hunched over and huddled together as if for protection from the storm.

Either that, Dylan Barnes thought grimly as his left boot departed moistened sand for the outer edges of the stone porch, or he was about to run head-on and unarmed into a death-match from which escaping with his own hide intact might prove impossible.

Fourteen

Diagnosis Mayhem

The slender, muscular man, the soaked remains of his dark red tee hanging from his taut, chiseled shoulders in tattered shreds, held the larger figure in a textbook sleeper hold, driving his squirming form first to his knees and releasing him only when all signs of struggle had ceased.

Slumping to the water-logged tile with only the whites of his eyes showing, the larger man rested on his left shoulder as his co-combatant—wincing and wide-eyed—slumped away while favoring the left side of his ribcage. Blood leaked from his right nostril and lower lip, mingling with a steady mist of rain wafting in from the open front door to run down his cheeks in separate, blackish trails.

Given a final, forceful push by the squall trailing his every step, Barnes rumbled in, skidding to a clumsily executed, wind-milling halt and immediately splashing down onto all fours. Shaking the excess from the raingear, he reached up and peeled back the hood to find he knelt within reaching distance of Liza, who appeared paralyzed—the shock-baton frozen in strike mode over her left shoulder—save her neck, which whipped back and forth as if on a timed cue.

"Wh-what the h-hell, d-Doc?" Barnes literally spat, his teeth coated in sandy grit that altered his speech to that of a lisping stutterer, "Wh-what g-gives?"

"Yes, what does...*give*, Doctor Graham?" Liza chimed in breathlessly, teeth gnashing while still shifting her focus from the facility physician to her fallen spouse and finally over to Barnes through narrow slits. "I'd say you've got about...three ticks to explain precisely why I walk in on you choking out the love of my life before I...do my dead-ladder best to...return the favor."

"Dead *letter*, babe," Barnes said, unable to resist despite highly questionable timing.

To that, Liza flashed him a look that, if possible by the laws of physics, would have literally melted his face.

In turn, Barnes gestured with a thumb in her direction while regarding Dean Graham with an expression of similar, if not quite as lethal, disgust.

"What *she* said, Doc..."

Graham leaned against an overturned couch, a forearm parked underneath his nose in an apparent attempt to cut off or at least show the free-flow. Perhaps a yard away to his left, lying on his back with his head propped nearly flush against the lower portion of the cracked closet door, a nearly nude Tate Hawkins' eyes fluttered sporadically, the fingers of his left hand dancing and tapping like the legs of a spider in the throngs of a final death spasm. To his right at the center of the flooded living room, Zack Gorman lay tucked in a fetal position with a portion of the left side of his face, including the majority of one closed eye and the whole of one nostril submerged in the flowing waters. The right sleeve of his uniform shirt had been ripped away at the shoulder, showcasing a muscular bicep and attached forearm, both riddled with various tattoos in the early stages of age-fading.

"Calm do—...j-just take it easy...you...you t- two. B-back off a sec-second and...give me a chance to...explain," Graham managed between strained gasps, his voice comically nasal due to the forced blockage of both nostrils. "Your...t-timing is both unfortunate in some ways and so very...v-very *welcome* in...others."

Tip-toeing over to her fallen spouse with her sight trained exclusively on Graham, Liza kept the baton cocked firmly in place while using her free arm to gently roll him over onto his back. In response, Zack instantly coughed out a glut of seawater while a separate pool streamed from his previously semi-submerged nostril.

"Explain on, Doctor," she spat, seemingly on the verge of hysterics as her accent held a pronounced Filipino slant, her jaw set tight with the masseter muscles working overtime. "And without all the flowery cow fertilization, if you please."

"She means cut the bullshit, Doc," Barnes injected with a sneer of his own while peeling away the raingear to reveal a gravy-stained white muscle-tee underneath. "In case ya needed a translation."

Graham waved him off with his own unrestricted appendage, the forearm of the other still tasked as a fleshy bandage. Meanwhile, the solid stone walls were fast losing their sense of invulnerability, as if on the verge of buckling like the thinnest balsa wood from a most unmerciful barrage.

"Unnecessary, Dylan, but thank you. I understand Liza's enunciation just fine, despite the dramatic alteration in accent caused by her present state of uncertainty."

After carefully folding the bulky gear, Barnes laid it on the underside of the overturned couch and began vigorously rubbing both arms—each as pasty as freshly fallen snow with the biceps adorned with separate, unidentifiable tattoos—as if severely chilled.

"Uh-huh, well, I personally *define* the lady's present state as mighty fuckin' pissed off and even though I don't really know her that well, Doc, I *do* know enough that you wouldn't like her when she pissed."

Graham briefly eyed the commotion outside the hut entrance, blinking rapidly from invading gusts, before turning and facing Liza exclusively, dropping his elbow to reveal a grotesquely swollen, blood-crusted lip and nostrils lined with crusting seepage. Perhaps as a cautionary measure to the impending reaction, he slid back a single step.

"Liza, I…know this is going to be…extremely difficult for you to…accept as truth, but your hus—…Zackary has…seemingly committed the vilest of human atrocities."

Her searing, unblinking gaze did not waver, nor did her stance other than using her weaponless hand to gently massage her fallen mate's moistened scalp.

"G-Go on…" she croaked, following a strained swallow, the otherwise murky room lit up by the occasional lightning strike.

"I…take it you two paid a visit to…our late commander's office before departing Atlantis. I mean, otherwise your presence here amid such potentially…catastrophic conditions and in such a personal state of…frenzy, is, well, without logic."

Stepping over to stand just to Liza's left, Barnes' eyes drifted just past Graham to the kitchen tile—a shade darker than the living room's—where a mystery object lay between overturned dining chairs, half-submerged in flowing floodwaters.

"Yeah, Doc, we both got an eyeful of both Captain C and the fuzz-cheeked CO," he replied, alternating glances between Graham and the bizarre item, careful as not to lock on the latter in case it was more than simply a dislodged shard of debris. "Needless to say, they'd both seen healthier, happier days. As far as our…frenzied presence as Mama Nature pisses in our collective Wheaties, I could and will ask you the same question."

"What…*he* said," Liza added blankly, regarding the two lone men standing with separate glances after having finally dropped the baton to one side, propped against a bent knee, in order to dedicate her full

275

attention to Zack, whose head rested in her lap. As Graham had torn off a section of his shredded tee and began dabbing his bloated lip during pauses in dialogue, he resumed almost immediately following Liza's snide reply, almost as if cued to do so.

"I obviously made the discovery perhaps a half-hour before you. And, much like you, made a choice that did not include notifying the second in command."

Still hugging himself tight, Barnes took a step forward until he fronted the Gormans while flashing the occasional peek at the semi-submerged, enigmatic item that, slowly, began to take shape as something other than an irrelevant floater amid so many of the same.

"How do you know we *didn't*?" he shot back with a wink meant as anything but playful, "Fact is, we did drop by the Com Center at some point before slippin' and then shippin' out."

"Indeed we did," Liza murmured, barely audible over the surrounding chaos.

Graham shrugged, seemingly undaunted by the inquisitory line of banter.

"No doubt *before* dropping by the commander's office on your way to the dock. I highly doubt you took the time to double back and report in, fearing…much like myself, of being ordered to remain on land as the dock gates prepared to slam shut.

"As it is, I'm surprised you two beat the lockdown order when I had doubts of my own successful exit."

Barnes nodded in apparent agreement while, from his newly obtained position, was able to better scrutinize and at least somewhat define the object then nearly fully engulfed by the flood's continual intrusion.

"Yeah, well…I get the distinct feelin' we're gonna highly regret doin' so. Last radar shot I saw had the eye of this baby makin' a bee-line for our present loca—…"

"Hey!" Liza suddenly shrieked, her cheeks glowing red and her teeth bared anew while regarding both men with equal disdain. "I couldn't give…a…st-steaming shit about *how*…we got here or…what protocol was broken in doing so. All I ne—want to know at this moment, before we're all swallowed up and spat out to sea is…of what human atrocities do you speak, Doctor Graham, and what th-the fuck they have to do with…my husband?"

Graham folded chiseled arms across an equally taut, muscular chest and sighed deeply, focusing solely on the fallen senior correctional officer.

"Officer Gor—Liza, it should be obvious, even staring through rose-colored blinders as coke-bottle thick as the ones you've donned this past month."

"Zack did not…do that to Carmi—to the captain and that…boy. Did not…" she paused just long enough to peer downward as she gently stroked her lover's scalp, "…*could* not."

Though his overall deportment was of someone not the least bit shocked at a particular accusation, Barnes nodded in agreement without speaking.

"I'm…not just referring to the…those specific homicides."

Liza and Barnes exchanged a bewildered glance as Graham—arms folded at the pit of his back—began to pace the length of the room, the interior lit by the occasional lightning strike.

"All the mysterious …suicides of the incarcerated."

"Yeah, what about 'em?" Barnes asked, wincing with each sporadic thunderclap, distant or near. "Bunch'a murderin' wackos ate up with guilt…done in by the isolation and loneliness. I don't claim shrink status, amateur or otherwise, but ya gotta figure their collective consciences came callin' with one hefty bill in tow that none of 'em had the cash to cover, so to speak."

"R-right," Liza agreed, reclaiming her grip on the shock-baton, her free hand noticeably shaking as it continued to pet and soothe her husband's fevered flesh. "Suicides, Graham, plain and simple. No evidence of…" she paused, struggling for the right words, "…foul play. None that I heard of. You…know something we don't?"

"Perhaps," Graham replied, a brow raised suspiciously. "Perhaps not. Remains to be seen. I myself…" his turn to pause to regard Barnes with a mild shrug, "…do not claim to be a sleuth or barrister, amateur or otherwise, but there was…*is* proof of the foul play you speak of, Liza. It was, in fact, sitting in plain view inside the office of your… our dear departed facility CO."

"Y-you mean the…pipe cleaner and those glass tu—vials?" Liza retorted defensively as Barnes, eyes distant, stood in silence while recalling the mentioned items as a familiar fog threatened to cloak the details of any specific memory of the past forty-eight hours. "Other than Marquez Chandler, how the hell is either of those…reve…reval…releven—"

A particularly nasty gust threatened to reposition all present, forcing Liza to lean over Zack's prone form like a protective parent over a weak, vulnerable child.

"*Relevant?* Well, first off those glass vials you speak of were preloaded with a powerful hallucinogen normally used to treat the extremely psychotic. They can, and often cause …suicidal tendencies if not teamed with other medications.

"An extensive inventory check started approximately six weeks ago hinted at their theft from the infirmary.

"Secondly, didn't you yourself divulge to me that Zack would often provide unauthorized doses of medications to certain inmates?

Thirdly, and perhaps most damaging of all, both the generic Drano and the drug in question were found and retrieved from your and Zack's assigned abode."

Snatching Barnes' discarded raingear from the upturned couch, Liza folded it gently beneath Zack's head before not quite standing but hopping to her feet, her petite frame slouching slightly; a coiled serpent prepped to strike.

"Wait…*Patawad*…Ex-excuse m-me? Re-retrieved from our….retrieved wh-when and…by whom exactly?"

Perhaps in an attempt to calm her obvious frustration and nip the impending rage squarely in the bud, Graham purposely altered his tone from guarded apprehension to a low, soothing monotone while also adjusting his body language—head and chin lowered a smidgen, shoulders visibly slumped, palms turned upward and exposed—to that of professional counselor and healer of damaged psyches.

"All *I* know is what Carmichael divulged to me inside his office approximately twenty-four hours before his murder," Graham explained timidly, the words nearly drowned out by an assortment of thuds, thumps, whistling winds, thunderclaps and lightning strikes that crackled and sizzled like live wires kissing over standing water.

Meanwhile, Dylan Barnes shook his head vigorously from side to side as the swirling fog gripping his subconscious begin to magically lift at the conclusion of Graham's shocking revelation. A memory, once so deeply suppressed, pushed and shoved its way to the forefront like a battering ram, the sensation so overwhelming he was on the cusp of taking a knee from a sudden wave of dizziness.

"Not my place to question the good captain's motives or procedures in obtaining said evidence, Liza. Obviously, there was…extreme concern of Zackary's possible involvement in…well, some sort of premeditated mission of personal eradication."

With this, Liza's frame began to tremble and shake; her lips pursed and shaded dark purple from intense pressure.

"Pre—personal erect…" she babbled, slowly raising the baton to shoulder level.

Graham resumed his earlier pacing, though at a more deliberate clip and with an eye turned cautiously forward with only the overturned couch as a buffer between him and any forthcoming acts of aggression.

"Zackary 's many…gambling debts were mentioned, and, well, we've all endured the mandatory briefings on the many outside factions willing to pay those in power to extract revenge for a fee."

"Horse-shit, Doctor. Try again. Not a chance," Liza growled, eyes ablaze as the full-body tremor appeared to ease a degree.

"Liza, if not Zackary, there can only be one other, well, *viable* suspect in face of such damning evidence." "It was *you*," Barnes spat just loud enough to be heard through the bedlam, his choice of words perhaps the true catalyst in drowning out both Graham's latest accusation and what sounded like a portion of the reinforced, steel-tiled roof being slowly peeled away like a ripe orange beneath a straight razor.

"You…sent me th—…made me…*ordered* me to…confiscate the…" he continued, strolling casually to the left as if to circle the couch and meet the doctor halfway. "No wonder I've been moppin' around like a cadaver since…since *you* hooked me up with that trifecta of mind-foggin' happy pills, am I right? Fuckin' puppet on a string…and guess who was pullin' the wires?"

"Dylan, you're delusional. When did you last medica—"

"*BULLSHIT*, Graham! Just stow the malarkey already, pal. I ain't quite at total recall just yet, but its gettin' there."

Even as Graham paused in mid-stride, resting his chin atop a clenched fist, Tate Hawkins released a garbled cough that resulted in dark maroon leakage from his left nostril that streamed over his top lip and into the partially open chasm below in a pencil-thin line.

"Wait…w-ait…a-are you saying I…had something to with Carmi—…the captain and…these…those other deaths?" Liza suddenly blurted, as if the preceding dialogue had bypassed her completely. "H-how…dare you even…*mayabang* fucker! What g-gives you the right?"

"Liza…" Barnes insisted, side-stepping over and placing a hand gently atop her shaking right shoulder, "…didn't you hear me? Doctor Forked-Tongue here doped me up and…hell, I dunno…put me under hypnosis maybe…and sent me into your guy's hooch on a search and retrieve mission."

"Dylan, Liza," Graham injected calmly, having assumed full counselor mode complete with creased brow, pronounced hand gestures and ultra-patronizing tone. "We are all professionals here. We must focus on facts, not wild conjecture or…pardon the expression, *chemically-enhanced* speculation.

"Tate Hawkins is alive, that is the important thing, as is his attacker. The facts, however shocking, will surely come to light in the aftermath of our own survival of this damnable storm. Now, let's work as a team and see to it we all arrive alive back at *Atlan*—…"

"Put in sock in it, Graham," Barnes shot back angrily, his perpetually pasty cheeks turning beet red. "The lady and I are havin' a discussion. Feel free to listen in but kindly speak only when spoken to, ya dig?"

As if sensing the mention of his name, Hawkins coughed again, this time finding the energy to reach up with a groping hand and covering his blood-coated lips. His eyes fluttered twice before resealing.

Liza turned her head toward Barnes, though her semi-crouched body remained directly in-line with Graham.

"He…sent you? Where…so you did find those…the Drano and meds inside *our* digs?"

"Yeah, yeah, they were, damn, gimme a sec," he replied, scratching his head vigorously as if direct trauma might transform a foggy memory into crystal clear high-definition.

"It…they were both hidden behind a stack of t-paper under the kitchen sink. It was…almost like I knew exactly where to look, ya know? Like I was bein' jerked along on a leash."

Practically leaning over the couch, within reaching distance of them both, Graham's eyes took on a ruddy gleam, his arms flexing across his chest like banded steel.

"Um, guys, this is all very fascinating, but seriously, given the circumstances, there is a desperate, *immediate* need for us, as a group, to fortify this hut and properly hunker down…"

"Awww, a weak, croaking voice exclaimed, triggering a trio of double-takes from those within earshot.

Having repositioned onto his left side, Zack winced in obvious pain while using the opposite hand to massage the back of his neck.

"Zack," Liza mouthed, a throaty whisper easily drowned out by the storm's continuing fury. She practically levitated over, the baton tucked to her left thigh as she knelt over her spouse and gently gripped his right forearm, "Are you…can you move? I mean, is anything broken?"

"Ju-just my pride, babe," he replied, staring up at her through leaden eyes that strained to focus. "Been lis—able to overhear a decent p-portion of the manure…h-he's been spreading."

"Liza," Graham practically bellowed, his neck riddled with thick, freshly hatched veins. "I would strongly suggest you move away from Za—from your husband. You, most of all, simply cannot fathom how dangerous he actually is. I know this is…*extremely* difficult for you to accept, but he *is* responsible for the recent carnage of which I spoke…"

Dylan Barnes blared out in a tone just as authoritative, if not downright threatening.

"Two sides to every story, right Doc? Well, we've heard a big hunk of your version. Time for the other side."

"*Time*, Dylan? Truly, just how much more of that certain commodity are we going to be allowed before these hut walls crumble inward? Take a listen, yes? I'd say we'd bet—"

"Flood room contains a grand total of three life-pods, genius. You gonna volunteer to take your chances up top?"

"Well, I…it's a matter of rank then, I presume…"

"Meaning Hawkins ranks as an involuntary slab of drowned meat, then Liz and myself."

At this, Barnes cupped his chin in an open palm and cocked a brow as if in deep thought.

"So basically you *prefer* to ride the storm out inside a four by six tomb with a man you've all but tried and convicted as bein' as dangerous as the murderin', soulless scum we're paid to serve?"

Seemingly deflated, Graham threw up both arms before twisting around to face the open hut door, which hung precariously from either badly bent or completely shattered hinges.

"Fine, Dylan, we'll draw straws. Perhaps a quick game of 'Trivial Pursuit?' Whatever, but we'd better decide before it's a woefully moot point."

With that, the doctor strode purposely to the left as to circle around the couch and join the others, only to freeze in mid-step in the face of twin reactions, each similarly stern but delivered in opposite extremes.

"W-wait. He...it's a distraction. He wants us...off-guard and in easy....s-striking distance," announced Zack, sitting up with his knees pulled to his chest and muscular arms tucking them ever tighter "J-just give me a second to...ca-catch my breath."

Liza's pronouncement wasn't nearly as subdued—more akin to the rage-fueled barking of one highly-perturbed drill instructor—as she lunged toward Graham with the baton in prime striking position.

"Just hold position, Doctor. Stay...right...*there.*"

Eyes darting about the room to scan various objects that floated about, most at least partially submerged and spinning about like fish-bobs in a whirlpool, Barnes suddenly felt a great need to secure a weapon, any weapon.

"Liza...Dylan," Graham pleaded, ankle-deep in flowing seawater with an elbow resting at the far west end of the tipped couch, "I've stated my case. It can...*will* all be worked out once this damnable storm is no longer a viable threat. Please, we must decide on a plan of action that is...fair to everyone involved."

A booming thunderclap, so close it seemed to rattle and reverberate off the hut's interior walls, punctuated the doctor's desperate appeal.

"H-hey…is th-this a pr-private r-roasting or c-can any…anyone j-join in?" echoed a voice so weak, so muffled, it was lost on everyone save those closest to its bone-weary vibe, that being Liza and Zackary, each of whom turned toward the source with similar expressions of wide-eyed awe.

"*Jesus*, Hawkins…I…figured you for a…well, a concrete slab," she blurted, a shameful roll of the eyes indicative of an immediately regret in her choice of words.

Barnes followed their lead, twisting around and peeking over Liza's right shoulder in order to pinpoint the object of their sudden attention.

"Well I'll be…already given *him* up for packaged chum," he muttered, joining the Gormans in a state of distraction so complete, none were privy to Dean Graham's catlike departure from the living room into the kitchen, where he began rummaging through drawers, the storm serving to drown out all accompanying noise.

Meanwhile, Liza had temporarily abandoned Zack—breathing easily while slowly regaining the gist of his senses—to scoot over and aid Tate Hawkins, who appeared to be taking a leisurely tub-bath save his exposed head, shoulders and upper chest. A large black and blue shaded knot, easily the diameter of a regulation golf ball and nearly as bulky, protruded from just above his right eye socket, while a thick line of bloody mucus dribbled forth from his left nostril.

"You…are you able to move at all? Can you see?" Liza inquired while placing a hand atop his bared chest as if checking for an active heartbeat, the man's blank, slightly cockeyed gaze prompting the latter query.

"I c-can't quite s-see you, d-doll-face, but I…can sure de-detect that sw-sweet s-southeastern…Asian a-aroma of yours. A hea…heavenly scent it…is, I m-must say."

Liza snorted, rolling her eyes in disbelief.

"Save it, Romeo. I'm going to lean you up against the wall before you drown, okay? Brace yourself and just...breathe easy, okay? We're...we'll get you some help."

"I...hear...th-though I h-heard o-others. A-are we...alone?"

"Shhhh, just stop talking. I'm here to help."

She did so with the professional skills of a veteran nurse as Hawkins' pained grimace clearly showcased the anguish such movement triggered, however gentle the technique.

"Yeah, just...take it easy, Hawk," Barnes echoed with the occasional stammer while assuming the unfamiliar role of optimist. "Once Mother Nature ceases her bellyachin', we'll see you're transported to the mainland for a nice, soft bed in the infirmary."

Staring blankly in the direction of the source, Tate Hawkins' complexion was ghostly-white, a fading phantom whose ghastly visage had been dipped in flour.

"Appre...most o-obliged. Tooth...truth be t-told, I've...f-felth better."

Once assured he wasn't about to keel back over into the flowing floodwater, Liza rejoined Zack without actually turning around and thus still had no clue of the Dean Graham's conspicuous absence. Ditto Dylan Barnes, flashing a mischievous grin as he reached down to deliver a mild slap to Zack's right shoulder, whose hoarse whisper was barely audible.

"He's...Tate needs immediate help. We...can't let him nod off, not if...it was...is a concussion."

"Understood, big guy, but outside of teleportation, I see no way to speed up the pro—"

"Damn it! I...feel responsible for his...state, Barnes. If I'd just...got here a few minutes earlier. W-we have to...I have to get him to...safety."

Barnes bristled as if goosed in the rear.

"Swell. Maybe you two lovebirds can even bunk together. Meanwhile, those of us still standin' upright had damn well better begin fortifyin' this cement tomb before we find ourselves back-strokin' it back to HQ. I for one can't swim for shit but can sure as hell sink like a stone…"

Graham's sudden appearance within their personal space—barging past in a blur, so stealth-like and graceful as to leave no possibility to prevent same—caused all but Tate Hawkins, staring into the rock ceiling through shiny, glazed eyes—to physically cringe as a trio of jaws dropped and eyes grew wide in almost perfectly-timed synchronization.

"What…Graham…what are…get away fr-from…" Liza blurted, lurching back and nearly tripping over a shattered chair leg and forced to use the shock-baton not as a weapon but a crutch in order to regain her balance.

"Li-Liza…s-stop that…that c-crazy bastard!" Zackary spat, spinning around on his hips and collapsing onto his back in the aftermath, his empty palms frantically slapping the surrounding water into a frothy foam.

"Hey, Doc…wha the fu—" Barnes stammered, actually lunging forward and whipping out his right arm, his grasping fingers nabbing a handful of blowing, mist-filled air and nothing else.

Shirtless after apparently ripping away the sparse remains of his shredded tee, Graham slid to his knees just to the right of Hawkins' prone form before executing a graceful turn with both arms held high in mock surrender.

"Good lord, just *relax,* damn it. I *am* a doctor, remember? And this man is, as you can plainly see, in dire need. If we are to perish together, it won't be from a lack of effort on *my* part to avoid said fate."

"W-who's t-there, da-damn it?" Tate Hawkins warbled in full panic mode, reaching up weakly with both hands to grope the air in front of his face only to have them repeatedly knocked down by a nonstop barrage of gusts.

Graham loomed over his squirming form, grasping a blue wash cloth in one hand and what appeared to be a dark brown ice pack in the other.

"Relax, Tate...you've more than likely suffered a dilly of a concussion. From the brutal punishment I saw you endure..." he paused to regard Zack with the coldest of glares, "...it's nothing short of a miracle we're able to communicate at all."

Zack's croaking exclamation cut off any and all prospective replies, having risen to his knees, from which churning waters swirled almost to the upper thighs.

"L-Liza...d-don't listen. He came here to...kill Tate. Mas...m-must've p-parked the medevac c-cutter on the...so-south end of the isle. I ...walked in on...the aftermath of...the beat...the a-assault. Sub...due the bastard. Dylan," he shot Barnes a desperation-filled glance, "don't let that d-deranged son of a bitch get near H-Hawk or...Liz. I...there's...no time to explain j-just now, but...tr-trust me...I'm not...blowing smoke. He's...as dangerous as...he is...cunning."

"D-damn tooting...he...is," Hawkins babbled incoherently, his eyelids half-closed and his hands dropping weakly to his sides.

"I came here to save you, Tate," Graham sneered with shaky, pleading hands held airborne. "Risked my own life, and *this* is how I'm repaid."

Even as Dylan Barnes remained frozen in place, his bottom lip trembling while struggling mightily for the appropriate reply, Liza took immediate action, striding forward with feline quickness despite the double handicap of ankle-deep water and consistently pelting winds.

Dean Graham turned and regarded her through comically wide eyes. With a mere split-second's preparation, he was able to duck just a hair in order to avoid the full impact of the ascending baton across his exposed skull, instead taking the brunt behind the right ear and upper shoulder.

Reeling back, the doctor was able to deflect the follow-up blow with an upraised forearm while executing an off-balance leg-sweep that caught Liza across the ankles and effectively flipped her head over heels to land face first with a muffled splash.

"Shi-shit....Liz!" Zack shouted as both he and Barnes plunged forth in her direction, the former scrambling on all fours and the latter in a gawky lurch. Reaching her splayed form at precisely the same moment, each grabbed the nearest appendage and rolled her gently onto her back as Graham back-pedaled away.

Her bottom lip had split down the center upon impact with the water-logged tile, while her left eye had immediately begun to swell, resembling a battered, punch-drunk pugilist.

"W-where...di-did you...did y-you g-get...ta-take him down, bi-big 'un?" she asked between garbled coughs that spewed forth varying amounts of ingested seawater.

Zack pushed a thick strand of matted hair from the left side of her face before stealing a quick glance Graham's way, the doctor having dropped to one knee just inside the opened entrance with his head bowed and a fine mist blowing in to add a fresh coat of moisture to his already glistening frame.

"Soon, Z, soon enough. Just...catch a breath. How's...a-are you hurting anywhere but...th-the obvious?"

"N-no time for...a damn p-physical, y-you b-big lug," she countered with a forced smile while already attempting to squirm and wriggle herself upright. "Wh-where's...where's the baton?"

As if previously awaiting that precise cue, Barnes leaned over and down, displaying said beating-stick in a double-fisted grip.

"It's here when ya need it, Spitfire," he grinned, periodically redirecting his own focus from Graham's slumped form to the mystery, semi-submerged object floating just outside the kitchen entrance that had so effectively piqued his curiosity since their arrival.

Without pause, Zack reached up and snagged the baton at its slightly thicker end and pulled it gently from his grasp.

"I'll...gladly procure that....particular persuader, Mister...Barnes. Got some...pressing unfinished business, you might say."

Standing with Barnes' considerable aid, Zack then stepped past the smaller man and used his free hand to shove the overturned couch to one side, leaving less than a dozen feet between himself and the target of his ire.

"There is, after all...the matter of apprehending and...taking into custody a certain...rogue physican."

To that, Dean Graham did not so much as rise but leap to his feet and assume a defensive posture straight from the definitive book of taekwondo.

"Enough, Gorman!" he barked angrily, the emotionally stilted façade of icy coolness having finally peeled away to reveal an inner shell that sheathed with a pulsing, red-hot rage.

Zack Gorman, meanwhile, effortlessly slipped into the doctor's former role—both tone and expression equally bland and utterly void of emotion—his chin dropped and eyes upraised in full accusatory mode while playfully tossing the baton from palm to palm.

"I read your file, Doctor. Carmichael gave me access, no doubt just hours before you entered his office and, well, what you *know* I don't have to tell you, right?"

Almost pleading, Graham cocked his head to one side while simultaneously lowering his voice back to a more characteristic level.

"It's not going to fly, Zackary? You have to *know* that. As delusional as you may be in the face of this...rather unexpected series of interruptions, you must realize there can be only one outcome," Graham paused, nodding to the open entrance and swirling chaos at his back. "Well, two, if one counts being washed out to sea as a viable option."

"He was onto you, Graham. Told me as much while sitting in his office with all that damning evidence piled at the center of his desk. Evidence you'd so clumsily planted in my…in *our* room."

"Who exactly are you performing for, Zack? Officer Barnes? Your wife? Probable Oscar nomination aside, they will have…they *have* their doubts. As I've come to discover countless times over during the duration of my relatively short career, humans are the ultimate chameleons. One never truly knows another, no matter the passing of time or supposed closeness and intimacy involved…not *completely* anyway."

"So says the King of sleight of hand. Nice touch with the crutches, by the way. Damn shame about that kid. Barely a week on station and his reward is a boat ride home inside a glorified garbage bag.

"Collateral damage, I suppose, huh Doc?"

Graham didn't seem to hear, or simply chose to ignore the larger man's continuing spiel.

"So, tell me, Zackary . No, tell us *all*. What is the going price for a human life in that blackest of markets? Enough to wipe out all those pesky gambling debts and ensure that luxurious retirement I'm sure you'd long-since promised both yourself and a spouse who clearly despises her chosen profession?"

Returning the favor, Zack acted as if he were spotlighted in a one-man play.

"Carmichael found the chink in that shiny armor, Doc. Buried so deep within the tiny cracks and fine print of your personnel record it must've taken the Hubble telescope to spot it. That he…or someone higher up the command echelon didn't see it before really seemed to…well, embarrass the man something fierce. Pissed him off royally, I'm sure, but moreover, just made him feel damn foolish for not putting the pieces together sooner. After all, who was it making all those extra…island calls to better counsel and treat the most mentally disturbed within the ranks of the incarcerated? Why, good old Doc Graham, that's who! Kind, caring, understanding ….he of the big heart and even *bigger* syringe. Tell me…*us* true, Dean…how exactly did you finagle this assignment? Must've burned the ol' midnight oil doing research on all the convicted child killers assigned to Atlantis, am I right? Losing a kid sister to a deranged maniac at such a young age probably even steered you into the profession, I'd surmise. In the end, it was never about helping them…treating them, was it? It was about…*eradicating* those responsible, which was, in your mind, every…damn…one of them."

A particularly nasty gust penetrated the seven-feet high by three-feet wide hut entrance, accompanied by a large mass of twisted palm fronds, the latter slapping the back of Graham's knees and nearly toppling him backward.

"*Jesus*, Gorman. Enough with the fictional motives!

"This is all about saving your own skin, so by all means you three pack into the flood room and…I'll just…fend for myself."

"My ass you will, mister."

Graham's face twisted; a contorted horror.

"E-excuse me?"

"You really think we're about to…" Zack paused, sucking wind as if ascending an icy mountainside "…lock ourselves in that stone pit and be trapped inside…while you wait out the storm up here and then sail away at your convenience?"

"Yeah," Barnes added defiantly, though with a just a twinge of uncertainly in both his tone and expression. "I'll take my chances up top, if ya don't mind…or even if ya do."

Bear-hugging his own naked flesh as if from a sudden chill, Graham turned to the entrance and raised both forearms as a shield from incoming shrapnel.

291

"Great. Fantastic. Whatever. Believe what you will, then. Needless to say, this isn't the time nor the place for the kangaroo court and public hanging you so obviously pine for."

He turned back, eyes ablaze, his chest and arms flexing periodically, making it appear as though he had donned a glistening muscle-suit pulled from a Hollywood effects rack.

"For now, could those of you up to it please assist me in first barricading this front entrance and then in securing the kitchen windows and back door?"

Barnes and Zackary exchanged a worrisome glance before turning toward Liza, who merely shrugged indifferently before refocusing on Tate Hawkins.

Still leaning hard on Barnes for support, Zack glanced around at the sparse collection of floating debris and laughed heartily before coughing harshly into a curled palm.

"Pray tell, ye of the multiple college degrees and countless diplomas, what are we supposed to use to fortify said breaches? That is, unless you know the location of a secret stash filled with an unlimited supply of tools, lumber and tarp."

As if to second the motion, Barnes performed a similar scan of the general area, wearing a mask of comical befuddlement, before regarding Graham.

"Yeah, what're we supposed to use to board up the holes, Doc? Maybe fill up some sand bags?"

This time, both Gormans laughed aloud.

"Unbelievable," Graham spewed between lips pursed so tightly they'd turned a light shade of purple. "So-called trained professionals with absolutely no fathom of improvisation."

Muscles bulging at his neck and upper back, he grasped the overturned couch by two of its metallic caster wheels and literally pulled it from the shallow floodwaters like some ancient, giant god

SEA OF BONES

plucking a disabled battleship from raging seas, slinging its considerable bulk—in addition to what appeared to be several gallons of soaked-in seawater—around in a single, graceful twist.

The water-logged couch at his back, he then turned to the entrance, wrestling briefly with the semi-detached oak door before fitting it into its intended groove minus several broken hinges, only one of which still clung loosely to its otherwise undamaged host.

A graceful, athletic hop over the couch ensued, followed by a single, forceful shove that pinned it snugly against the bottom portion of the loosely propped door.

Exhaling nosily, Graham backed away several steps with hands on hips to survey his handiwork and also to test its resilience. Satisfied it could and would endure the harshest of impending gusts, he twisted about in a fluid, flawless rendition of a military about-face and faced the others with a wry grin stretched across his usually stoic visage.

"It isn't rocket-science, people. Now, what say we decide once and for all who remains up top to take their, ahem, chances."

"Trapped prey are the easiest to slay, right, Doc?" Barnes answered, for perhaps the first time since he and Liza's arrival at the hut, without even a minute trace of humor, sarcastic or otherwise. "For one, I'm done listenin' to your tap-dancin' pyschobabble, pal. My days of playin' your stooge, doped up or otherwise, are history. Fact is, the more I stand here stewin' on it," he paused before lunging back and to his left—temporarily leaving a staggering Zack Gorman to fend for himself—and snatching the shock-baton from Liza's loose grip, much to her wide-eyed shock, "it's time I did some *improvisin'* of my own. As in, takin' you into custody until the unvarnished truth I already strongly suspect can come to light inside a proper courtroom. Until that time, you murderin' skull-fucker, it's about shuttin' your pompous ass up 'til we're able to depart the premises."

Grinning maniacally, Barnes had yet to take his first step toward the intended target—Graham having already repositioned his upper body in a defensive, blocking pose—when his left shoulder fell victim to a Vulcan-esque pinch and he was yanked backward almost to the point of toppling head over slippery boot-heels.

"Whoa there, Sergeant Rock," he was shocked to hear Liza whisper near his right ear, having logically but mistakenly assumed such a display of physical prowess had come courtesy of her hulking spouse. "You're in no shape to take on Doc Muscles by your lonesome. Probably what he was counting on; to take us one at a time."

"What do *you* propose then, woman? We wait for the bastard to drown?" he replied, leaning down to deliver his own, barely audible mumble.

"Zackary's in no shape for a rematch," she scolded, staring up at him through an eye so swollen it appeared completely sealed. Barnes glanced briefly toward her lesser half, who had dropped to one knee and appeared to have a hard time catching his breath.

"Yeah, he takes us out...the weasel runs the table for sure. Locks himself in the flood room and waits out the storm with plenty of time to stage our deaths as accidental...storm-related."

"Exactly. We...have to do this right. Remember our training. He's strong, Barnes. Deceivably so. I...I'd *never* seen Zack bested in a one-on-one before today."

Despite the severity of the situation, Barnes was tempted to correct her latest malapropism—the word *deceptively* literally balanced on the tip of his woefully parched tongue—when a loud thump smacking the hut roof instantly reset his priorities.

"I don't know what misguided, pot-bellied scheme you two are cooking up over there, but if it involves an impending physical confrontation, allow me to speculate on such a dreadful mistake's probable outcomes," Graham bellowed, a necessary evil in order to be heard over the surrounding bedlam—a building mishmash with elements of both a roaring freight train and a thousand, ear-splitting whistles, the kind most commonly used by a sports referee—having hardly flinched at the resounding crash from just moments before. "First off, one or possibly more of the combatants are likely to inherit injuries of a potentially fatal nature. On the bright side, they won't have to worry about surviving the storm while already playing the part of human flotsam. Quite the waste, considering such an attack is based on wholly circumstantial evidence."

He gestured past the sulking pair toward Zack, who had managed to hoist a comatose Tate Hawkins into a sitting position.

"Circumstantial, and may I state in my own defense, totally *fabricated* by the lone member in your troop apparently unwilling to risk his own neck in my apprehension. A man who was, with God serving as my only fully coherent witness, mere moments from completing his latest assassination before I strolled in and surprised him into a moment of recklessness, wherein I was able to gain the upper hand. As far as motive, our late commander's hunch appears to have been sadly prophetic."

Barnes took a half-step forward, the baton clutched at both ends and tucked snugly against his breastbone.

"I say again, Doctor, and for the last time...*horseshit*. Senior Officer Gorman is about as likely an inmate slayer as my Aunt Fannie."

"Enough chat-chit already," Liza injected in what continued as a muffled whisper that gradually added decibels until mutating into a full-blown scream. "Let's take him out before this concrete septic tank crumbles around our ears."

Having hooked Tate Hawkins' limp right arm around his shoulder and neck, Zack had managed to stand upright while facing the kitchen.

"Z, just hold your position, damn it! I'm taking Hawk to the flood room. Wait on me, understand? *Do not* take action until...if or *when* I give the word. You reading me, Barnes? Both of you, consider that an order."

Tossing his head back like a baying wolf, Dean Graham's echoing howl mimicked the same.

"Oh, that's priceless, Zackary. By all means, flee the scene and secure your own safety above all else, knowing full well your two charges here, each wired up, fired up, smelling blood and itching for a fight, aren't about to adhere to such a half-hearted, half-*assed* command."

"Clam up, psycho," Barnes growled, never taking his eyes off the doctor while pausing to address the senior officer. "You got it, big guy, though if he gets frisky in the meantime, all bets are off."

"Make it snappy, Zack," Liza chimed in, arms curled upward and fists tightly clenched in the classic pugilist style. Like Barnes, her focus remained solely on the opposition while addressing her spouse. "Banged up or not, I…want you here when the time comes for a takedown."

Trudging slowly past the posed duo, Zack had an arm coiled around Hawkins' waist, the thinner man's blood-smeared feet slicing through the ankle deep waters atop their respective arches.

"Just do as I say, Z. Soon as Hawk's tucked inside, we'll be back to full strength. Also give…gives me a few extra clicks to clear away the cobwebs."

Just as the two men cleared the kitchen threshold—Zack Gorman's pained grunts fading with each subsequent step—Dean Graham briefly broke his blocking stance in order to wave them off with both hands.

"That's it, Gorman…run away! Leave your wife and a half-crippled subordinate to do your dirty work. All part of the plan, right? Better hope they're up to the task, mister, or you and I will be conversing again reeeeeaaaalll soon."

Apparently having waited for Zack and his limp passenger to stroll through the kitchen entrance and soon vanish from sight, Barnes leaned back and whispered out of the left corner of his mouth, his soggy mustache bobbing about like an electro-shocked caterpillar.

"Before I rush 'im, I'm gonna backhand the baton your way. Once I get the bastard's arms pinned, step in and turn out the lights."

Leaning forward until her swollen, blood-crusted bottom lip practically massaged his earlobe, Liza keep her one working eye focused on Graham, who had already reassumed the combat-ready pose of moments earlier.

"Wha—? Thought we were supposed to wait on Za—"

"Face it, babe, the big guy is no better than a disability at this point. Graham gets his hands on 'im again, it's a stalemate with no end in sight...at least nothin' resemblin' a happy one. It's you an' me...now or never."

"B-but what if...he manages to...how are *you* going to manage to pin *his* arms? Cracked egghead or not, the man is strong as an ox and quick as a greased feline."

"Greased fe—" Barnes grinned despite himself. "...Never quite heard it worded quite that way."

"He gets past you, or worse, holds you hostage, our advantage..." she paused to gesture with a forefinger toward the baton, lying flat across Barnes' left shoulder, "...will be lost."

"Don't let the flabby gut fool ya, babe. Two-time state wrestlin' champ back in the day, and a few extra pounds aside, this boy ain't lost a step. Mr. Olympia over there won't know what hit 'im. Just don't leave me hangin' too long before ya crack his skull."

"Barnes, seriously, I don't think we shou—"

He gently tapped the fatter end of the baton against his shoulder.

"This bad boy's set on incapacitate and ya figure all the moistness will add an extra kick. I'm just hopin' the secondary shock doesn't toss me into the nearest stone wall."

"Zack really needs to be here..."

Briefly breaking contact with Graham, Barnes pointed the baton toward the ceiling, its wet, gleaming finish splitting his view of Liza's desperation-filled glare as the two stood boot-toe to boot-toe.

"Where your husband needs to be is where he's squattin' right about now...tucked inside that flood room for a little R and R. He's of absolutely no help here, Liza. I know ya see 'im as your big, bad bodyguard, but I'm tellin' ya, Doctor Kill-dare already kicked his behind once. In Zack's present state, I wouldn't exactly be pinin' for a rematch.

"Basically, Officer Gorman," he turned back toward the doctor, who in turn cocked a brow inquisitively, "it's up to us or the only one paddlin' off this dune with a workin' pulse is gonna that murderin', slick-talkin' bastard with all the PhDs."

Her bloated lower lip noticeably trembling, Liza nodded with obvious reluctance.

They turned as one, Barnes' having tucked the baton snugly against his left thigh; Liza in a slight crouch with both fists upraised once again.

"You…we don't *have* to do this," Graham pleaded, legs firmly planted, shoulders and biceps bulging.

"Should've thought of that before ya turned judge, jury and executioner," Barnes replied with a stern nod before lunging forth, kicking and splashing through the calf-high waters like a charging bull while reaching back and passing the baton to Liza's waiting palm like a pair of relay racers.

Utterly motionless, Dean Graham stood his ground until Dylan Barnes was literally on top of him, the manic flurry that ensued a vicious, swirling blur that would, in a mere matter of seconds, decide the fate of all present.

Fifteen

Low Tide

Forced to pause every few seconds to prevent passing out from severe waves of dizziness, Zack was eventually able to properly tuck Tate Hawkins in the first of three life-pods, the man's limp, motionless frame adding a dead weight element that more than once brought the big man to his knees with black dots littering his vision.

Once ensured the inner air-filtration system had been successfully powered up, he'd sealed Hawkins inside the thick, crystal-glass tube with a low click and immediately crouched to a knee, his forehead and jowls infested with pellet-sized sweat bullets and his breath coming in hoarse, rattling gasps.

Cocking an ear toward the room's narrow, v-shaped entrance, he picked up faint rumblings he realized had little to do with the storm.

"Well t-then, take him…down, Dylan. Please l-lord," he muttered between sucking in additional gulps of air, bowing his head slightly as if in prayer. "For Liza's sake…grant th-that…farm-fed c-country boy strength he never knew h-he possessed."

As the commotion intensified—barricading walls aside—from no more than perhaps eight to nine yards away, Zack inhaled one final time as if to prep for a deep-sea dive and rose unsteadily to his feet, only then becoming fully aware of the toll Graham's choke-hold had taken.

"S-suck it up, s-soldier," he growled, reaching inside his disheveled uniform shirt to retrieve an object that, upon first inspection through floater-riddled eyes, appeared strangely alien lying flat atop his open palm.

"Son of...a bitch c-caught you off-guard once. N-never have trusted those...damn martial arts fre-freaks. Fine...golden rule...severely violated but...hey, survived f-for a reason. Nobody ever...said sealing...one's fate was going to be easy, even for...those for whom...destiny smiles."

A trio of lengthy, thundering strides saw his hasty, surprisingly agile exit from the flood room, the door of which slid smoothly with a faint whoosh.

Left to peacefully vegetate within the dimly lit space—a single LED light preventing total darkness—Hawkins stirred amid a fresh series of quakes racking the stone structure beyond, his breathing shallow but consistent, his left eye occasionally twitching as if experiencing a particularly vivid dream. By the time he'd fully awakened, at first wide-eyed with panic at the unfamiliarity of the glass tube sealing him in, all save the occasional rumble of thunder and the sound of unknown shrapnel bounding off the surrounding walls had grown eerily silent.

Upon seeking out and finding the hatch's inner release, he'd leaned up and forward with his upper body poking from the smooth glass opening as if hatching. The life-pod's inner filtration system's low hum and typhoon commotion aside, there was no indication of human interaction beyond the flood-room's admittedly thick walls, nor evidence of any movement whatsoever other than the storm-related type.

A full minute ticked away… then two…then the majority of a third before Hawkins was able to muster up the physical strength to completely vacate the pod, his arms and legs visibly shaking from the effort, his entire torso coated in a fresh cloak of sweat.

He'd managed nary a single step toward the exit before it whisked open, the narrow threshold instantly filled by a roving shadow whose originator would soon be revealed. Gasping aloud upon said reveal, Tate Hawkins reeled back with a sudden, overpowering wave of total recall, the effect instantly transforming his already weak, frail frame into a trembling husk.

~ * ~

Dylan Barnes' screeching rebel yell had ended abruptly in mid-howl, the required oxygen to complete its climax cut off at the source via a forceful kick to the gut that essentially creased his spiraling form in mid-air.

In the aftermath of delivering the perfectly executed side-kick, Dean Graham's clumsy, flailing follow-through—arms wind-milling and bare feet splashing wildly to regain balance—served as a positive as the tip of an ascending shock-baton barely grazed his chin with a crackle of electric static.

Dropping instantly to all fours, his upper back absorbed the brunt of Liza's overzealous lunge as she went sailing overhead, her knees thumping into his rib cage as, for the second time in less than five minutes, she was flipped head-over-heels onto the water-logged tile.

Graham stumbled up and back, favoring his battered ribs while keeping separate pegs on his erstwhile attackers, both of whom flopped and squirmed away in opposite directions: Barnes toward the kitchen and Liza the barricaded entrance, the former on his hands and knees and the latter performing a soldier's crawl with both hands conspicuously empty and her bowed head barely treading the frothy floodwaters.

Kneeling, Graham scooped up the shock baton and stumbled back into and then onto the soggy confines of the couch while studying the handle's minute controls.

To his right, Liza had wriggled and squirmed her way to a far wall, just past the closet door. Tate Hawkins' pile-driving skull had fractured some time earlier, wheezing and gasping as thin streams of sea water flowed freely from each nostril.

To his left, Barnes leaned half into the kitchen, balanced on his knees with arms outstretched and his hands groping in the lathered waters for some unseen object, his labored exhales birthing a raspy whistle intermingled with shrill cries of anguish.

Pushing himself from the couch, Graham held the baton chest level while trudging purposely toward the kitchen, lifting his bare feet knee-level to avoid undo splash along the way.

"He has some cracked ribs, perhaps even broken," he announced apparently to no one in particular, posing behind the man's crouched frame with the baton cupped at each end and positioned horizontally at neck level.

"Y-yeah, well, y-you're a ca-cracked *e-egg*, d-Doc," Barnes shot back in a guttural croak, snatching the squared edge of a nearby cabinet in an attempt to haul himself up, his entire frame shuddering from the effort. "So t-there. J-just gim-give me a sec to re...regroup and I'll...have ya...writing pain m-med prescrips to...yourse—"

Reaching up, over and down with machine-like precision, Graham cleared the slumping man's head and hooked the baton beneath his chin, a single, forceful jerk serving to meld their bodies as one.

In first yanking from side to side, Graham was able to achieve the desired amount of leverage, though with far more resistance than he'd expected if his wide-eyed response were any indication.

"My god, but he is....is indeed.....as self-proclaimed...strong as...the...proverbial enraged bull."

Following a quick repositioning of his feet, Graham released a power lifter's pre-jerk growl before heaving up and back with such savagery his quarry's perpetually kicking, booted feet were temporarily displaced from the floor. Meanwhile, at precisely the same moment Dylan Barnes went airborne, Liza pushed herself from the wall and proceeded toward them in a weaving, drunken sprint.

The object had flown from Barnes' grip just as he'd gone weightless, an unidentifiable, wind-milling blur that landed with a resounding splash in the exact spot his government-issued steel-toed combat boots had previously occupied.

Bug-eyed, grunting and growling, having managed to hook both hands underneath the center of the baton, Barnes attempted in vain to yank Graham off-balance and perhaps loosen the extreme pressure at his neck. Several attempts at driving the heel of his boots into the strangler's ankles or shins had resulted in bar-jarring whiffs, mainly due to a woeful lack of leverage. Though his eyes brimmed with tears, he caught a hazy glimpse of Liza sliding to her knees just to his left, perhaps no more than a yard away, and pulling the object he'd lost from the gradually ascending floodwaters. Between rapid blinking jags, he could just make her out dancing wildly from his left to his right. She would often reverse fields in an apparent attempt to get to Graham, whose constant repositionings were effective enough to keep her at bay.

Perhaps from her efforts to save his bacon, Barnes experienced a sudden rush of adrenalin shoot through his fatigued frame like a nesting of live wires—ironically just as it felt as his assailant had eased up just a mite—resulting in first a shift of leverage in his favor and finally a textbook over the shoulder flip that concluded with Graham lying nearly completely submerged in knee-high seawater and the baton in the double-fisted possession of its original carrier.

"G-great goin', b-babe. N-now....w-what s-say...we...f-finish off...this...fuckin' quack?" Dylan Barnes beamed, stumbling back a step as Liza stepped between him and a frantically splashing Dean Graham.

Exchanging frantic glances between the standing man and the prone one, she held the object cocked back over her left shoulder, a piece of improvised, abstract weaponry from the undeniably warped genius that was Tate Hawkins.

As Graham rolled and flopped about in a spastic frenzy, Barnes busied himself first shaking excessive saltwater from the baton and then resetting the miniscule gauge located atop the flat edge of its insulated handle. Meanwhile—standing in a fast-rising, knee-high flow, the source of its rapid intrusion easily identified as the front entrance had been pushed partially ajar despite the makeshift barricade—Liza remained frozen in place, her lone functioning eye staring down Graham between thin strands of fully saturated, pitch-black hair.

"Hey…don't feel ya…gotta wait…wait on me, woman. Go ahead…get your jollies 'fore…he gets a…second wind. I'll…gladly take…sloppy seconds," Barnes croaked, flashing a hideous grin while obviously still straining to complete a full, unobstructed breath.

Kneeling with one hand submerged to the elbow and the other raised in a blocking stance at face level, Graham bit into his lower lip while peeking just beneath his forearm to meet Liza's stare.

With a grunt and disgusted roll of the eyes, Barnes lunged forth, using a free hand to gently push her aside.

"Well…shit then, I guess if…a man wants somethin' done…right, he has to do it himse—" The first blow was of a glancing variety, slicing off the pinky and ring fingers of his right hand—previously cocked with baton firmly in tow—before shaving off the majority of his right ear, the severed lobe bouncing off the entrance door before landing with a soggy plop in the center section of the couch.

Miraculously able to maintain a loose grip on the baton, Barnes regarded his mutilated appendage with comical shock, mouth hanging agape and eyes saucer-wide.

"Wh-what…t-the f-f-fu—"

The brunt of the second so perfectively halved his face it was as if it had been surgically dotted from forehead to chin. Dylan Barnes stumbled back a single step, arms falling to his side as the baton splashed down next to his right combat boot, briefly maintaining a surprising steady stance despite the makeshift tomahawk handle sticking from the center of his face like some bizarre, recently birthed bone. He convulsed but once—a shuddering body-spasm so viciously executed it jarred the tomahawk free from the bloody crater it had so expertly rooted—before collapsing back in a heap, a volcanic eruption of blackish fluids spewing upward to dot the ceiling before cascading downward as if to reunite with its now-lifeless source.

"Well, *good grief,* my lady," Graham scolded, smirking sourly as he stood and began twisting his naked torso from side to side to shake off the excess "I was beginning to seriously ponder your loyalties. I must say, you surely believe in taking one for the team."

Reclaiming the crudely-constructed but surprisingly effective war-club from the swirling, crimson-shaded waters, she gently sloshed its ax-end back and forth into same to clear away the fresh build-up of shredded, bloodied flesh.

"Don't d-dare, Slick," she growled angrily. "Not…now."

"Face it, Liz," he replied tactfully, exposing open palms. "Some simply cannot be saved. No one can say you didn't give it the full Ivy League try and then some. You must know and accept there was no other way."

Shoulders slumped, voice cracking, her head slowly bowed.

"I…didn't want this. *Awa*…god knows I…wanted to save him …save them all. Dim bulb that he is…*was*, Barnes is…*was* still a physical threat."

With a tentative reach toward her, Graham resumed in full patronizing mode, only to be cut off in mid drivel.

"Indeed he was. You did what you had to do. Nothing less, nothing more."

"Tossed your perfectly-chiseled black ass across the room easy enough, right?" she snarled, her head snapping up and back—thick strands of sopping wet hair slapping his extended hand away with the effectiveness of a well-aimed backhand. "Meanwhile, you've managed to half-blind me with that all that fancy, fag-fighting."

"We had discussed the possibilities of your…plan faltering and the potential repercussions, Liz. What's done is done," he countered coldly, stepping over the dead man's floating frame while taking obvious pains to avoid viewing the extreme mutilation incurred.

"In case you hadn't noticed, Mother Ocean is very gradually swallowing this dune whole, and the old girl's appetite appears, if anything, to be growing increasingly voracious."

"Fact has not eluded me, fancy-pants," she sneered, shooting a glance at the hut entrance, standing semi-ajar as to allow a hazy view of what had been a fairly spacious beachhead just a half-hour earlier— presently, an-ever widening, ever-expanding lagoon awaiting official christening as just another blip of ocean-space.

Submerged to just past the knees, Graham stepped past her toward the kitchen entrance.

"To the flood room then. There's still the rather nasty business of elimin—"

He halted in mid-stride, nearly tripping over a block of squared, wooden debris that once might've served as a lower cabinet door.

"Well Zackary, you're moving about quite well, I see," he nodded solemnly, folding chiseled arms. "I know this must come as quite the shock. Can *only* imagine, actually."

Zack paid no mind, staring past Graham to Liza through a floss-thin squint, jaws set tight and sporadically flexing. He stood at the outer entrance to kitchen, a single boot breaking the threshold as he leaned against the wall for support.

In silent response, Liza met his penetrating gaze with an unblinking glare of her own, her posture as defiant as her chest-out, shoulders-back pose.

"Really? You with...*him*?" he mouthed, the overall effect no better than a muted whisper, nodding weakly toward Graham, who had instinctively taken a step back just as Liza seemed to levitate forward to take point.

"So, you rushed here through a tropical storm not to...for me, but...*for* him."

"So, this is...really that hard for you to accept?" she countered, head thrown back and bloated bottom lip beginning to tremble. "Hard as it is to believe, I'm not now or was *ever* your indentured servant. *You* turned down the offer, but *not* for the both of us."

As the hungry sea continued its unstoppable takeover of a soon-to-be extinct Hawk Island, climbing nearly to Liza's thighs and Graham's knees, the normally bland stone walls took on a ruddy sheen, as if breaking a healthy sweat from the extreme humidity.

"Liza, my dear, as potentially therapeutic as airing such marital dirty laundry might be, there simply isn't the time," Graham chided, gesturing past Zack, who had entered the kitchen and stood at its flooded center amid various forms of flotsam with hands on hips and head slightly tilted.

"The concept of greed I can at least understand," the senior Gorman declared at full roar, paying no heed to either the doctor's dialogue or very presence. "You've always...hinted at a thirst. But...cold-blooded murder in its name? I mean...the thought of an eternally damned soul didn't at least give you hesitation?"

Pumping a fist, she simultaneously cocked the crude tomahawk with the other arm as if prepping to sling it forward once her building rage reached a crescendo.

"Guilt-free as can be. Sadistic, child-murdering scum...got...what...they...deserved. You *truly* think I accepted this assignment in order to cow down and serve their kind? I'd have happily participated for free. So, why not take early retirement to do so? Besides," she paused, lowering the war club to shoulder level while pointing toward the doctor with her free hand, "I would think any sort of husband might be a bit more peeved at the probability that his wife just might've been balling the facility physician."

Liza winked, sucking her own index finger seductively.

"I mean, do you *really* think all those headaches were sincere?"

"Oh, my lady, that nasty little barb is an ice-spear direct hit to not only a man's soul but also his *groin*, am I right, Senior Officer Gorman?" Graham injected between hitch-pitched giggles, side-stepping over until he stood directly to Liza's right, where he leaned down, extended an arm and coiled it gently around her hunched shoulders.

Ignoring the doctor yet again, Zack casually brushed away a chunk of busted window frame that had wedged itself between his soaked thighs and regarded Liza with a raised brow.

"Why then…why the act? Was all…that necessary when it basically boiled down to Dylan and me against you two? Why not just team up and attack us on sight once you and Dylan arrived?"

Liza spat out a mouthful of blood and shrugged, but otherwise remained mum as if unsure of the proper response.

"Allow me, my lady," Graham interjected smugly, an arm cocked and forefinger duly raised, the other arm tucked tightly at his lower back as he began a slow, gradual pace of minimal square-footage. "Your soon to be ex-wife is quite the romantic, Zackary. She begged, no…*commanded* me to play along with that quite ludicrous charade in the hopes that you or Barnes might never discover our secret or know of our fiendish intentions. This was the sole reason I merely chocked you out and did not just snap your fool neck and be done with it. We were to eliminate Tate, of course, but only after you and Dylan were temporarily put down. The two of you would awake in the flood-room none the wiser, with the only logical explanation being that all involved drowned in your absence. Of course, you'd face numerous charges back at base, but Liza preferred you alive, and possibly incarcerated, over deceased. As for Barnes, she seemed to categorize him as sort of a…well, the loyal canine type; good-hearted but dumb and thus not deserving of euthanization. Sentimental hogwash, I say…but then, it's all a moot point now. Dylan's bloodlust was most distracting, as was Mister Hawkins' penchant for survival. Alas, the whole shebang can now end as fate would have it end."

He paused as he and Liza briefly locked eyes.

"Sorry, my lady. What's true *is* true. Zackary's weathering the storm would only have complicated the…our future plans."

Tilting his head slightly forward, Zack regarded his wife with a sour, squinty-eyed expression that screamed utter disbelief.

"So *all* are inevitable expendable, is that it? Dylan, Tate and I go down with the island, so to speak, while you two…lovers, presumed dead as well, paddle off into the sunset with a wealth of riches. Compensation for a murder spree well done."

"Look at it this way, Zackary," Graham interrupted again, resting his chin atop a clenched fist in a mocking variation of *The Thinker*. "At least perishing at sea is preferable to infinite incarceration."

Zack growled, nostrils flaring and teeth gnashing.

"Lock the lips, asshole. Not talking to you."

"You…shouldn't have come…followed him here," Liza added blandly, her face a blank slate of Vulcanesque proportions. "Never could leave things well enough alone. Just…stay on site, the worst you'd suffer is a bit of embarrassment, possibly serve some time, but probably be acquitted on lack of evidence. But no, not you…Mister Squared-Away braves the storm in order to spare his latest pet project: The assassin with the heart of gold."

She sighed heavily, wading aimlessly forward several steps and cutting the distance between herself and her spouse to less than ten feet.

"Stiff-shirted, square-jawed *Mr. Clean* to the very end."

Purposely jutting said jaw, Zack began peeling away his uniform shirt, so glued to the flesh underneath it appeared more a forced shedding.

"Your partner's absolutely correct about one thing anyway. I'd much rather die here, fighting against injustice, than be tried and convicted of a...of Carmichael's murder."

Graham waded forth until he stood at Liza's side and directly across from her husband.

"If it'll sooth matters between you two somewhat—I simply despise conflict—the commander's set-up was all my idea."

"As was the planting of evidence, no doubt, using Dylan as your hand-picked zombie. Tell me, Doctor, is your part in this really revenge-based from the trauma of your childhood or, like Liz here, purely greed related?"

"The facts of my...upbringing are just that, Zackary, and I must congratulate the good captain for uncovering juvenile information I thought long-expunged and thus quite secure from prying eyes, even those with the highest government clearance."

The rushing water massaging his groin, Zack stood his ground, bare-chested save a dull chain and gleaming set of dog tags, with bulky arms crossed over same. He soon fought to maintain a semblance of composure upon obtaining a clear, unobstructed view of Dylan Barnes' lifeless corpse float past in the background, the gashed section of the man's maimed visage bobbing just above the surface and resembling some grotesque, two-face sculpture.

"So your kid sister being abducted and murdered by some unknown assailant justifies all this, in your professional opinion? Once Carmichael finally made the connection—that each of the inmate suicide victims had been convicted in child homicides and your own preteen family tragedy—it was a short leap toward the man in charge of both face-to-face counseling *and* the facility medicine cabinet. Shit, Graham, always thought you people were bound by an oath."

Graham snorted, not quite a laugh and not quite a growl but a strained, forced hybrid of each, his apathetic gaze suddenly flaring to life.

"She...Marisa was six years old—taken by force, held for over ninety days while no doubt being bludgeoned and raped repeatedly, and...ultimately...finally...perhaps mercifully...burned alive...the charred remains tucked inside a popcorn tin and buried in a shallow grave discovered less than five miles from our home. I was her senior by less than two years, as the file no doubt correctly states.

"Yes indeed, to answer your rather simplistic inquiry, I do feel a sense of justification in ridding the world of those such as Tate Hawkins, born predators who serve no other purpose. Through the years, as was my duty, I...did attempt to counsel...to treat, that is, until I resolved myself to the futility of such efforts. As for the monetary reward to which you refer," Graham revealed a wide, toothy, slightly warped grin, ironically of the same ilk as those he might initially diagnose as criminally insane. "As laymen such as yourself are so fond of spouting, we'll just call it...*the icing on the proverbial cake*."

"Their dreams, the nightmares and hallucinations—midnight visions of past victims returning from the grave for retribution—all due to some carefully administered medications, I take it?"

"Indeed," Graham replied with a slight bow. "The emotionally fragile are so easily steered down a path of self-destruction."

"Well then," Zack concluded with a casual smirk, "other than some really shitty planning for what I surmise was your final planned sanction, I'd say that wraps it up, that is, other than the identity of the mysterious Sugar Daddy behind it all."

A sudden surge of plunger break strength slapped Graham and Liza in the lower and upper backs, respectively, nearly toppling the latter face-forward as the couch barricade was first shoved and subsequently flipped until it rotated in a gradual spin away from the front entrance, which blew open and hung by a single, bent hinge.

"Specifics are not provided, Zackary, as men and women in such positions of power aren't about to divulge their true identities to peons such as you and me. Let's just say, our…benefactors share in my own personal opinion concerning those such as Tate Hawkins living the relatively carefree island life at taxpayers' expense, and that the offer placed on the table was, to say the very least, extremely generous."

Liza rolled her lone remaining functioning eye while regarding Graham with obvious disdain.

"*Ikulong!* Enough, already. Damn, but you just adore the sound of your own voice."

Shooting the senior Gorman a playful, sarcasm-fueled wink, Graham gestured toward her with an extended thumb.

"Women, right? Can't live with them…can't fit them into mason jars."

"Real charmer, Z," Zack countered, wading back a half-step as the rising waters swallowed his six-foot-plus frame past the belly-button. "I'm sure you two will find true bliss in whatever off-the-grid South American rain-forest you call home."

Paddling ever-so-gradually forward, pushed along by increasingly stout waves at their backs, Liza and Graham bantered back and forth without ever dare breaking eye contact with Zack.

"Strictly your call, my lady. I'm sure this is…quite the stressful ad-lib, but there's no more time to waste."

"Simple math, really. Flood room built for three, with the same number of filtered chambers."

"Those are the facts, indeed, though I beg to differ on the simplicity of said scenario. Sparing Za….your soon-to-be-former spouse under the…these circumstances is the most foolhardy of risks."

"You suggesting we spare Hawkins instead?"

"I'm suggesting nothing of the sort. Hawkins will soon be tossed out with the rest of the driftwood. I highly suggest Senior CO Gorman join him in…taking their chances. Perhaps Zack, in his devotion to saving convicted murderers at any cost, can serve as a sort of human flotation device."

"Not necessary. We seal him in first and I short-circuit the inner hatch release. Once the storm passes, we exit and leave him for the rescue team."

"We… you short-cir… you mean… scout's honor…. truly know how to accomplish this?"

"Men," she snorted indifferently, her bloated lower lip curled upward like a purple, coiling slug.

Once stationed inside the narrow hall, Zack backed past the hut lavatory—the door sealed with water markings near its diamond-shaped knob—to approximately the halfway point toward the flood room and braced his booted feet. He twisted around briefly to eye the metal ladder while scanning the waters below for anything to utilize as a weapon.

Dean Graham entered the hall first, baton resting across a tightly muscled shoulder and tilting his head like a stalking Mantis.

"C'mon, big fella, do we really have to *insist* on a bit of cooperation here? I mean, isn't it enough that your former life-partner has convinced me to spare you? No need to make this more difficult than it has to be. After all, we were once, at the very least, confidants of a sort."

Zack shrugged before raising both fists, flexing massively pumped biceps and gesturing the other man forward.

"All *faux* sentimentality aside, Graham, rest assured I *will not* make this easy."

Graham turned to address Liza, still standing out of Zack's line of sight.

"You heard the man, my lady. He's leaving me no choice but end it here and now. As you oft said, the man is nothing if not stubborn to a fault."

"Would you please just stop talking and *finish* it then," she barked harshly in reply, the tone utilized so utterly alien, so blatantly out-of-character, it struck Zack like a right hook to the gut that he'd truly been sharing marital space with a complete stranger for the better part of five years.

Waving the baton back and forth like the rotating hands of some colossal grandfather clock, Graham nodded sternly and trudged forth through the waist-high waters with renewed vigor.

"Yes, dear. Whatever you say…dear."

The initial tremor was hardly noticeable, no more than subtle tilting beneath their feet that was further trivialized by the sudden intrusion of a new voice amid the chaos—a high-pitched wail from a vaguely familiar source—originating from behind the closed bathroom door.

"T-that you out there, Doc? Hey, how about that…final jawing session you promised? God knows I…I need to clear the air now more than ever!"

Wading over and tentatively planting an ear near the door's mist-saturated surface, Graham's visual focus remained glued to Zack, who in turn inched ever closer to the latter while cursing under his breath at Tate Hawkins' apparent recklessness. With the storm's increasing fury and the very distinct possibility of an island-swallowing riptide, he'd seriously considered bypassing the rematch with Graham in lieu of sealing himself and Hawkins into the flood room and taking his chances.

"Hawkins? That you in there, old boy?"

"Very astute, Doc. No wonder you rate the varied diplomas. I know…my timing is a might questionable, but…you got a minute? I really…need to get a few things off my chest before this damn burg is relocated to the ocean floor."

Undaunted, Graham sneered and moved away from the door while delivering a series of playful taps to its center with the thick end of the baton.

"My apologies, Hawk, but I'm a tad *indisposed* at the moment. I suggest you make peace with whatever deity you deem highest in the celestial pecking order and hope for leniency."

"At the end, I *saw* you, Doc. Saw you...heard you in High-Definition crystal clarity. Oh, Clint Winslow made a brief appearance, no more than cameo really. Little Gina, well, she was little more than a phantom blur...hardly convincing. Being an amateur master-mixer of hallucinogens myself, I'd say you got lazy with the formula. Maybe even omitted an ingredient or two along the way. "

Graham froze in his tracks, ear cocked, sneer firmly intact and accompanied by the periodic twitch near his left cheek.

"Whatever voodoo you *did*, chemical-alteration-wise, the dose administered didn't quite cut the cheese. I guess recklessness in the face of insatiable greed and/or lust is understandable, to a degree."

Zack watched Liz turn the corner into the hall just as Graham inexplicably treaded in reverse, his teeth visibly gnashing between tightly pursed lips.

"Tell you this, Slick, if not for that chicken-shit surprise attack, I'd have surely skinned your preppy ass alive."

"Dean, what the hell are you doing?" Liza blurted, biting into her split lower lip and wincing in the aftermath as a fresh stream of dark crimson trailed onto her chin.

"Is that so, Tate? Well, as it turns out, I believe I can work you in for that final session after all," Graham shrieked, pointing the baton directly at Zack.

"Don't run away now, Zackary. This won't take but a jiff."

"Stupid a-asshole," Liza ranted between bloody spats, hanging on to the hall entranceway doorframe with her free hand as the rushing waters pooled at her upper back, "He's gon…going to seal himself in a-and…l-lock us out!"

"Not a chance, my lady. Senior Correctional Officer Extraordinaire Zackary Gorman would much prefer to, pardon the mob-life pun, *swim with the fishes* than save his own rear end at the expense of a colleague, right Zack?"

"Wha-the hell…has c-college got t-to..."

Graham snorted, reaching the door and curling a palm around its deep blue knob, which sat mere inches from being fully submerged.

"He won't lock himself in or us *out* without Tate Hawkins in tow, understand?"

The second tremor was stouter and noticeably longer in duration; a full three-second terrain shake that instantly widened all eyes save Dean Graham's, whose own remained squinted in a gradually seething rage.

"Di-did you feel t-that, Professor Know-it-All? I'd say we've got about two minutes before this dune capsizes! Forget Hawkins and let's secure the flo—"

The doctor's head twisted about briefly, just long enough to showcase a predatory snarl that triggered an involuntary flinch from his usually unflappable cohort.

"With all undue respect, my lady, kindly clam up or by all means, you're perfectly welcome to secure the room on your own. As previously stated, I will be brief."

"Hey, what's the holdup, Doc? That *yellow streak* up your back not waterproof?" Hawkins bellowed from behind the sealed door a split-second before Graham twisted the knob and barreled forward with as much quickness as the swirling, waist-high waters would allow.

Hanging back with her grip on the door frame growing increasingly weak, Liza was allowed a fairly clear view of the miniscule john's interior, though split in puzzle-piece fashion by the splayed limbs of her partner.

Afforded a temporary respite as surrounding flood waters temporarily receded upon greeting the lavatory's bone-dry space, Graham took a single, free-moving step inside before being engulfed up to the groin once more.

"Hawkins…" he nodded, slapping the fat end of the baton into the flat of his left palm, "…stomach cramps, I presume?"

Tate Hawkins sat balanced atop the hard plastic toilet seat, bowing forward with his face hidden and arms extended downward over a squared object of light brown shading that was swallowed so quickly by the surge that proper identification had been virtually impossible.

"Well, not to worry, old boy. This is your classic good news, bad news scenario. The former? I have just the prescription to end such petty discomfort. The latter? Alas, it is quite the permanent fix with the unfortunate side effect of certain death."

"Sounds more like a promise than a threat, Doc," Hawkins replied, head still slumped downward and arms submerged to the biceps as his upper back, shoulders and neck visibly tensed.

"Personally, and feel free to take this personally…"

His head gradually arose until the two men locked eyes. One haggard, lanky, ghostly pale; his demeanor astonishingly calm. The other coiled to spring—a sleek, meticulously chiseled specimen of flawless physicality who grasped the shock-baton in both fists like a miniature Louisville Slugger.

"…I'm of the sincere belief you simply don't have the balls."

"Tate old man," Graham bellowed over increasingly savage winds that whistled through the gutted hut from various entry points, "I will now proceed to prove said theory incorrect…doctor to patient."

"Dean, j-just forget about him, for shit's sake!" Liza shouted through a cupped fist, though the effect was severely diminished amid the continual roar—akin to standing between passing freights or perhaps being slowly sucked into a jet's thrusting engine—her gut abruptly tightening with an inexplicable dread.

"Damn it…something's not…right," she concluded, silently lipping the final refrain while reaching out her free hand as if to magically pull him back without actually making contact.

Two steps into the bathroom's cramped confines—the baton sufficiently coiled to deliver a single, potentially fatal blow—Graham froze, the smarmy grin melting away as his eyes widened with a sudden realization that came several ticks too late.

The object sailed forth from the frothy swill like a rising leviathan, thrust upward with shocking force by a man the doctor had mistakenly labeled as hapless.

Though he'd instinctively flung his head and shoulders back while simultaneously tilting slightly to the right, his semi-tucked chin took the brunt of the impact, a sickening crunch clearly audible despite the surrounding uproar.

Tate Hawkins had released his secret weapon—a granite sledgehammer weighing upwards of eighteen pounds— chiseled over a four-month span using smaller, sharp-edge rocks and oyster shells in an impromptu homage to the *Hand of God* he'd once so effectively wielded. Despite the obvious handicap of being forced to swing away from two and a half feet of churning seawater, the blow's effect was brutal beyond all expectations, its upward trajectory shattering Dean Graham's jaw and driving a half-dozen spiked bone fragments first into his nasal cavity and eventually into soft, moist brain matter. In the aftermath, the doctor was slung back with arms flapping—the shock-baton spinning end-over-end into the adjoining hall—a single, pencil-thin shard of bone protruding from his right eye socket like a bony quill.

The doctor splashed down in a heap, his mangled, weirdly bloodless face completely unrecognizable as his shattered jaw, mashed grotesquely inward, appeared to be in the process of literally cannibalizing the remainder of his lifeless visage, perhaps in a desperate, last-ditch effort to survive.

"DEAN!" Liza cried out in sincere anguish, releasing the door frame to come to her lover's aid and in her haste, discarding the tomahawk with a casual flip of the wrist.

The third tremor was, conservatively, two-fold its predecessor's strength, a rumbling pre-shock that was either threatening to split the island into assorted, indistinct sectors, or worse, force it down like an sand-crested anchor.

Liza was the first to feel the immediate effects, her legs pulled slightly apart as the concrete foundation cracked and split beneath her booted feet. Wind-milling both arms as if to take flight, she was first hoisted upward and subsequently shoved back as the battered stone elevated like some long-dormant, fossilized prehistoric species jostled to life. Dancing a clumsy, comical jig, she managed to keep her footing even as a sizeable portion of the wooden door frame she'd used for balance peeled from its stone base, which had begun to splinter and spread like a freshly-spun web throughout the structure.

Having briefly dismissed the idea of scaling the ladder, however tempting, Zack had instead opted instead to play chaperone to Tate Hawkins, managing but a single stride toward the lavatory before being hurled into the nearest wall with such force the sharp snapping of his left shoulder all but ensured a complete separation. "Booo-yah, you uppity motherfucker," Tate Hawkins exclaimed, clapping enthusiastically overhead while utterly ignoring a sudden swell of floodwater that buried him to the neck. Having already discarded his granite version of *Mjolnir* following its undeniably spectacular one-shot debut, he dove headfirst into the rising waters and swam just inches above the stone surface and just beneath the doctor's floating corpse.

Gasping and instantly exhausted from the sudden excursion, he surfaced at the center of the hall to a high-pitched shriek he initially mistook, crazily, for a wailing klaxon.

"Y-you murdering…s-son of…a BITCH!" Liza howled, using the pounding waves at her back to lunge forth with hands clutching and clawing.

"Tate! M-move your ass! G-get out of there!" Zack exclaimed weakly between choking gurgles of inhaled seawater, crouched neck-deep and clutching his damaged shoulder with an infestation of floating black dots littering his vision.

Obviously underestimating his new assailant's strength and accompanying rage, Hawkins didn't realize the scope of such a mistake until the first raking of fingernails dug a trio of deep gashes into his left cheek, followed quickly by a vicious right hook that mashed and bloodied his nose despite making only partial contact.

A shrill, continuing cry spewing forth from her pursed lips, the bottom grape-sized and caked in her own spilled fluids, Liza leapt from chest-high waters like a rising, retribution-driven Phoenix and clamped both hands atop Hawkins' naked shoulders before forcing his head down into the frothy swirl.

"H-Hawk! D-damn it," Zack shouted, pure instinct dictating he reach out with his good arm to render aid despite the fifteen to twenty foot distance between himself and the melee.

As fate would have it, the third and final tremor to rock the island served notice that a fourth would not be necessary to ensure compliance to whatever drastic makeover the storm had in mind.

First and foremost—foreboding-wise—the hut's supposed hurricane-proof walls, a full foot-and-a-half thick and possessing a rod-iron exo-skeleton coated in granite, folded inward like a crumpled tin can between a heavy work boot. Secondly and equally disastrous was the mass upheaval from below, the tiled floor and foundation beneath cracking and splitting, forcing stony shrapnel shooting to the surface in jagged clumps.

Despite such a catastrophic unraveling, Liza maintained a virtual death-grip on Hawkins' shoulders, nails digging bloody trenches into his traps and deltoids beneath a sudden influx of fresh seawater whose depths had abruptly risen to just below her chin.

"Li-Liza! For g-god's s-sake, le-let him...be," Zack pleaded between hacking coughs, clinging to the ladder's middle rung after being bludgeoned back by the sudden swell. "Th-this...the whole pl-place is...going under. We have to secure the flood room be-before it's...too late!"

Forced to extend his wounded arm to wipe away a fresh splashing of stinging saltwater from each eye, Zack ceased any further attempt at civilized dialogue in the stark realization that he no longer recognized the target of the banter.

Blood-stained teeth bared, top lip curled upward and single, undamaged eye pulled saucer-wide, the woman he'd years earlier placed high on a pedestal to friends and family alike as the 'kind-hearted, calming influence' he'd so sorely missed in his younger years (and previous two marriages), then resembled no less than a dozen similarly deranged maniacs he'd helped house in a twenty-plus year career in the corrections field.

"J-Jesus, L-Liza," he mumbled wearily, peering upward for a final, forlorn glance at the open flood room door while preparing to release the rung in a last-ditch attempt to save a life other than his own, be it that of his psychotic wife, or a man likewise labeled by both society and the justice system.

He hesitated, tips of his fingers still gripping wet metal, upon hearing Liza's garbled scream and watching her arms sail upward as if peeling both hands from the surface of a red-hot oven eye. Tate Hawkins' head shot upward a split-second later, choking, gagging and spitting while executing a surprising effective backstroke that quickly separated him from his attacker.

"T-Tate, over h-here," Zack barked, descending the ladder until he hung from the lowest rung, "Pump it h-hard, man...we're fa-fast running out-outta time."

Moments later, as his outstretched hand curled around Hawkins' right wrist and began to pull with what meager energy remained, Zack was afforded a lingering glance at the source of his beleaguered spouse's sudden, inexplicable panic.

Hoisted upward by the raging sea's continuing influx until the tip of her scalp nearly scraped the stone ceiling, Liza had been besieged upon from both front and back by floating corpses. Slapping the surface with both palms to ward off their respective assaults, she literally appeared to be staving off being purposely drowned.

The former Doctor Dean Graham, his lower jaw flopping about like a broken shutter and his left eye open and bugging as if on the verge of popping free, had somehow managed to reach up and curl dead fingers into the wet tangle of his former partner's hair.

To complete the ghastly dance, the splayed legs of Dylan Barnes had wrapped around her midsection like coiling tentacles, the right side of the man's horribly mutilated face sporadically surfacing like a mangled fish-bobber.

Forced to turn away while assisting a weak, barely coherent Tate Hawkins to scale the ladder, Zack heard the north end of the structure buckle and implode. Allowing himself a final peek before climbing upward, he would later pray to *somehow, someday* be granted the mercy to forget what would be his last glimpse of a woman he still loved despite her recent actions.

As the hallway walls had literally begun to fold in from both sides—the thick stone splintering at the middle as the ceiling drooped dangerously downward—he stood frozen with hands clamped on the metal ladder as Liza reached from the neck-high waters directly toward him, shouting his name between wet, gagging hacks as the twin corpses appeared to close ranks.

In retrospect, Zack would have preferred she point an accusing finger, perhaps even damn him for allowing her impending death with some clichéd, curse-ridden death speech straight from a B-grade horror flick. Instead, she chose to beg his assistance as her head was gradually being forced under and directly toward the disfigured, cave-like maw of her former lover as if to join lips—or *lip* in the singular sense in the good doctor's case—for all of eternity.

A split-second before the ceiling collapsed and the adjoining walls creased, he saw the trio sucked beneath the lavatory doorframe, Liza's final garbled words only partially audible but as haunting and unforgettable as if delivered with crystal-clear clarity into otherwise dead air.

Though the *"Forgive"* had been communicated with surprising distinction, the concluding *"me"* had stretched out like a faint, ghostly echo spewed forth from the deepest pit imaginable, delivered as she'd shot beneath the doorframe with the speed of live ammunition through a smoking barrel.

Utterly breathless and besieged by sudden sharp pain that punctured his breastbone like a flaming arrow, Zack hung suspended half-way up the ladder—slack-jawed and unblinking in his utter disbelief—that is until what had been a stone foundation several feet thick began to surge upward and the entire structure as a whole commenced to tilt severely to the right, wherein he cleared the final six rungs as if magically levitated by the primal power of fear.

Crawling belly first into the flood room and assisted by a sudden, extreme shift to the left as what remained of the hut continued to implode, he triple-rolled until halting suddenly as the left side of his skull impacted the hard glass cylinder at the center of the three available life pods.

He heard Tate Hawkins bellowing from the pod to his immediate left—the words rendered woefully inaudible by the surrounding rumble of rock walls transformed to jagged gravel—pulling himself upright by gripping the edge of the open pod. It wasn't until he'd managed to plant a booted foot inside, the room decidedly warped but temporarily stable, that the intended message was visualized and a wave of panic clouted his gut with jackhammer force.

Upon completing his clumsily executed, terror-filled entry into the flood room, he'd overlooked a rather vital key to their survival—that being to properly *seal* the waterproof door. Having been rotated and spun hard to the left, the room, moreover the cylinder within, sat horribly askew, though with the temporary lull in movement, Zack was able to shove himself from the pod and crawl on all fours toward the open entrance while obtaining sustainable handholds on the assortment of thick, insulated cable that ran along the tile flooring.

Scrambling to the very edge of the opening, he peeked back over his right shoulder toward Tate Hawkins, who was nodding and gesturing wildly as if suffering a major seizure while jabbering silently away at warp speed.

Zack's response was a mild shrug as he groped to obtain a workable handhold on the smooth track of the circular opening, re-shifting his focus downward and instantly shrieking aloud as a blackened blur shot forth from the rising waters to rake the bare flesh of his right forearm from wrist to elbow.

Reeling back, he managed to maintain a loose hold while collapsing to the tile with his wounded left shoulder taking the brunt. Grimacing from this newfound anguish, his vision cloaked in tiny, dark spatters that soon mutated into a billowy cape of blackness, Zack fought a stout temptation to surrender to impending unconsciousness, instead focusing on the source of this latest malady.

With a vigorous series of head-shakes, he was able to secure a quarter-sized tunnel from which to peek in order to better diagnose the stinging numbness enveloping the whole of his right arm.

Strange, in light of such garish horror, that he should feel less terrorized than slightly amused. Perhaps it was the absolute ridiculousness of the scene itself—a logical sense of unreality that accompanied such abstract lunacy by proxy—that effectively diverted whatever fear might naturally follow.

Lifting his arm out and away from his body as far as physically possible while somehow maintaining a firm grip with the other, despite a connecting shoulder that was at least partially if not fully dislocated, Zack openly snickered at the mere sight, a snicker that soon evolved into a grinning snort and then a full-blown, rib-rattling guffaw.

Hanging from the meaty, muscular top-edge of his forearm, Liza had apparently chomped down bone-deep, as only her pale, puffy lips were visible, the upper propped atop the hairy flesh just below the crook of his elbow. Suspended in mid-air like a hooked catfish, her bare arms were pinned to her sides, wedged firmly into place by a duo of familiar corpses that clung to each like flesh-seeking parasites. Regarding Zack through the single eye facing him, so monstrously bloated it leaked thick streams of yellowish pus with each sporadic blink, there was a sense of desperation trapped within its bloodshot dimness that appeared to be fading by the second, as if her inner life-source was on the verge of blinking out.

A sudden vicious tug downward and her grip weakened substantially, revealing a top row of badly-chipped, blood-soaked choppers. A second jerk and she was pulled free with a weak, pathetic cry that, despite losing a sizeable chunk of flesh in the bargain, triggered in Zack such a resounding wave of pity that all other pains were easily dismissed.

The swirling seawater in which his wife had vanished, along with the uninvited houseguests serving as her personal anchors, had turned a dark crimson that bubbled and churned like a witch's cauldron. In the aftermath, driven by reckless instinct, Zack had reached down and penetrated the maroon swill with the same torn appendage, the splayed fingers of which instantly coiled into what he could only deduce was a drifting patch of seaweed.

Instead, upon reeling his mystery catch to the surface, accompanied by a great swell of ocean spewing forth like a hot, frothy ejaculation akin to that of Yellowstone's Old Faithful, Zack found he was no longer amused, but utterly freaked out.

"Let 'er go, big guy," the Dylan Barnes corpse exclaimed with a playful wink, Zack's spread fingers having dug deep groves into his balding, partially fleshless scalp. "Cheatin' bitch got greedy and is payin' the market price. Not your fault, dude. Just let...it...go. Lots of pus...uh, *quality* chicks out there to whom loyalty ain't just a word.

"Despite all the familiar trappings of a marriage on the rocks, just remember this, boss, she was the traitor, not you. *Dig it*...you deserve better than what ya got."

"Crudely put, as usual, but I have to admit, well-said and painfully honest," a wet, gurgling voice chimed in, surfacing only afterwards. Strangely, despite his shattered lower jaw flopping about like a broken wing, Dean Graham's speech was not affected in the least. "Though you might not feel it...*appropriate* to take the advice of a newly sworn enemy, I'd at least take heed of Dylan's words. You need to, as quickly as possible, discard the baggage of your failed coupling with the late little missus.

"As it stands," he continued, the left side of Dylan's Barnes' perfectly halved face staring him down with a single, milky eye, the right side attached only by a single, inch-thick shred of pulpy flesh which hung so comically askew it appeared on the verge of peeling away, "the upcoming accusations of murdering a major correctional facility's commanding officer will no doubt suffice in filling anyone's personal stress quota."

Lifting a pasty hand from the rolling waters, Dylan laid it gently atop Zack's right wrist—its cool, clammy feel not lost on the source, who openly flinched.

"Doc Shit-heel has a point, big guy. Don't let 'em bury ya. Hold your ground."

Dean Graham nodded in silent agreement, the effort causing his right eyeball to squirt free from the socket and swing back and forth like a fleshy pendulum from a string of optic nerve.

"Hell, big guy, don't just lie there like chopped chum. Save your own ass, for shit's sake!" he head Dylan say, the words strangely garbled and with a faint echo as if spoken from beneath the water.

A sharp pinch to his wrist—a deep, throbbing he logically tied to Dylan—shook him awake, the flood room's cylinder-like door parked firmly atop his upper arm and tapping metal against bone as additional seawater filled in a few salty gallons at a time, accompanied by small chunks of stone and a single, spear-like twist of metal pipe. Shaking the cobwebs with a fierce series of head-shakes, he could hear Tate Hawkins bellowing in the background while slowly rising off of his damaged shoulder. Removing his hand from inside the hatch opening, he soon realized the twisted metal pipe was serving as the true barricade and quickly deduced it had also been, conversing specters aide, the genuine source of his sliced forearm.

Up on one knee, he reached down, gripped the pipe and shoved it down and over before forcing the door shut over an increasingly rabid water swell, sealing it in place with a trio of clockwise turns of its slick, round wheel.

Zack stood gingerly, pausing a full moment to ensure the door had properly sealed before turning toward the life pods.

He'd completed three of the four full steps necessary to reach his destination, Tate Hawkins clapping and cheering him on like some haggard, maniacal cheerleader, when the flood room first shimmed and shook before being flipped top to bottom, capsizing like an overturned hourglass sand-timer.

Hoisted head-over-heels, Zack landed feet first with a pained groan, severely twisting his left ankle and further jarring his dislocated shoulder while also smacking the back of his skull. On the cusp of surrendering to unconsciousness again, he peeked through bleary eyes in expectation of lying spread eagle atop what had been the flood room's smooth, stone ceiling. Instead, just as the room first spun hard to the left before braking abruptly and then twisting in the opposite direction like some short-circuiting carnival ride, Zack found himself tucked snugly inside his designated life pod, having somehow—against all conceivable odds of gravity and physics—been tossed up, over and directly *into* the narrow, circular entrance.

That final, vicious twist ensued just as Zack had pressed a shaky thumb to a tiny keypad located just underneath the pod door, a faint whooshing sound accompanying the sealing process.

Briefly titled upward to strike a perfectly vertical pose amid the deafening sound of granite being crushed, squeezed and pummeled into jagged specks of gravel, Zack secured a combination waist/shoulder strap and, poised as if at attention, peered over at Tate Hawkins' pod to his immediate right.

Despite similarly dazed, disheveled states, the two shared a knowing nod—Hawkins even managing to produce a weak, warped but sincere smile of apparent appreciation—before their supposed watertight, triple-reinforced stainless steel and stone safe-haven spun free from its granite base with a echoing groan, as if somehow bemoaning the loss of the mother ship.

The veteran correctional officer, tightly secured inside an unbreakable glass cylinder casing being flung about like an industrial washer on spin cycle, would soon enough succumb to the strangely soothing darkness, but not before a thought inconceivably blacker attached itself to his subconscious like a feeding, pulsating parasite. Equally depressing and oppressive—like twin anvils pressing at his breastbone in hopes of crushing his heart like overripe fruit—it screamed validity despite the high level of self-pity involved.

In light of such an unthinkable, unfathomable betrayal from the most unlikely of sources, was survival really, truly necessary?

Additionally, bellowed his inner drama-king, why the fuck bother? Worst-case scenario: Possible federal prison time loomed, a life sentence perhaps served out atop similarly secluded dunes as those under the guileless watch of Atlantis Correctional.

A life sentence to do nothing but ponder *why*; to grow increasingly bitter and enraged; to focus on the once-trusted, greed-distorted faces of utter disloyalty that had possibly sealed his fate as they had their very own.

As his parasitical muse wisely bypassed around the tiny but integral segment of gray matter that controlled logical and practical thinking; instead punching, jabbing and gouging unmercifully at the soft tissue in charge solely of *raw, impractical emotion*, Zackary Gorman, despite an outer blissful, deepened state of near-comatose unconsciousness, might well have reached up and torn out his own throat.

Epilogue

A Clean Slate

"SCO Gor—…can you….ear me? Inhale deep—…exhale slowly. Take it slow…deep breaths…in and out…going to give you…—jections, the first a mild -dative and…shot of B-twelve, okay? Just relax…you're going to…fine."

Flickering in and out of consciousness, Zack could only be certain of one specific aspect of this latest in a string of resurrections: His wildly flaring nostrils and mouth were cloaked by an oxygen mask that was pumping in cool, fresh air as sweet and refreshing as any icy liquid he'd ever ingested amid stifling heat.

The presence of others nearby, scrambling about and mumbling incoherently, became obvious and he soon felt faint, twin stings at the inside of his left elbow, delivered just seconds apart. The hum of a chopper's whirling blades—most likely a Coast Guard Medevac MH-65 or equivalent as these were common in air-to-sea scenarios—served up the perfect rhythm for nodding out again.

"How are we feeling, Officer Gorman?" the deep male voice echoed from somewhere overhead. As if weighed down by separate anchors, Zack discovered the act of lifting his eyelids quite the laborious task. He felt a full-body shiver cloak every appendage, as if he were lying completely nude inside a walk-in freezer.

"Vitals are approaching normal levels, Doctor," a female voice chimed in from apparently the same deep, dank cave, "BP at one-ten over sixty-two. Pulse at fifty-eight. Breathing has stabilized."

"This initial grogginess is normal, Officer Gorman," the doctor resumed after an undetermined passage of time, the flat, echoing tone now crystal clear. "Still, it's going to take another half-hour or so before you can be properly briefed. Just relax and someone of a more…official nature will join you soon. I'll then drop by for a final debrief on your condition before you're flown back to the mainland."

"Th-the m-main…loan?" Zack croaked, his own voice—hoarse and cracking like a prepubescent teen—unrecognizable even to himself.

"Yes indeed," the female answered, and he felt a warm hand land atop and briefly tap the back of his left hand. "The duration of your recovery will take place at Yokota Air Base. They know of your situation and are prepping a room at the base hospital as we speak. Now, you just lie back and nap. Allow the medication to naturally wear off."

His tongue a swollen lump of sandpaper, Zack attempted a final inquiry despite a fresh wave of dizziness birthed from the effort. His eyes fluttered but were unable to focus past a gray, pulsating wall of blurriness.

"Whu…wha…'bout Tape…T-Tate…Huck-H-Hawker-kins?"

A short hesitation ensued, followed by a noisy throat-clearing and the doctor's stiff, rather curt reply.

"You'll be briefed extensively upon your arrival at the base, Mist— Officer Gorman. For now, just know you are a very, very fortunate man."

"Yo-ko-daaa...Air Sp-base..." he stammered, the smell of antiseptic suddenly overwhelming. On this particular occasion, it was the droning of unfamiliar voices that successfully greased the skids of his latest and lengthiest powernap.

~ * ~

Standing in a semi-parade rest pose with his dislocated shoulder tucked into a tightly wound sling and both ankles wrapped to inhibit movement from twin sprains, Zack's squared chin had collapsed at the news, his eyes instantly glazing over in apparent disbelief.

"The... entire facility, sir? I mean, wasn't it... reinforced to withstand... for any possibili—"

The man whose massive desk he faced leaned back until it appeared his high-back leather recliner might overturn.

"Indeed it was, as are all such sites. Then again, the blueprint did not include oceanic earthquakes of the eight-plus Richter scale level or the massive tidal wave that soon followed. Sixty to seventy feet high and untold miles across," the silver-haired man shrugged wearily, his shiny gray suit reflecting the sun rays through the parted blinds of a nearby window directly into Zack's squinting, overly sensitive eyes. Though the two men shared similarly high-and-tight buzz-cut styled haircuts, Zack was ten years the other man's junior and roughly twice his size.

"Sixty to...*damn*. Were there...any survivors, sir? I mean, um, as far as Atlantis? I know there are specially designed holding areas similar to the flood rooms built into the inmate huts."

His gruff voice as haggard and worn as his rugged visage, Ronald Ford, former CO, longtime stateside warden and current chief executive officer of Pacific Corrections, bowed his head and sighed.

"Two made it. Two blessed souls spared out of the thirty-six present when the lockdown was ordered. Not the best percentage by far, but at least the...devastation wasn't complete, at least in a human sense.

Facility, stone, steel and reinforced glass, was crushed like a Styrofoam cup. I…toured the area just yesterday. Nothing left but tons of floating debris."

As Zack cleared his throat through a cupped palm, the older man typed aimlessly atop a black keyboard at the center of the desk.

"As of just minutes before your arrival, they've recovered but eighteen bodies."

"Sir, if I might…who…could you divulge the names of those who…did make it?"

"Com officer named Flores and a newly assigned inventory clerk…Jason Markum. They had taken refuge…sealed themselves into the Command Post's inner storm shelter just as the wave was impacting. Only by the grace of God did they survive such a pounding, though each did sustain major injuries and are currently listed in critical but stable condition."

"What of the inmate islands? Did…were there others that suffered the same…damage as Hawk Isle?"

"Nine reclaimed by the angry sea; six others still afloat but with considerable repairs in order. Before you ask, ten of the incarcerated were lost with but one body recovered. It may sound a bit callous, but when compared to Atlantis…a miniscule loss at best. One of my…*the* better rated facilities within the sector, manned by a fine, dedicated staff."

"Yes, sir. And what of Captain Carmichael?"

"Sad to report the commander's body has yet to be found, nor will it be, I'm afraid, without divine intervention. That damnable storm scattered the facility and its inhabitants over a two-hundred mile radius. Early estimates place the monetary loss to the corporation at just over two billion dollars. Needless to say, our shareholders are…sure to discuss possible dismantlement of the program as it stands, at least in the Pacific region."

Wincing from the constant throb from an assortment of pained appendages, Zack nodded in silence.

333

"Um, it goes without saying, Officer Gorman, *Zackary,* that all personal belongings are...were lost. I realize that might sound woefully trite in light of your wife's untimely passing. I do apologize. It's merely a mandatory portion of the debrief. Of course, it goes without saying that reimbursement, to include, well," CEO Ford paused, having strolled over to the window to peek through blinds he gently parted with openly shaky fingers, "That is to say that all corporation life insurance policies will be honored. Again, Zackary, for what it's worth, I offer my most sincere condolences for your loss. Liza was, as I understand it, a fine CO with an unlimited future."

"Thank you, sir. She..." Zack briefly broke contact with the CEO, instead peering downward at his glossy, spit-shined boots, "...was indeed."

Stepping from the window, Ford shuffled back over to his desk to be engulfed within the cushiony confines of the recliner.

"I see from your own record that retirement is imminent. It goes without saying we'd love to have you stick around as long as you desire. Senior COs with your experience are few and far between."

"Appreciate the offer, sir. I...in truth the specific plans I had are, well, on hold for now, for obvious reasons. Still, at the present moment I'm thinking a little personal time is in order, just to get my head straight, if you can understand."

"I can only imagine. I lost my wife two years ago to liver cancer. She fought tooth-and-nail for many, many months before succumbing, so her passing held no such shock as what you are now enduring."

Zack nodded wordlessly again before extending a hand over the desk to apply a firm shake to the older man's own.

"Bless you, Zackary, and God speed."

Departing the CEO's office on knees of the most pliable rubber, Zack exited the administrative building of Pacific Correctional Corporation with a certified schizophrenic's worth of conflicted emotions. He'd overheard rumors in the eight days he'd spent recouping at Yokota, though nothing could be confirmed until the official debrief with Bowen. He had, of course, perused the internet and watched countless video newsfeeds from the disaster site, all providing little detail except to paraphrase the painfully obvious in calling it the worst such tragedy in oceanic-based corrections history. *No shit, Sherlock,* he'd moaned silently at each proceeding report, one more stupefying than the other in terms of confirmed details or numbers.

He'd requested and been granted an early release from a scheduled two-week rehab for just that reason, finding the daily psychological grind much more difficult to stomach than any physical discomfort a dislocated shoulder and two severely twisted ankles could match. Every waking hour, between pain med feedings, hot tub sessions and sedative-induced, thrice-daily power naps, he'd half-expected PCC internal affairs agents to bulrush into the room and slap on the cuffs, charging him with numerous counts of dereliction of duty, misuse of corporation equipment, and of course, multiple charges of homicide.

Instead, Mother Nature had seen fit to wipe the slate, at least his personal dish, whistle-clean. The same temperamental *Wicked Witch of Weather Catastrophe* that had seen fit to banish nearly every living soul within a fifty-mile radius to Davey Jones' locker had simultaneously buried all evidence of Dean Graham's fiendish plot to frame him for not only the commander's murder, but the inmate spree as well.

Tucked in a far, darkened corner of a local watering hole just a few scant miles from the headquarters building, Zack further pondered the historical disaster of Atlantis Correctional Facility over several cold bottles of brew and a bowl of semi-stale pretzels. A disaster that had served, or so it seemed, to save his bacon, though at a tremendous personal cost to almost everyone else. Families would grieve; lawsuits would be filed. As far as the former went, he would not escape completely unscathed, as Liza's mother (her father had passed nearly a decade ago) and family surely expect his personal take on her passing via Skype within the next coming days. As he sipped and chewed in equal measures of dazed indifference, Zack's moods alternated by the minute from one extreme to the next, depending on the thought dwelled upon. Teeth-gritting rage to a tranquil calmness—unbridled joy to sadness—elation to dread—sweet relief to bone-jarring guilt.

At the twilight of one of the longest days of his life, freshly-showered and half-asleep while lying spread-eagle atop a hotel bed that threatened to swallow him whole, Zackary Gorman experienced an epiphany of sorts, perhaps birthed more from mental fatigue than practical logic, but an epiphany nonetheless.

Accept it. Without guilt. Without remorse. Fate. Kismet. There must be a reason. A reason only the good Lord is currently privy too. In the meantime, make good on it. Justify it. Period. Amen.

Epilogue II

The Fate of Tate

Despite the extreme circumstances of their reunion, the two men felt a similar comfort in each other's presence that stone walls and unbreakable glass did little to diminish, and though it had been just over seven months since the sinking of Hawk Isle, each could conjure up the memory in painstaking detail as if mere days had passed.

"Appears you've been afforded some better chow in your new digs," Zack quipped, a tiny audio mic secured to his denim jacket's collar. Though the unit's heating system infused the confined space with a continuous supply of tepid air, North Dakota in late January was quite the unrelenting, unbeatable foe in terms of finding consistent warmth. Despite tucking both hands into the folds of the fur-lined parka folded at his lap, a lingering chill stung each curled finger.

"Yeah, well, the tropical climes make up for the grub, however tasty and/or filling. Quite a change from our previous stomping grounds, yeah?"

"I'll say. Almost had my flight cancelled for the third straight day. As it was, it took me three and a half hours to steer a rented Pathfinder from Grand Forks. Forty-nine blessed miles. Pretty damn certain I could've skied it in under two."

Tate Hawkins leaned back wearing a sly, slightly warped grin so very familiar to his visitor despite the glaring absence of his trademark facial hair, the omission of which showcased a trio of shiny, pencil-thin scars trailing his left cheek.

Meaty of torso, clean-shaven and short-locked, he appeared a decade younger despite a noticeably paler complexion easily chalked up to his new surroundings.

"Perhaps, but they would have had to free your frozen carcass with a pick-axe. Truth be told, I prefer chillier surroundings these days. Got my quota of heat and humidity at that other stop, I guess. Hear you've got a new gig: Zackary Cain Gorman, Security Consultant for Manskar Incorporated. Congratulatons, Doc."

"Um, thanks but…but how did—"

"This isn't Devil's Island. Even us victims of permanent administrative segregation are allowed sporadic television and internet access.

"Your celebrity status might've been short-lived until the next disaster victim grabbed the spotlight, but the media has seen fit to provide an update now and then.

Hey, it's only a few short months before the one-year anniversary, so you'd best gird your loins and prep for the vultures."

"Ditto yourself," Zack sighed wearily. "Speaking of which, does the name Chris Fields ring a bell?"

Tate's laughter came across the surrounding speakers as ringing bursts of static.

"Wanna-be documentary producer sporting the *faux* Brit accent and Snidely Whiplash 'stache? He's been sniffing around these grounds for months, yes sir. Smarmy little prick—about as sincere as most of his ilk, I'd imagine. Kind of reminds me of a certain correctional physician I had the misfortunate of knowing."

"Cannot disagree in the least. From what I hear, he's going on with the project with or without our cooperation. Latest working title is, brace yourself, *Atlantis: Lost Once More*."

Additional bursts of static-filled guffaws ensued.

"Classy, and not the least bit melodramatic. Big-budget fictional version will soon follow, I'd wager. As far as casting goes, I'm hoping for the most current of today's cinematic heartthrobs—ruggedly handsome, ultra-charming and with torsos chiseled from the statues of the Greek gods. And you?"

Zack shrugged as the guard stationed at his back paced back into view from behind a glass door.

"As far as I'm concerned, Tate, they can omit my character all together."

"Snidely offered the moon, I surmise."

"Not up front, no. Severe budgetary restrictions, or so he said, though certain monetary percentages were mentioned concerning future box-office and DVD sales. Told the weasel to take a long stroll off a short pier. Truth be told, there isn't a price tag high enough. Besides," he paused, lowering his voice a degree, "I've started to misremember some of the lies, if you get my drift."

Tate raised a hand, flashing a thumb and forefinger salute.

"Same here, big guy. Same here."

The two fell silent for several moments while exchanging a knowing glance.

"In all seriousness, and this might sound damn callous, I'm…glad it worked out for you the way it did. Death and devastation aside, if those trumped-up charges of Graham's would have come to light, we might not be having this conversation, except maybe with both of us perched on *this* side of the glass. As lone material witnesses go, Doc, I'm exactly nobody's first choice."

"I...still struggle with it, Tate," Zack countered, suddenly appearing old and haggard beneath the glaring fluorescents, "daily. I'll go through streaks of feeling, well, fortunate for the second chance. Then there are those other, darker days, when guilt intercedes. I hope and pray, over time, the positive will outweigh the negative. Currently, they're running about even."

"Do you ever mull the distinct possibility of the...those mystery solicitors of the island murders coming clean someday, be it via guilty conscience or criminal confession? If so, chief, we might find ourselves shoulder-deep in reporters for an altogether different reason."

"Mulled it over quite often, as a matter of fact; the positive spin being that evidence would be virtually impossible to obtain at this point. I also find some solace in the hopes that Graham was their lone contact and Liza was savvy enough to remain a quiet partner throughout."

Tate nodded as another brief silence followed. Once he did resume their verbal folly—the facility limited individual visitation times to ten minutes maximum, and they had but a few precious few remaining—it was with a loud, enthusiastic clap that caused Zack to flinch back, albeit with a wide smile creasing his rugged visage.

"Hey now! That'll be enough of the *black cloud floating overhead* garbage. I hear through the grapevine, actually TMZ online, that you're getting hitched soon, Doc."

The nappy dressed man with the broad-shoulders, crew-cut coif and box-shaped jaw practically beamed, the transformation in expressions assisting in realigning his overall appearance back the decade he'd previously lost to solemnness.

"Guilty as charged, though the official ceremony isn't 'til next spring."

With that, Hawkins' grin grew ever wider.

"Fast moving type, are we?"

"Nina's idea, not mine, well, not entirely."

"Nina. Nice name. Quite the looker too, if I may be so kind. Of Cuban descent, is she?"

"Yeah, immigrated to the US as a pre-teen. Worked her way from admin assistant to lead production designer at Manskars in less than a decade. A real firecracker."

"And ethnic to boot. Definitely your type, chief." Hawkins' smile wavered as the last word trailed off.

"Oh, yeah. That came out kinda awkward. I surely didn't mean…well…um…sorry, big guy."

Zack quickly waved him off.

"Forget it. If Nina does remind me of *her* at times, it's the Jekyll version, not the Hyde. I…do sometimes wonder if I'm allowing myself to be rushed into this just to erase those final, bitter memories as quickly as possible."

"Hey, why wait, right? Days might just be numbers, Doc, but those numbers are limited. Now, to be fair," Hawkins' leaned toward the glass as if to deliver a muted whisper, "aren't you gonna ask about *my* love life?"

Zack's lips parted—eyes pulled wide and darting in obvious befuddlement—before eventually shrugging in silent defeat.

"Got'cha," Hawkins' said with a wink. They shared a hearty laugh, interrupted at its conclusion by the posted guard tapping on the outer door to signal the ten minute duration had nearly expired.

"Hey, thanks for the DVDs and reading material, chief," Hawkins concluded, pushing away from his chair with the mic pinched between two fingers, "and don't bother denying it was you. It's not like I have a lengthy checklist of possible suspects."

Zack replied while turning briefly to flash the guard a 'just a second' gesture with forefinger raised.

"Not a problem. I take requests. All *you* have to do is ask."

They stood facing one another and, sharing a casual, comfortable vibe that no further dialogue was necessary, merely nodded in unison before Zack turned away to be led from the unit's visitation center.

Minutes later, upon exiting through the sally port's sliding chain-link fence, he strolled purposely toward the section of unit parking specifically marked for visitors, a cold, brisk wind chiding him to don the parka's thick, fur-lined hood approximately midway to his destination.

Standing at the passenger side with the rental truck's keys poised in a gloved hand, Zack paused for a lingering glance at the unit, so similar to many he'd worked himself. As with all such facilities, usually located as far away from large, populated areas as feasibly possible, there was an overwhelming sense of desolation …isolation…hopelessness.

Peeling away the parka hood despite temperatures so frigid the flesh of his cheeks stung as if instantly freezer-burned, he was abruptly, inexplicably, taken back for a fleeting moment in time. A memory so vivid and crystal clear it surpassed any mere flashback—so realistic and drenched in *déjà vu* that he briefly lost all sense of reality—literally transported, ever-so-briefly, into a scene from the recent past.

The heat and humidity are suffocating, inhumanly oppressive. Still, the vibe is remarkably positive. He totes a suitcase in each hand and she an aged, dingy-gray duffel, stuffed to the max, tossed over her left shoulder. As tufts of sand kick up from the heels of her boots and playfully spatter his own, the familiar sound of her cackling laughter— joyous and wholly genuine—pierces and subsequently twists within his midsection like a razor-sharp stiletto.

She whirls about as they near a winding, paved walkway leading off the beach and flashes her best smile—wide and toothy—and pouts seductively.

"So this is the paradise you promised me, big 'un? C'mon he said. It's the tropics he said. Your kind of weather, he said. New

assignment…state of the art technology, he said…live on the beach and work on the beach, he said…blah blah blah," she chides good-naturedly, "Well, rest assured I'm going to make you keep that vow of unabashed happiness." She winks and flips back around, shaking her hips seductively beneath a pair of skin-tight spandex shorts. "Starting tonight, lover-boy."

The employee barracks building, marked 'Atlantis Base Housing' looms. She vanishes into its darkened interior just as Zack feels the air depart his lungs in a dry, hot rush. The suitcases collapse onto the sand; his knees grow weak. He tries to speak her name, scream out, perhaps reset time and verbally warn of the dreadful events to come…even as he sucks in a bitterly cold refill comparable only to sucking down a mouthful of crushed ice.

His face masked in a whitish cloud of condensation, Zack completed the strained, extended exhale while leaning against the Pathfinder's frost-coated door for support. Peeking into the nearby side mirror, his complexion appeared as pale as the sporadic drifts of snow lining the mostly deserted lot.

Keying the door while hoping no one had witnessed the episode, he practically collapsed inside, suddenly exhausted in both a mental and physical sense. He cranked the engine, engaged the heater and waited for both to properly warm. In the meantime, a quick check of the rearview mirror revealed a frozen tear, no larger than a pin drop, lodged halfway down his left cheek.

Removing his gloves, Zack reached up and gently poked at it with a shaking forefinger. It instantly melted away, much like the surreal daydream that had birthed it.

He mumbled silently to himself while steering slowly away as shards of packed snow and ice cracked and snapped beneath churning, chain-covered tires, mouthing an altogether new promise to both himself and his maker.

A promise. A fervent vow.

A solemn pledge to file away the immediate past and exist solely for the now, regardless of climate. He asked for help in maintaining this particular oath and hoped it wasn't too late, at least in his case, for such divine intervention.

As if provided his answer, the North Dakota sun soon broke through considerable cloud coverage and instantly warmed his face.

Unlike the sun he'd last known, this was a kinder, gentler version, and Zack couldn't have been more pleased with the difference.

Meet

Terry Vinson

Born and raised in Northern Alabama, Terry Vinson is an Air Force veteran and former corrections officer who is the author of over a dozen published novels. Having previously resided in five states and overseas, he currently homesteads in Hendersonville, Tennessee with his wife Liza.

VISIT OUR WEBSITE
FOR THE FULL INVENTORY
OF QUALITY BOOKS:

www.books-by-wings-epress.com

Wings Press, Inc.

Quality trade paperbacks and downloads
in multiple formats,
in genres ranging from light romantic comedy to
general fiction and horror. Wings has something
for every reader's taste.
Visit the website, then bookmark it.
We add new titles each month!

www.ingramcontent.com/pod-product-compliance
Lightning Source LLC
Chambersburg PA
CBHW070902030426
42336CB00014BA/2301